WHERE
FLAVOR
WAS BORN

WHERE FLAVOR WAS BORN

BY ANDREAS VIESTAD

PHOTOGRAPHS BY METTE RANDEM

RECIPES AND CULINARY TRAVELS
ALONG THE INDIAN OCEAN SPICE ROUTE

CHRONICLE BOOKS
SAN FRANCISCO

PAGE 2: A market in the Krabi region of southern Thailand. Not only is the produce fantastic; you can also have a lot of fun trying to figure out the logic behind the displays. What do a soccer ball and bananas have in common?

FACING PAGE: A woman bringing bananas to market on Bali. Carrying things on your head takes sure footing and a bit of practice, but when mastered, it makes it easier to carry heavy loads a long way.

Library of Congress Cataloging-in-Publication Data available.

ISBN-10: 0-8118-4965-1
ISBN-13: 978-0-8118-4965-4

Manufactured in China

Designed by Marc English Design
Food styling by Magnus Castracane
Typesetting by Rebecka Anglander
Set in Sol, Mrs. Eaves, and Gill Sans
Photographs on pages 49, 66–69, 77, 119, 239 by Silje Sibel
Photographs on pages 150, 206, 230–231 by Andreas Viestad

Distributed in Canada by Raincoast Books
9050 Shaughnessy Street
Vancouver, British Columbia V6P 6E5

10 9 8 7 6 5 4 3 2 1

Chronicle Books LLC
680 Second Street
San Francisco, California 94107

www.chroniclebooks.com

TO VIBEKE-LIFE IS AN ADVENTURE

CONTENTS

13   **INTRODUCTION**

19   **THE SPICES OF
THE INDIAN OCEAN AT A GLANCE**

CUMIN

37   **DESERTED BY ALL BUT ONE**
41   Tomato and Cucumber Salad with Cumin Salt
42   Lemon-and-Cumin-Grilled Fish
43   Fresh Yogurt-Cucumber Soup with Coriander and Cumin
45   Cumin-Curry Tuna Salad with Dates and Chickpeas
46   Cumin-Carrot Soup with Almonds and Nigella
47   Cumin Toasted Chicken Drumsticks with Honey
48   Nan with Cumin, Raisins, and Onions

SIMPLY SPICY

51   **WITH OR WITHOUT**
53   Spicy Pineapple Skewers
55   Pineapple with Minced Shrimp and Peanut Topping
56   Pepper Tandoori Potato Chips
57   Spicy Honey Bread
59   Spice-Dusted Avocado with Mango and Crab
61   Melon with Pepper
62   Oysters with Malay Masala and Cucumber Relish
63   Grilled Tuna with Zanzibar Spices
65   Spicy Deep-Fried Vegetables

PEPPER

73   **WHERE EVERY TRADE IS GOOD**
79   Indian Pepper Chicken
81   Spicy Beef Salad with Green Peppercorns
82   Pepper-Crusted Fish with Watercress and Spring Onion Sauce
83   Black Pepper Crabs
85   Cubeb Pepper Figs Cooked in Red Wine
86   Lemon Pepper Chicken
87   Chocolate Pepper Cookies

GINGER

	89	**SO GINGERLY**
	91	Grouper with Ginger and Spring Onions
	93	Goan Fish Cakes
	94	Stuffed Onions with Ginger and Lamb
	95	Carrots with Ginger and Soy Sauce
	96	Potato Croquettes with Ginger and Honey

CHILES

	99	**STEP OUTSIDE, SIR**
	103	Chicken Piri Piri
	104	Soothing Clove and Yogurt Dip
	105	Piri Piri Sauce
	106	Shrimp Piri Piri
	107	Chiles with Hot Tuna Stuffing
	108	Chili Potatoes
	109	Green Papaya Salad

CARDAMOM

	117	**I HAVE HEARD THE SONG OF CARDAMOM**
	121	Cardamom Mangoes
	122	Chicken Cardamom Masala with Cashews
	125	Bananas with Coconut and Cardamom
	126	Coconut Pancakes with Cardamom
	127	Aromatic Cardamom Lamb with Saffron Carrots

CURRIES

	129	**IT IS ALL IN THE MIX**
	131	**THE BEST CONFUSION I EVER HAD**
	137	Sor Patel
	138	Fish in Coconut Curry
	141	Rice Noodles with Squid, Shrimp, and Chicken
	142	Mussaman Curry Paste
	143	Slow-Cooked Leg of Lamb
	145	Kerala Spicy Beef Curry
	146	Lamb Korma
	147	Coconut Curry Cake
	149	Mussaman Beef Curry

CORIANDER

151	**IN GOOD TASTE**
153	Kerala Jewish Fish with Green Herbs and Spices
154	Pearl Onions with Coriander and Mint
155	Coriander and Mint Sauce
156	Coriander Lamb Skewers with Grilled Peppers
157	Squab with Coriander, Cumin, and Apricots
159	Grilled Green Fish with Red Rice
160	Green Curry with Chicken
161	Green Curry Paste
162	Red Coconut Rice

TURMERIC

175	**WHY GOD TAKES A BATH**
179	**WAITING FOR MY BABI**
183	Balinese Suckling Pig
185	Mauritian "Bouillabaisse"
187	Simple Shellfish Stock
188	Réunionnaise Yellow Chicken and Banana Curry
189	Yellow Rice
191	Oven-Baked Cape Malay Curry

LEMONGRASS

193	**STEP ON THE GRASS**
195	Steamed Fish with Lemongrass and Herbs
197	Pork and Shrimp Meatballs with Lemongrass and Ginger
199	Mussels with Lemongrass, Chiles, and Holy Basil
200	Spicy Lemongrass Fish Cakes
201	Lemongrass-Coconut Soup with Shrimp
203	Lemongrass Tea
204	Coconut Panna Cotta with Lemongrass, Turmeric, and Passion Fruit

TAMARIND

207	**DANGER AHEAD**
209	Tamarind-Glazed Fruits with Star Anise
210	Entrecôte with Onion, Ginger, and Tamarind
211	Sweet-and-Sour Vegetable Soup with Peanuts
213	**ZANZIBAR — LIFE AQUATIC**
217	Turmeric Squid with Tamarind Sauce
219	Octopus Curry
220	Shrimp Balls with Tamarind Sauce

NUTMEG & CLOVES

235	**MISSIONARY OF SPICES**	
241	Persian Rice Pilaf with Saffron and Pomegranates	
242	Farmer's Sausage with Cloves and Coriander	
243	Rice Pilau with Cashews and Coriander	
245	Kingfish with Orange, Cloves, and Ginger	
246	Nutmeg-and-Ginger Spinach Soup with Soy Sauce–Baked Sweet Potato	
247	Stewed Oxtail with Nutmeg Sauce	

VANILLA

249	**HEAVEN CAN'T WAIT**
253	Trout with Rum and Vanilla
255	Curried Duck with Vanilla
256	Flambéed Bananas with Vanilla and Rum Caramel
257	Bourbon Vanilla Ice Cream

CINNAMON

259	**COOKING UNDER PRESSURE**
263	Rice Flour Dumplings in Sweet Coconut-Cinnamon Sauce
264	Grilled Sirloin with Pepper and Cinnamon
265	Lamb with Spinach and Cinnamon
267	Rhum Arrangé
268	Oranges with Cinnamon
269	Zanzibar Coffee
271	Baked Almond Custard with Cinnamon and Raisins

272	Sources: Where to Buy Your Spices
273	Further Reading
274	Chart of Scoville Units
275	Table of Equivalents
276	Thank You
277	Index

INTRODUCTION

By lunchtime on my second day in Thailand, my sunglasses had already been at the bottom of the sea for several hours, having gracefully but inconveniently slipped off my sun lotion–shining nose and into the azure-blue ocean just before the boat landed on the beach. The tropical sun was so bright that I could hardly see. Through my squinting eyes, the waiter who brought me lunch was no more than a silhouette, and the surroundings were tropical but nondescript, with all the culturally and geographically defining details blurred. Like overexposed film, the whole scene had a dreamlike vagueness to it.

My lunch was a simple fish and vegetable curry: vegetables, fish, and spices cooked in coconut milk. When I started eating, I allowed my eyes some rest, and with my eyes closed, I savored the flavors of a country that was still new to me. The dish allowed me to taste what my eyes were too sore to see, and the food instilled in me a feeling of really being in Thailand. The aromatic lemongrass and the freshness from the signature Thai combination of soapy cilantro and fresh lime juice left no doubt of where I was.

Still, I had a strong feeling of recognition. The sweet spiciness from the coriander and cumin in the green curry paste reminded me of encounters with Arabic and Persian cuisines, and the rich, sweetish coconuts, infused with a plethora of seemingly contradictory flavors, had the same effortless elegance I had enjoyed in similar surroundings on the island of Zanzibar, thousands of miles away. The reinvigorating bite from the tiny red-hot chile peppers was very much like what you get when tasting food from Mozambique and southern India. The fresh galangal and kaffir lime leaves could just as easily have been served in Malaysia. With some small but all-important adjustments, I could have been anywhere along the Indian Ocean.

The Indian Ocean — stretching from South Africa, lining the coasts of eastern Africa, the Arabian Peninsula, Iran, Pakistan, India, Myanmar, Thailand, Malaysia, and Indonesia, all the way to the western coast of Australia — is a world of its own. The ocean belongs to so many peoples, so many countries and cultures, that it is easy to think that they do not have much in common apart from the body of water that separates them. But there is more to an ocean than just water, and the elements that keep us apart can also

A woman trader waiting for customers at the spice and vegetable market in Ubud, Bali.

bring us together. For millennia, the vast Indian Ocean has been the stage for hazardous explorations and vigorous trading, a trading route for spices that connected peoples and cultures, giving common flavors to the otherwise disparate food traditions of the countries around the ocean. Whether in a restaurant in Durban, South Africa; a food stall in Zanzibar; a home in Kerala, India; or on a remote island off the coast of Thailand, there are many similarities. I like to think of the different cooking styles of the Indian Ocean as clearly distinct but comprehensible dialects within one large and complex language.

It was the quest for spices that made the world as we know it. Had there been no spice trade, Marco Polo would not have known where to go — or why to go; Columbus would not have seen any reason to search for the seaway to India; and several of the world's great civilizations — including those of the West, one could argue — would simply not have existed as we know them today. Almost all of history's great societies were founded on trade, and the spices of the Indian Ocean were among the first global commodities. The spices that did not originate in the region were soon to be cultivated in the fertile tropical climate around the ocean.

More than anything else, the spices of the Indian Ocean made food what it is today. Whenever you grind pepper over your steak or add a pinch of saffron to make the French bouillabaisse fiery red, tuck into a temperamental curry or sprinkle cinnamon over your cappuccino, whenever your appetite is whetted by the sweet aromas of vanilla from the ice cream parlor, it is a testimony to the omnipresence of spices that were once so rare and expensive that men would risk their lives, and countries would risk their very existence, in the struggle to get hold of them. One may find oneself musing that perhaps the reason we take spices for granted is not that man won the battle, but, rather, that man was conquered by spices, lured to expose his weaknesses and follies and venture beyond the limits of the known world, thereby realizing, for better or worse, that the world and humankind are one.

I first experienced the cooking of the Indian Ocean on the island of Zanzibar, off the coast of Tanzania, in 1992, and the first sweet smell of cloves lingering over the island and the sensation of the intense yet gentle flavors of Swahili cooking will always be a part of me. I can leave the island longing for the conveniences of life in the developed North, where shopping for groceries does not feel like an expedition, and I never, ever, have to haggle with the police. But once I am home again, I feel that a part of me is left behind — shoulders up, a quicker pace of life, not constantly using all my senses to navigate everyday life. And I always return.

Since I first caught the whiff of spices and saw the reflection of the sun dancing in the waves of the Indian Ocean, I have traveled extensively in the region, from South Africa to Indonesia. I have worked and lived in Zimbabwe, Mozambique, and South Africa, and for a short period I lived on Zanzibar, where I wrote my first food-related articles, and, more important, learned enough Swahili to do a decent bit of haggling and enough cooking to invite friends over for dinner without embarrassment.

Writing and researching *Where Flavor Was Born* has been a long and laborious process — and a dream come true. I have spent the last three years traveling to eleven of the countries around the Indian Ocean — Indonesia, Malaysia, Thailand, India, Oman, Egypt, Réunion Island (still a French overseas *département*), Mauritius, Tanzania, Mozambique, and South Africa — trying to go beyond the hotel restaurants, in order to find the soul of the local cooking. I have sought out all kinds of people who could help me to broaden my perspective: home cooks, chefs, food historians, and street vendors.

I have tried to seek out meeting points, old trading posts where some of the ambience of the spice trade can still be found. And in many of the places I have visited, I have sought out minorities, for it is often there that the creative confluence of different traditions can be seen most clearly. The cooking of Muslims of southern Thailand is clearly Thai, but at the same time there is also a familiarity with other Muslim communities in the region. In Kerala, India, I was able to visit the place where two of the most important spices, pepper and cardamom, originated, and also to get to know a society most definitely Indian, but with strong influences from large Christian and Muslim minorities and a small but historically important Jewish community. And then there are the places that are nothing but minorities and the meeting of cultures. Zanzibar, Mauritius, Réunion, and South Africa are, each in their own way, melting pots, or salad bowls, or, perhaps more accurately, masalas of people and cultures, each group bringing its own flavors to the table and sharing them with others, who might use them in vastly different ways.

The cooking of the Indian Ocean has many temperaments but only one soul, and the soul is to be found in the spices. In *Where Flavor Was Born*, the different cuisines come together for the first time. The similarities are so many and the familiarities among some dishes so strong that it is often hard to tell them apart.

I hope this book can inspire you to travel to these fantastic places. But most of all I hope that you will be inspired to investigate, discover, or rediscover the spices you already know, to use them in new ways. Why not try to use pepper in a dessert, as they do in South Africa, where the chocolate chip cookies actually bite back?

A few of the ingredients in the book may be hard to come by — I have listed specialty stores and mail-order sources that should be able to help you — but the central ingredients, the basic spices, are all widely available. They also keep well — that is the reason behind their success as a commodity in earlier times. And, by investigating the soul of the spices, getting to know their flavors and histories, you will discover that it is easier to improvise and find suitable replacements if one ingredient is lacking for some reason.

The cooking techniques called for in this book vary, but they are related and always simple. Some cuisines call for stews that are simmered for a long time to extract the full depth of flavor from the spices, while others may use the same spices in a quick stir-fry, bringing out other flavors, a different temperament.

The more I learn about the cooking of the Indian Ocean and the spices at the heart of the cooking, the more I appreciate its openness and flexibility. I strongly believe that cooking is more about inspiration and interpretation than authority and authenticity. When you or I re-create a dish from Zanzibar or Malaysia or Bali, it will not taste the same as it did in its place of origin. Our ingredients are different: the chicken we use is store-bought — it has not lived in a backyard, eating scraps; the ginger is not fresh from our own garden, but may have traveled a long way. Our utensils are machine-made, and our ovens are more likely to be powered by electricity or propane gas than firewood. Our hands and bodies confront the tasks before us in ways that are both individually and culturally conditioned, and probably quite different from those of a cook in the place where the recipe originated.

That said, once we get the hang of it, when we manage to establish a trustful relationship between ourselves and the cooking we are about to commit — that fine sense of communication between hands, palate, and mind — then the struggle for "authenticity" is no longer the most important. What is important is to create a dish or a meal that tastes good and resonates the idea of the dish. There are hundreds, if not thousands, of different ways to make a *pilau*, for example, dramatic or minuscule variations according to where it comes from and who makes it. Perhaps tomorrow you will make a *pilau* that will suit your palate perfectly, with your own little twist, a dish that will partake in a culinary tradition that has always been on the move, and will always continue to be so.

I believe that such freedom and openness extend beyond just the cooking. I enjoy combining dishes from different places in the region — an Egyptian salad, a main course from India, and a side dish from South Africa — but I also like to combine the cooking of the Indian Ocean with that of other areas if I think they go well together. When grilling a steak, I may choose to flavor it the way they do in Oman, with cinnamon and pepper, but serve it much the same way people in Western Europe and the United States do: with potatoes, a fresh green salad, a French-style sauce, and a good hearty glass of red wine. It is hardly how it would be presented in Oman, but it is wonderful nevertheless. You cannot call this crossover cooking, because there is no line to cross. Flavor was born when flavor started to travel. And it lives because it continues to do so.

Where Flavor Was Born is a combined cookbook, travelogue, introduction to an exciting region, and the story of the spices we all use in our everyday cooking — and how these spices have affected our common history. It is meant as an encouragement to travel and to experience the world, but most of all, to bring the world into your kitchen.

A man drinking coffee at a market in Ubud, Bali. All around the Indian Ocean, coffee is often spiked with spices — cardamom, cinnamon, or ginger, or a combination.

Spices are, and have always been, global commodities. Therefore, not all the spices typical of the Indian Ocean originated there, and some of the spices that are indigenous to the region are not much used in everyday cooking. (For spice shops and online sources, see page 272.)

How to buy, store, and treat spices is crucial. Most spices have extremely fragile "top notes" that will disappear soon after harvesting or grinding. Common to all spices is that, once cured or dried, they should be kept in an airtight container and not be exposed to light.

What constitutes a spice is still, after more than two thousand years, open to debate. Spices can be fruits, seeds, rhizomes, roots, bark, flower buds, pods, herbs, or, as is the case with tamarind, the pulp inside a pod surrounding the seeds. Whether or not something is a spice may depend on usage: A fresh red paprika pepper is a fruit used as a vegetable and is not, in itself, considered a spice. Once dried and ground, though, it is undoubtedly considered as such. But processing is not the only thing that determines the status of a spice. Although it is true that most spices are processed in some way, they do not have to be. It is natural to view a bird's-eye chile, botanically a close relative of the red paprika pepper, as a spice even when it has just been picked, and fresh ginger is just as important as a spice as the dried and powdered stuff. Coriander seeds are spices and fresh coriander (cilantro) is an herb, but when used together, as in a Thai green curry paste, they complete each other and become interchangeable. And what, really, is lemongrass?

The original Latin name for spices, *species*, means nothing more than "of a specific kind." It later came to mean "goods" or "merchandise," so one wide and well-rooted definition of spices may be a flavoring commodity that is or has been traded — that has been a part of the spice trade, which indeed is the main topic of this book. That the use of certain spices has changed over time, as the spices reached new users with different ideas, or as modern greenhouse technology and changes in the trade routes made it possible to use both the dried and the fresh spice, as with ginger and lemongrass, is just an added bonus. This book is meant, to paraphrase Darwin, as an investigation into the origin of spices, and in order to do just that, it is also important to see how they have evolved.

A typical presentation of spices for a Balinese curry. On Bali, the aesthetic side of cooking is tremendously important; even the prep should look beautiful. Clockwise from top left: black peppercorns, kaffir lime leaves, red chile, coriander seeds, lemongrass, ginger, red chiles, nutmeg, cinnamon, turmeric, galangal.

ANISEED

The dried seed of an herb native to the Middle East, aniseed has a distinct licorice flavor and is said to have digestive properties. The seeds release their flavors easily when cooked and can therefore be used whole. Aniseed should always be bought whole, as ground anise will lose its flavor quickly.

CARDAMOM

Cardamom pods contain three small chambers, each with two to six seeds inside. They can be green, off-white, or dark brown. The green is the "normal" cardamom. White cardamom pods have gone through an artificial bleaching process. The larger brown cardamom is technically not the same type but a close relative. It is sometimes referred to as bastard cardamom, which is rather unfair, as it is simply another member of the family, less pungent and sweet but still very good in savory dishes.

It is never a good idea to buy ground cardamom. As with most spices, the aromas are fragile and the fine top notes are lost relatively soon after grinding. I crush whole cardamom pods using a mortar and pestle, removing the husks as I go along. In many curries and sauces, it is not necessary to crush or grind the pods; bruising them using the botton of a pot or a heavy skillet, or simply your hands, is enough to open them up, and they will release their fine flavor as they cook.

CHILES AND CHILI

All chiles originated in the Americas, but once they reached India and the rest of the Indian Ocean at the beginning of the sixteenth century, they became an integral part of the cuisines of the region. Today, India is the world's largest producer of chiles.

The world of chiles is a world of its own, containing hundreds of different varieties with different flavors and vastly different levels of pungency and hotness. The level of hotness is determined by the presence of the crystalline substance capsaicin, which is measured in Scoville units (see page 274). The heat can be anything from around 200 Scoville units for mild peperoncini chiles or 600 for El Paso chiles to around 75,000 for Thai chiles, 100,000 for bird's-eye chiles, and the record 500,000 for a special type of habanero called Red Savino. It is advisable to wear protective gloves whenever working with chiles. Capsaicin is found mainly in the seeds and the white, fleshy material that connects the seeds to the fruit; hence the pungency level can be reduced drastically by removing these. Crossbreeding and regional differences make it difficult to assess the pungency merely by looking at a chile, or even knowing the name of the variety; it is therefore advisable to always add chiles a little at a time. If you experience a painful capsaicin overdose, drinking water will not help much — it can even make it worse. The best remedy is a spoonful of yogurt or sugar.

Green chiles are unripe; red chiles are ripe and have a sweeter flavor (some chiles turn yellow, brown, purple, or black). Fresh chiles should be smooth and shiny and firm. If they are wrinkly and soft, it can mean that they have started to rot or decompose from the inside. Smaller chiles tend to be hotter than larger specimens of the same type and batch.

Chili powder is ground dried chiles, often mixed with paprika and salt, and sometimes other spices and herbs. There is no standard for chili powder, and it can be difficult to find out how it is composed just from looking at the packaging; when you find one you like, stick to it. I like to use a relatively pure, hot, but otherwise "neutral" chili powder. If I want it to be milder, I mix it with some paprika.

Chile flakes, or crushed red pepper flakes, are chopped, crushed, or coarsely ground dried chiles that can be used much the same way as chili powder. They have longer durability and you can be sure that they are not mixed with other spices. As with chiles, the hotness of chile pepper flakes varies greatly: add a little at a time.

CINNAMON AND CASSIA

Cinnamon and cassia are both the dried bark of tropical trees, and they are both marketed as cinnamon – in powdered form, the two are often blended. The distinction is important, as true cinnamon has a sweet, woody, mild flavor, whereas cassia is somewhat more obtrusive, highly perfumed, and slightly pungent.

Whole cinnamon is most frequently found in rolled-up quills that look like sticks at first, but on closer inspection turn out to be made from many layers of paper-thin bark. Cassia bark, from larger trees, is thicker. The two can usually be used interchangeably, but in desserts and other mild dishes, the finer aroma of true cinnamon is preferable. Cinnamon and cassia lose most of the top notes soon after grinding, so I suggest buying whole sticks or quills and crushing them in a spice grinder or using a mortar and pestle – or using them whole in soups. While commercially ground cinnamon tends to be finely powdered, I prefer to coarsely grind or crush the spice; small pieces of cooked cinnamon in a stew can be quite pleasant "sweet explosions." I do not recommend using ground cinnamon, but if that is your only option, make sure the cinnamon is newly bought.

CLOVES

Cloves are dried unripe flower buds with a high concentration of essential oils. The oils are pungent, with a soothing, almost numbing effect, and can overpower other flavors. Cloves should always be used in moderation. Extracted clove oil was once prescribed for toothache and is still sometimes used as a mild anesthetic. Cloves can be used whole or ground; they keep well until crushed or ground.

Cloves originated on the Spice Islands of the Moluccas, in what is now Indonesia. Since the nineteenth century, Indonesia has shared the role of top producer with Zanzibar, off the coast of Tanzania in East Africa.

CORIANDER

Coriander seeds are small and round, with a papery husk. In ancient Greece, the spice was thought to resemble a bedbug — *corys* is Greek for "bug." The seeds have a sweet, dusty flavor and go particularly well with fish. As coriander combines well with both sweet and pungent spices, it is often used in spice mixtures, where it serves to amalgamate other flavors, rather than to stand out itself. When you want a distinct coriander flavor, I suggest you crush the seeds lightly and sprinkle them over the dish just before serving.

Fresh coriander — often sold under its Spanish name, *cilantro* — is highly popular in Thai and Indian, as well as Southwestern American, Mexican, and Peruvian, cooking and has a strong, fresh taste that is often described as "soapy." The flavor, although by no means discreet, is fragile, and will evaporate when boiled. It's best to buy fresh coriander on the root, preferably in a pot with some soil.

Coriander roots have a mild, slightly sweet flavor and are often used in spice pastes. Coriander grows well in temperate to tropical climates, and where it is grown seems of little importance to the quality.

CUBEB PEPPER

Cubeb pepper, or tailed pepper, is an Indonesian relative of the common black pepper from India. The peppercorns are slightly larger than regular peppercorns, with a short stalk at one end, making them look slightly like a small cartoon bubble. They do not have a white core. Cubeb is hot and pungent, with a smoky pinelike flavor. It can be added, in small quantities, to black pepper in all dishes where black pepper is used, for a more interesting flavor.

CUMIN

The dried seed of an herb in the parsley family, cumin probably originated in the Mediterranean region but is now grown all over the world, mainly in temperate and subtropical areas. It is one of the most important spices in Middle Eastern cooking, where it is the main flavoring for a whole range of stews and meat and vegetable dishes, and it is also a frequent and prominent component in Middle Eastern and Indian spice mixtures; it is common but less prominent in Far Eastern cooking.

The flavor of cumin blends well with other flavors during cooking, so that it is difficult to distinguish; if you want a distinct cumin flavor, I suggest adding a sprinkle of freshly ground cumin seeds just before serving. Cumin is also sold under its Indian name, *jeerah*.

Whole cumin seeds yield a milder flavor than ground cumin. Ground cumin loses its flavor quickly and can develop a dusty, slightly bitter taste. I suggest only buying whole cumin seeds.

CURRY LEAF

The young green leaflets of a small tree remotely related to the citrus tree, curry leaves are highly aromatic, with a flavor that, like that of allspice, may be reminiscent of several spices, including cumin, pepper, fenugreek, and dried lime. In French-speaking areas around the Indian Ocean, the leaf is referred to as *kari-poulet*, "chicken curry," as its acrid flavor adds an interesting touch to the local curry dishes. Use fresh curry leaves if you can find them. Dried leaves may also be used, but they tend to lose their flavor when exposed to air, so keep them in an airtight container.

GALANGAL

There are two main types of galangal. Greater galangal, which is the most popular variety, originated on the island of Java, in what is now Indonesia. It has a sharp, fresh flavor and is popular in Thai, Malaysian, and Indonesian cooking. Lesser galangal, which originated in China, is mostly used for medicinal purposes. A third variety of galangal, *kenchur*, has a mild, dusty, peppery flavor and is popular in Balinese cooking.

Galangal is closely related to ginger. Fresh galangal, at least greater galangal, is available in many Asian markets. It has paler skin than ginger and a similar knotty shape, and it should be plump and firm. Before using, scrape off the skin with a spoon or a knife, then chop or grate. Dried sliced galangal lacks the same freshness but keeps well. Powdered dried galangal loses its flavor quickly.

GINGER

Ginger is the rhizome of a lush tropical plant. The flavor is highly pungent, with a camphorous note and tangy freshness, more cooling than hot. It has been credited with a whole range of medicinal qualities: it is said to alleviate indigestion, help circulation, and boost the immune system.

Fresh ginger has a knotty shape, with lots of "fingers," so the whole rhizome resembles a strange-shaped hand. It should be plump and firm, and the fibrous flesh should be creamy or white. Fresh ginger keeps well when stored in a dark, cool place. Some supermarkets offer minced fresh ginger, but many of the volatile top notes and much of the aroma are lost soon after chopping or mincing — a high price to pay for being spared the simple job of scraping and chopping or grating.

A moderate dose of fresh ginger is a good way to ensure the freshness of a dish and to neutralize "fishy" or off flavors in seafood dishes. For extra pungency and freshness, add a small amount of freshly grated or chopped ginger to a dish just before serving. The best fresh ginger is grown on Bali and Jamaica.

Dried ginger has a very different flavor; it is less fresh tasting, often sweeter, with more lemonlike aromas, and sometimes quite hot. Ground ginger has limited durability and should always be stored in an airtight container, away from light. The best ground ginger comes from Kerala, India.

Anyone who has tried to peel fresh ginger will have seen that there is a whole lot of waste. Trying to get around all the wobbly parts with a knife or a peeler can reduce the rhizome by as much as a third. But if you use a spoon instead of a knife and simply scrape off the thin skin, it is quick and simple, with hardly any loss.

Ginger can also be preserved or pickled in syrupy or acidic solutions. These preparations are normally made with younger, less fibrous ginger rhizomes and are often preferred in Eastern desserts.

KAFFIR LIME

Kaffir lime, or *makrut* lime, is a tropical evergreen tree closely related to the ordinary lime, with similar-looking fruits, albeit more bumpy and wrinkled. However, unlike that of lime and other citrus fruits, the juice of the kaffir lime is not of much interest. The flavor is to be found in the zest and the leaves. The grated zest is used in East Asian fish and poultry dishes; the leaves are used in seafood dishes, soups, salads, and curry pastes, such as the Thai green curry paste. The leaves are normally removed before serving or placed on the side of the dish, but they can also be eaten; in that case, they must be very finely shredded. If fresh lime leaves cannot be found, dried leaves may be used in curry pastes and soups but not in salads; how much flavor they have depends on how they were processed.

LEMONGRASS

Lemongrass is a perennial tropical grass that grows in clusters. When bruised, it gives off a sweet lemony smell. The highest concentration of flavor can be found in the bottom part of the two- to three-foot-long stem, and it is common to discard the outer husks and the top green parts. To release the flavor, lemongrass should be bruised and chopped before adding it to a dish. For soups, the best method is to bruise it and tie it into a knot, then remove just before serving. Finely sliced lemongrass can be used in salads and stir-fries.

Lemongrass loses most of its flavor upon drying, and dried is not a good substitute for fresh lemongrass. If your supply of lemongrass is unreliable, it can be preserved by wrapping it tightly in foil and freezing, or by bruising it and placing it in a bottle of vinegar.

NUTMEG AND MACE

Nutmeg and mace are the two spices found inside the nutmeg fruit, from a tropical tree that, like cloves, originated on the Spice Islands of the Moluccas in what is now Indonesia. Along with Granada, those islands are still the main area of production. The nutmeg is the kernel of the seed, while mace is the aril, or cap, surrounding it.

Once dried, nutmeg is hard and dull brown; mace is bright red when fresh, reddish brown when dried. While nutmeg and mace share much of the same warm, intensely aromatic flavor, mace is often considered superior, with more earthy notes. Both are almost always used sparingly in spice mixtures, rarely as the main flavoring ingredient.

Nutmeg is the hardest of all spices and must be grated rather than crushed. It is also the most volatile of all spices; its flavor disappears soon after grating. Mace keeps somewhat better, but it is also best bought whole (see Sources, page 272).

PAPRIKA

Paprika is a powder made from several different types of capsicums, various peppers and chiles. The color varies widely from dark red to orange, and the presence of the heat element capsaicin is also far from constant, although true paprika should not be particularly hot. It is used both for its flavor — the best paprika is relatively mild, with a sweet, earthy taste — and for its lovely red color. Ground paprika loses its color and flavor easily when exposed to air and light. It should be bought in small quantities and kept in airtight containers in a dark place. Traditionally the best paprika was made in Hungary and Spain, but today Israel is also an important producer. Paprika is often used in chili powder mixtures.

PEPPER

"The king of spices" originated in southern India, where the best pepper is still produced. Black, white, and green peppercorns are all the fruit, or berries, of the same climbing plant, *Piper nigrum*, but have undergone different treatments.

Black peppercorns are picked while still green and unripe, then dried and cured in the sun. An enzymatic process renders them black and also helps develop the flavor of the black husk surrounding the white seed inside. Black pepper is a great flavor enhancer and can be used in both sweet and savory dishes.

Green peppercorns are also unripe berries, but here the enzymatic process has been stopped, traditionally by brining or by boiling them for a short time to kill the enzyme; nowadays this is most often done by freeze-drying. They will wrinkle up like black peppercorns but retain an attractive green color and a fresher, somewhat less complex flavor. Fresh green peppercorns can be bought in some Asian markets. They are also sold packed in brine, often tasting more of the brine than of pepper.

White peppercorns are allowed to mature before being picked, and then the husks are removed before drying, either by soaking in water or by rubbing. Lacking the outer husk, white pepper has some of the pungency but little of the mouthwatering earthiness of black pepper. I find that the only reason to use white pepper instead of black is if you do not want black or gray specks in an otherwise white dish; most often I use black pepper.

All dried peppercorns are best kept whole until just before using. Using a pepper mill to grind the peppercorns is convenient; however, I find that a mortar and pestle allows me much more freedom in deciding how fine or coarse I would like the crushed pepper. Also note that dried green peppercorns, and many of the other peppercorns found in decorative blends of "mixed peppercorns," are quite soft and have a tendency to clog up pepper mills.

Long pepper is a relative of *Piper nigrum*. The up-to-2½-inch-long spike consists of a cluster of small seeds. It is generally hotter than black pepper but with a somewhat less complex flavor. In earlier times, long pepper was as popular as black pepper, or even more popular, but it is now of only marginal importance.

Pink peppercorns are from a completely different plant, native to South America, *Schinus molle*, not related to *Piper nigrum*. They have a sweet peppery flavor, but their main advantage is their attractive pink color.

Szechuan pepper, sometimes referred to as anise pepper, is also unrelated to *Piper nigrum*; it is the fruit of a small Chinese tree, the prickly ash. It is hot and pepperlike, often with an herby, lemony flavor. It does not taste much of anise, despite its alternative name.

STAR ANISE

Star anise is the most spectacularly beautiful of all spices, the star-shaped fruit of a small evergreen tree. The star is formed by eight seed-holding segments, each section split open to reveal one shiny seed. Unlike most seeds and their bearers, star anise seeds actually have far less taste than the fruit itself. Star anise is not related to aniseed, but it contains some of the same chemical components; the flavor is warmer, with a lingering licorice-like aftertaste. Star anise is a popular spice in East Asia, especially in pork and seafood dishes. When used in soups or other stock-based dishes, it is often left whole as a decorative element. The guest may place it on the side of the plate, or, if one is interested in a mouthwatering, warming, and almost numbing explosion of flavor at the end of the meal, the almost-reconstituted star anise may be sucked after eating the dish (or, as is often the case in China and other places in Asia, it may be reserved and used again later). Star anise is best bought whole. When used in spice mixtures, it may be crushed using a mortar and pestle or the flat side of a heavy knife.

TAMARIND

The tamarind tree is an evergreen tree native to Africa that later spread to East Asia. Today tamarind is an important element in, among others, Indian, Thai, and Malaysian cuisines. The fruits of the tamarind tree are long pods with attractively shiny seeds, but neither the pod itself nor the seeds are eaten — the pleasantly sour pulp is the only part that is used. It is one of the most important souring agents in tropical regions that are too hot for citrus trees to thrive. Very fresh tamarind pulp is light brown, but it oxidizes easily, and after being dried and processed, it is very dark brown to jet-black. Tamarind paste is concentrated tamarind pulp, and it must be used in much smaller quantities than the regular pulp; how concentrated the paste is varies greatly. When using unrefined and unstrained tamarind pulp, it is best to first moisten it in a little hot water and then to remove the seeds. If in a hurry, you can add the pulp directly to boiling liquid, but make sure to stir until it dissolves, and remove the seeds before serving.

TURMERIC

Turmeric is a rhizome related to ginger and galangal, but where the flavor of ginger is intense and the color is dull off-white or cream, turmeric is mild and earthy, with an intense orange color that must be said to be its main quality.

Turmeric is indigenous to southern Asia, but it no longer grows there in its wild form. Now found all over the regions around the Indian Ocean, it is used in cooking, for dying fabrics, and for medicinal purposes; it is an important part of traditional Indian ayurvedic medicine.

In countries where turmeric grows, it is often used fresh, either grated or finely chopped. Fresh turmeric has a mild and rather complex earthy flavor with some sweet notes. It does not have an even distribution of the pigment curcumin, and finely chopped fresh turmeric creates a nice color play when stirred into a dish just before serving. Dried turmeric can be bought whole, sliced, or powdered. Unlike the case for most spices, I actually prefer to buy powdered turmeric, as the whole or sliced dried varieties are rather fibrous and hard to crush or grind, and it is also hard to estimate the color content. Powdered, or ground, turmeric should be kept in an airtight container away from light. The best turmeric comes from Kerala, in south India, and the island of Réunion.

VANILLA

Vanilla, the cured long pod of a flower in the orchid family, is the "queen of spices." It originally came from Central America, but much of the best vanilla is now grown on Réunion and Madagascar, in the Indian Ocean. Vanilla is a popular flavoring agent in desserts, but, as the cooking in vanilla-producing countries shows, it is also useful in savory dishes, particularly with fatty fish or meats. When fresh, the pod is flavorless; the complex sweet aromas only develop after a prolonged curing process. When used in cooking, the pod is normally split in half and the black seeds inside scraped out to be added to custards or sauces; these tiny black spots show the presence of true vanilla. It is worth noting that although the pod itself is not edible, it contains much of the flavor; it may be cooked to impart flavor and removed just before serving, or reserved for later use.

Vanilla used to be extremely expensive, and great efforts were taken to reproduce its flavor, or to get the most flavor out of every pod. Today vanilla is still among the most expensive spices by weight, but good vanilla is highly aromatic and goes a long way. You would have to have a very strained budget to make significant savings by using vanilla extract or artificial vanillin, which is not made from vanilla but is a by-product of the cellulose industry.

The best vanilla is Bourbon vanilla, from the island of Réunion (previously Île de Bourbon, hence the name), or Tahitian vanilla. Look for soft, flexible, plump pods, preferably stored in airtight containers.

THE BEST OF THE REST

ALLSPICE

Allspice is the dried unripe berry of a West Indian tree. When Columbus was presented with the spice in 1492, he thought he had found pepper, and therefore allspice is still sometimes referred to as Jamaica pepper — but to the modern cook, for whom spices are not a rarity, the flavor is more similar to that of cloves, cinnamon, and nutmeg. Allspice is often used as a substitute for any of these spices, as well as in spice mixtures; or it may be ground together with black pepper for a milder, more aromatic flavor. Allspice is still mainly grown in the West Indies.

DILL

Dill originated in Europe, and it is not a spice of great importance around the Indian Ocean. However, dill seeds are sometimes used in Indian spice mixtures, adding a sweet, mild taste, more similar to coriander seeds than to fresh dill.

FENNEL

Fennel is indigenous to Europe, where it is most often grown as a vegetable, but fennel seeds are also popular in Indian and Malaysian cooking, lending a sweet licorice-like flavor to many traditional curries. Fennel seeds are also served with small hard candies as a digestive aid after a meal.

FENUGREEK

Fenugreek is the seed pod of a small annual herb in the pea family. The seeds are small, golden brown, and irregularly shaped, with a small furrow on one side. The aroma is sharp and bitter, with nutty undertones. Fenugreek should be used in moderation, but it can add an interesting dimension to curries and spice mixtures.

GARLIC

Garlic is used all around the Indian Ocean, mostly in limited quantities. Look for fresh, plump garlic cloves, with no trace of green sprouts. Because of a chemical process that occurs between two of the main components in garlic when the whole cloves are disrupted, the taste of minced garlic is more intense than chopped garlic.

Dried garlic has a much more concentrated and bitter flavor than fresh garlic, as does garlic that has begun to sprout; I avoid both. Convenient containers of minced or chopped garlic are becoming popular, but the taste is inferior to fresh garlic.

MUSTARD

Mustard is a European spice little used in the cooking of the Indian Ocean, apart from Indian cuisine, where the seeds are sometimes used in curries or with vegetables.

NIGELLA

Nigella is sometimes erroneously referred to as black cumin, a spice with which it shares few similarities. Nigella seeds are beautifully jet-black, tear shaped, and about $\frac{1}{10}$ inch long. Smelling somewhat of petroleum and with a slightly metallic, peppery aftertaste, nigella is always used in limited quantity, mostly for decorative purposes.

SAFFRON

Saffron is the name of the spice and an orange-red coloring agent found on the stigma of a crocus flower. Saffron originated in either Europe or Asia Minor. It is known as the world's most expensive spice, and for good reason: each plant has only three stigmas, and it takes nearly 100,000 stigmas to make one pound of pure saffron. On the other hand, the flavor and the color pigment are so strong that only a very small quantity is needed — seldom more than a pinch, or a third or half of a gram. The flavor is earthy, and it has a slightly "dry" and bitter taste; when used in excess, saffron can be overpowering and even induce headache or nosebleed. It is worth noting that because of its price and rarity, saffron, in the words of the first-century Roman natural philosopher Pliny, is "the most frequently falsified commodity." I use only saffron threads, or stigmas, not refined powdered saffron. The best saffron is produced in Iran, Kashmir, and Spain.

The night market on Zanzibar is one of my favorite places. During daytime, the Forodhani Gardens is just a sleepy part of town; at sunset, the hawkers come with their food stalls, and when night falls, it is buzzing with life and the best street food in Eastern Africa.

LEFT: The fish market in Stone Town is not for the faint of heart. The many different varieties of fish can be bewildering. RIGHT: The House of Wonders is one of the most impressive buildings in Stone Town. Built in a combination of Arabic, European, and local building styles as a ceremonial palace for the sultan, it became the seat of the colonial administration, then a party headquarters after the 1964 coup. It is now a museum.

Who knows what kind of trades have been going on under the Big Tree in Zanzibar's Stone Town? Once an island dependent on the slave trade, and later the world's biggest clove producer, Zanzibar is now turning into a favorite tourist destination. The Big Tree is where you go to buy a hammock or arrange a trip to one of many beaches.

CUMIN

"IT IS VERY HARD TO IMAGINE MIDDLE EASTERN COOKING WITHOUT THE WHIFF OF CUMIN THAT SEEMS TO BE EVERYWHERE."

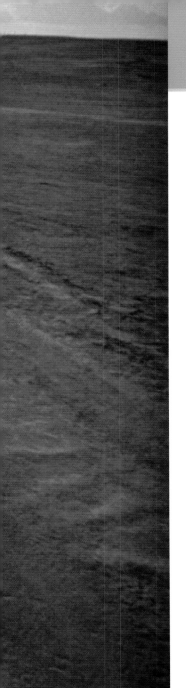

How the sand was won: Sometimes it can seem like the desert never ends, but with the help of a camel, the desert can be, if not conquered, at least survived.

DESERTED BY ALL BUT ONE

"Has flavor deserted me?" I wondered. After a few days in the outskirts of Egypt's Sinai Desert among tumbleweeds and Bedouins, I got the feeling that I was on a desert journey in more than one sense. Apart from the occasional date and strong, spicy coffee, I hadn't eaten anything that tasted of anything for days.

Others, of course, who had ventured here before me had not been so spoiled by choice as to complain about *how* things tasted; in the desert, food, water, and thus survival are not to be taken for granted.

I had intended to take the road less traveled, and what I had found was a vast emptiness. Far away on a cliff sat an old fortlike building. A few miles farther on, there was a small oasis with a cluster of date palms and a well with some not-so-clean water. And then there was not much more than sandstone and sand for hundreds of miles; land that had been used by caravans bearing spices and riches from faraway places to the markets of Alexandria and Jerusalem for millennia, but that now, in the post-camel age of other global trade routes, of airplanes and cars, is mainly just deserted.

So I turned back to where the desert meets the sea in the small village of Dahab, by the Red Sea. The Red Sea is a subsidiary of the Indian Ocean, and until the discovery of the seaway to India, it was one of the main routes from Europe to the East — a role it has regained over the last century and a half because of the Suez Canal. Dahab, however, on the eastern side of the Sinai, is quite unaffected by this. No ship makes this small, dusty village its port of call. State leaders and tourists do not flock here for peace talks and recreation, as they do to the sleek resort town of Sharm el-Sheikh a few miles to the south. In Dahab, Bedouins from nearby villages and hamlets come into town to stock up on food, gas, and water, with knives in their belts and camels or goats in the back of their incredibly beat-up pickup trucks. And fishermen bring their colorful catch to the market.

It is here that I experienced Egyptian cooking at its most basic, most pure. While Egyptian cuisine on the mainland is a showcase of Arab grandeur and hospitality, with an abundance of flavor and dozens of beautifully presented dishes laced with honey and spices, desert food is something quite different. The cooking of this small community eking out a living, squeezed between the desert and the sea, is predictably modest; survival, rather than opulence and innovation, has always been the main aim. There is fish, chicken, or camel meat to eat, depending on availability. There are also a couple of small vegetable gardens in Dahab, and, in addition, most courtyards sport a couple of tomato and cucumber vines that are fed a few drops of valuable water every evening — and in return give small mouthfuls that help one forget the harsh realities of desert life.

It did not take me many days to find my favorite restaurant in Dahab, and when there, I always ordered the same: a tomato and cucumber salad and the catch of the day. Not that I had much choice — that was about all they served, apart from the soggy French fries and sticky rice that did little to improve world cuisine.

But in these two dishes I had for lunch and dinner several days in a row, I sensed the essence of Egyptian cooking, and the transformative power of a single spice. The Egyptians love spices, and of all spices, they love cumin the most. In everything people had to forgo in Dahab, they could not live without cumin.

The salad was a simple affair: slices of cucumber, tomato, and onion, dressed with a little olive oil and a squeeze of lemon. I have had it hundreds of times all over the world, in the same kind of uninspired middle-of-the-road establishments that cannot even be bothered to make a proper dressing. But here there was one difference: just before serving, the salad was seasoned with a drizzle of homemade cumin salt. And that made all the difference. Such is the capacity of a single spice used the right way that it can make the rest of the ingredients taste more like themselves — the cucumber not only refreshingly watery and delicious but full of crispy confidence, the tomato not only sweet and tart but also complex and cooperative, and the onion not merely pungent but also revealing another, sweeter side. And it was the same with the fish — different fish nearly every day got the same treatment with this mild spice rub. It tasted not of honey and myrrh nor of the riches of the land. To me it tasted a whole lot better. I could sense a mild and sweet generosity, a human oasis on a small stretch of land between the desert and the sea.

Grilling fish at a market in Thailand, only a sprinkle of spices away from perfection.

TOMATO AND CUCUMBER SALAD
WITH CUMIN SALT

WHEN TRAVELING ON THE SINAI PENINSULA IN EGYPT, the way to determine whether a restaurant is good is to ask whether they serve the ubiquitous tomato and cucumber salad with a sprinkle of cumin or not. It is such an easy thing to do, but it makes all the difference. Most places use a mixture of cumin and salt, though some add a hint of coriander too, a small detail that makes the flavors sweeter and more playful. It is a salad that should be made immediately before serving to preserve the freshness of the vegetables, but the cumin salt can be made in advance. The salt is also good on chicken or white fish.

The transformative capacity of something as simple as cumin and salt makes this simple salad, which otherwise would be bordering on the boring, an interesting and nuanced taste experience. In Egypt, this is typically served as a starter, but I find that it works just as well as a side to other spicy dishes — and if you don't mind mixing food from different parts of the region, the fresh vegetables and the sweet cumin can be refreshing and soothing together with the flaming-hot dishes from India or Mozambique.

Typically the salad is arranged on serving plates, not mixed in a bowl, and just sprinkled with oil, lemon juice, and the cumin salt.

In Dahab, Egypt, where I had this first, the cumin, as in much of the Middle East, is relatively mild. The same mild cumin can be found in the West too, particularly in Asian shops. Unfortunately, some specialty stores stock a super-concentrated, super-cleaned variety that lacks much of the mild sweetness that makes cumin so good. If the cumin you have bought seems super-strong, you might want to dry-roast it for 5 to 7 minutes, in this case not just to release the flavor, but also to make it milder.

Serves 4 as a starter or side dish

1 to 2	tablespoons cumin seeds
2 to 3	tablespoons coarse sea salt
1	large cucumber, peeled and sliced
4 to 6	tomatoes, sliced
1	large onion, preferably a mild variety, sliced
¼	cup olive oil
¼	cup fresh lemon juice, or more to taste

1 Dry-roast the cumin in a small skillet over medium-high heat, stirring frequently, for 1 to 2 minutes, until fragrant. Using a mortar and pestle, coarsely grind the cumin seeds with the salt. The salt and cumin should not be crushed to a fine powder — allow for a little bit of texture. (If you don't have a mortar and pestle, you can mix the cumin and salt using your hands.)

2 Arrange the cucumber, tomatoes, and onion slices on four plates. Drizzle with the olive oil and lemon juice. Sprinkle the salads with a little of the cumin salt, and serve the rest in a small bowl on the side.

VARIATION *The cumin salt is a wonderful way to give flavor to simple steamed fish. You could also serve hard-cooked quail eggs dipped into cumin salt as a snack.*

LEMON-AND-CUMIN-GRILLED FISH

EGYPT **MIDDLE EAST**

Serves 2 as a main course

2	1-pound fish, cleaned, scaled, rinsed, and patted dry
2	tablespoons cumin seeds
2	cloves garlic, chopped
2	teaspoons coarse sea salt
2	tablespoons olive oil, plus more for serving
10	thin lemon slices, plus lemon wedges for serving
	Chopped mint or cilantro (fresh coriander) for garnish

THIS IS A DISH THAT EXISTS IN SEVERAL VERSIONS all over the cumin-loving Middle East. I prefer a simple version with cumin and lemon, but it can be expanded or elaborated upon to include paprika, chili powder, and coriander seeds. When grilling the fish, both the lemon and the skin of the fish should be slightly charred.

I find that this recipe works well with fish such as scrod, red snapper, trout, and tilapia. A tropical fish with relatively thick skin is the best choice.

1 Light a grill or preheat the broiler.

2 Rinse the fish in cold water. Remove the gills using a sharp knife, and make sure the cavity is clean, without traces of intestines or blood. Pat dry using a paper towel.

3 Dry-roast the cumin in a small skillet over medium-high heat, stirring frequently, for 1 to 2 minutes, until fragrant. Lightly crush using a mortar and pestle. Add the garlic and salt and mix well, but leave the texture somewhat coarse.

4 Using a sharp knife, cut a few slashes into the skin on both sides of the fish. Rub the fish with the cumin mixture, making sure to rub as much of the mixture as possible inside the slits. Brush with 2 tablespoons olive oil. Place 1 lemon slice inside the cavity of each fish, and place 2 on either side of each fish. Secure them with cotton string or wire, if necessary.

5 Grill the fish over high heat for 4 to 5 minutes on each side. Or arrange on the broiler pan and broil as close to the heating element as possible, turning once, for the same amount of time. The lemon slices and the exposed parts of the fish should be charred, but make sure the fish does not burn. Test for doneness by inserting a sharp knife or a fork into the thickest part of the fish; if it comes out warm, the fish is done. If necessary, move to a cooler part of the grill, or lower the broiler pan, and cook for a couple more minutes.

6 Garnish with mint and serve with olive oil and lemon wedges.

NOTE *If you cannot find small whole fish, you may use fillets, preferably skin on — or you will have to protect the fish with foil. You can cook the fillets in a grill pan or under the broiler.*

FRESH YOGURT-CUCUMBER SOUP
WITH CORIANDER AND CUMIN

YOU CAN MAKE THIS SOUP IN JUST A COUPLE OF MINUTES. You can serve it either as a starter or as a soothing side dish if the main course is very hot. Serve with toasted country bread or nan (such as one of the variations on page 48).

Serves 4 as a starter

1 Combine the yogurt, cucumber, tomatoes, coriander and cumin seeds, cilantro, lime juice, and lemongrass (if using) in a blender and pulse until almost smooth. Season with salt to taste. Cover and refrigerate for at least 30 minutes, or up to 1 day, before serving.

2 Garnish with cilantro leaves, onion, and paprika (if desired).

VARIATION *This is a dish that can easily be expanded by adding some cooked fish, such as salmon, or dusted with paprika powder, chili powder, salt, and a hint of cinnamon and baked.*

2 ½	cups plain full-fat yogurt
1	cucumber, peeled and chopped
2	tomatoes, finely chopped
2	teaspoons coriander seeds, crushed
2	teaspoons cumin seeds, crushed, or more to taste
¼	cup finely chopped cilantro (fresh coriander), plus whole leaves for garnish
3 to 4	tablespoons fresh lime juice
1	tablespoon finely chopped lemongrass (optional)
	Fine sea salt
	Finely chopped onion for garnish
	Paprika for garnish (optional)

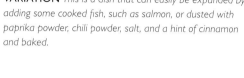

CUMIN-CURRY TUNA SALAD
WITH DATES AND CHICKPEAS

THE WATERS OFF THE COAST OF OMAN are one of the last areas where tuna is still relatively common, and in the port of Muscat, it is still a part of everyday life to see the fishermen showing off their catch, bragging about the almost supernatural strength of that most precious of game fish, with all the implications that has for their strength and manhood. Although Oman is today a relatively prosperous country, most of the valuable fish is exported.

Most Omani salads use purslane, a small salad green that is popular in the Arab world and the Indian subcontinent but not much used in the West. I substitute a variety of small-leaved salad greens, some bitter, like watercress and arugula, and some mild, like baby lettuce.

1 Season the tuna steaks on both sides with the ground cumin, curry, paprika, and salt to taste.

2 Heat a thin film of oil in a nonstick skillet over high heat. Add the tuna and cook for 2 minutes on each side. Transfer to a cutting board.

3 In a salad bowl, combine the remaining ingredients, except the flaky salt, and mix well. Adjust the seasoning, possibly using more lemon juice.

4 Transfer the salad to serving plates. Slice the tuna steaks and place on top of the salad. Sprinkle with flaky salt and serve.

NOTE *You can also make this salad using canned tuna. It is not as interesting but very good nonetheless. Just separate the tuna into large chunks and sprinkle with the ground cumin and curry.*

**Serves 6 to 8 as a starter,
2 as a main course**

2   8-ounce tuna steaks

2   teaspoons ground cumin seeds, plus
     2 teaspoons toasted cumin seeds

2   teaspoons curry powder, mild or
     hot, as preferred

1   teaspoon paprika

     Salt

     Oil for pan frying, such as canola

2   cups mixed salad greens

2   tomatoes, cut into strips

1   onion, sliced

1   large mild red chile, seeded and
     finely chopped

½   cup canned chickpeas,
     rinsed and drained

3   tablespoons chopped parsley
     (optional)

6   dates, pitted and quartered

⅓   cup olive oil

3 to 4   tablespoons fresh lemon juice,
          or to taste

     Flaky salt, such as *fleur de sel*
     or Maldon

CUMIN-CARROT SOUP
WITH ALMONDS AND NIGELLA

IRAN

Serves 4 as a starter

THE MARRIAGE BETWEEN SWEET CARROTS and sweetly aromatic cumin seems made in heaven. In reality, it is made in Egypt, Iran, and India. It makes a lot of sense that the two foods are closely related, the spice being the seeds of a cousin of the well-known root vegetable. The stylish jet-black nigella seeds are often incorrectly referred to as black cumin, as they bear a certain similarity to this rare variety of cumin. If you cannot find nigella, you can substitute cubeb pepper, black cumin, or black pepper, wildly different ways to preserve the visual appearance of the dish.

1	tablespoon unsalted butter or oil, such as canola
1	onion, chopped
1	pound carrots, chopped
2	teaspoons ground cumin seeds, or more to taste
1½	cups chicken stock
1	tablespoon slivered almonds
1 to 2	teaspoons nigella seeds
	Salt
	Yogurt for garnish (optional)
	Chopped cilantro (fresh coriander) for garnish (optional)

1 Melt the butter in a large saucepan over medium heat. Add the onion and sauté for 3 to 5 minutes, until soft. Add the carrots, cumin, and chicken stock, bring to a boil, and boil until the carrots are soft, about 15 minutes.

2 Meanwhile, dry-roast the almonds and nigella in a small skillet over medium-high heat, stirring frequently, until the almonds are starting to brown. Remove from the heat.

3 Transfer the carrots and stock to a blender and process until almost smooth. Season with more cumin (if desired) and salt to taste. Pour into bowls, sprinkle with the almonds and nigella, and garnish with yogurt and cilantro, if desired.

CUMIN TOASTED CHICKEN DRUMSTICKS
WITH HONEY

ALTHOUGH IT CAN EASILY BE SERVED AS A MAIN COURSE, I think of this flavorful dish as the perfect finger food. The honey is an important part of the dish, but I prefer to serve it on the side rather than dripping it over the chicken before serving. There is what seems like an awful lot of cumin in this recipe, and that is much of the point: the chicken should be saturated with spices (and some of them will fall off during baking).

Serve with sliced baby tomatoes, Potato Croquettes with Ginger and Honey (page 96), or Tomato and Cucumber Salad with Cumin Salt (page 41). However you choose to serve the drumsticks, they do need the company of some sliced tomatoes or a tomato salad.

**Makes 16 mouthfuls,
or a light main course for 4 to 6**

16	chicken drumsticks
	Salt
3 to 4	tablespoons cumin seeds
1	tablespoon coriander seeds (optional)
1	tablespoon finely chopped fresh ginger
1	tablespoon garam masala
1	tablespoon crushed red pepper flakes or chili powder, or more to taste
⅓	cup drained full-fat Greek-style yogurt
2	tablespoons fresh lemon juice, or as needed
2 to 3	tablespoons canola oil
⅓	cup runny, light honey
2	teaspoons ground ginger
	Sliced tomatoes or tomato salad for serving

1 Place the drumsticks in a bowl. Season them with a generous amount of salt, and set aside.

2 If desired, dry-roast the cumin and coriander seeds in a small skillet over medium-high heat, stirring frequently, for 1 to 2 minutes to release their flavors.

3 Combine the cumin and coriander with the ginger, garam masala, and red pepper flakes in a mortar and crush lightly with the pestle. Add the yogurt, lemon juice, and oil and mix well.

4 Rub the chicken drumsticks with the spice mixture. Cover and refrigerate for at least 2 hours, or up to 24 hours. Or, if you do not have that much time, add a little more lemon juice and marinate for 1 hour at room temperature.

5 Preheat the broiler. Place the chicken drumsticks on the broiling pan and broil for 15 minutes. Turn and broil for an additional 15 minutes, or until cooked through. Keep an eye on the chicken: the spice mixture should turn dark brown and may give off a little smoke, but it should not burn. To test that the chicken is cooked through, pierce a drumstick with a fork: if the juice runs clear, it is done; if the juices are still pink or red, the chicken will need more time under the broiler.

6 Combine the honey and ground ginger in a small serving bowl. Serve this dipping sauce with the drumsticks, along with some refreshing tomato slices on the side.

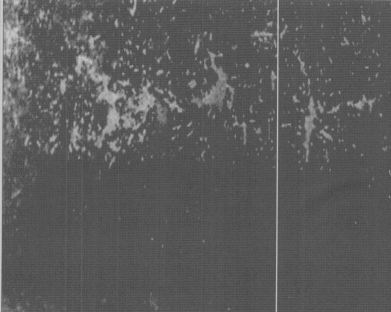

NAN
WITH CUMIN, RAISINS, AND ONIONS

Makes 6 breads

4	cups all-purpose flour, or as needed
1	teaspoon salt
2	teaspoons active dry yeast
1	cup plain full-fat yogurt
¾	cup whole milk
1 to 2	tablespoons butter or ghee
3	onions, chopped
3	tablespoons raisins
2 to 3	teaspoons cumin seeds
About 3	tablespoons vegetable oil

NAN IS THE PERSIAN WORD FOR "BREAD." Different versions of nan are served all over Asia, from Xinjiang Province in China to Afghanistan and Lebanon, and if one counts the closely related Greek pita and perhaps even the Italian pizza, it is obvious that this sort of flatbread is a member of a family with global reach.

The Indian nan that this recipe is based on is traditionally baked in a tandoor oven. I have modified the recipe for a normal household oven.

Nan can serve as an alternative to rice, as an accompaniment to dips or soups, or simply as something to nibble on before the meal. You can easily make different variations of nan with different spices, or fill the breads with cheese, fruits, vegetables, or meats (see the variations below).

1 In a large bowl, combine the flour, salt, and yeast. Combine the yogurt and milk in a small pot and heat until the mixture reaches about 110 degrees F – no more than 120 degrees F, or you risk killing the yeast. Stir the yogurt mixture into the flour, then knead the dough for 1 to 2 minutes; let the dough rest for a couple of minutes, and repeat the kneading and resting two or three times, until the dough is smooth and soft. You may need a little more flour, but make sure not to "feed" it too much, or the nan will be hard and tough. Cover and allow to rise for about 1 hour.

2 Meanwhile, melt the butter in a small skillet over medium-high heat. Add the onions, raisins, and 2 teaspoons cumin seeds and sauté for 10 minutes, or until the onions are brown. Season with more cumin to taste, if desired. Remove from the heat.

3 Preheat the oven to 450 degrees F.

4 Knead the onion mixture into the dough (alternatively, divide and roll out the dough, divide the onion mixture among the dough rounds, and fold each one over into a half-moon shape). Divide the dough into 6 pieces. Using your hands or a rolling pin, pat or roll out the dough to flat rounds (they don't have to be perfect rounds). Rub your hands and the rolling pin generously with oil as necessary to prevent sticking.

5 Place 1 or 2 breads at a time directly on an oven rack and bake until puffed up and with some dark brown patches, about 3 to 5 minutes. Pay close attention so the breads do not burn.

VARIATIONS
Nan with Spicy Ground Meat *Sauté ground meat, preferably lamb, with onions, chiles, cardamom, cinnamon, and turmeric. Divide the dough into 6 pieces, roll out, and fill and bake as directed.*

Nan with Dried Fruits *Sauté onions, mixed dried fruits, and cinnamon (to taste) in oil until the onions are soft and slightly caramelized. Divide the dough into 6 pieces, roll out, and fill and bake as directed.*

Nan with Sesame Seeds *Sprinkle the plain nan dough, or any of the other variations, with sesame seeds before baking.*

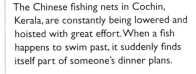

The Chinese fishing nets in Cochin, Kerala, are constantly being lowered and hoisted with great effort. When a fish happens to swim past, it suddenly finds itself part of someone's dinner plans.

SIMPLY SPICY

"IT IS SOMETIMES SAID OF SPICES THAT THEY ARE USED TO FRESHEN UP FOOD THAT IS SLIGHTLY OFF. THIS IS EXACTLY THE OPPOSITE OF MY EXPERIENCE WITH THE COOKING OF THE INDIAN OCEAN, WHERE I HAVE SO OFTEN EXPERIENCED THAT VERY GOOD INGREDIENTS, THROUGH THE SIMPLE ALCHEMY OF SPICES, CAN BE TRANSFORMED INTO SOMETHING MAGICAL."

The sweetest thing: Pineapples grow all around the Indian Ocean. It's hard to choose a favorite from among the Thai, South African, or Balinese pineapples.

WITH OR WITHOUT

"Yes, the pineapple is very sweet, of course. With or without?"

At first I didn't get the question. To quench my thirst and get my blood sugar back to a normal level after a long day on the hot streets of Durban, I had decided to purchase some succulent pineapple from a street vendor.

The asking price for the pineapple — huge chunks of juicy yellow fruit threaded onto a wooden stick — was one rand, less than a quarter, which I had just paid. It was a simple transaction if there ever was one. But now I was confronted with a difficult question.

"With or without?" the street vendor insisted.

"With or without what?" I asked.

"With or without spice, of course," the vendor said. It was hard to know whether he was annoyed or amused by my unworldly ignorance. He held out a wide bowl of an orange-colored spice mixture and lifted it all the way up to my nose, so that I had a tickling sensation, like a sneeze building up. When I, somewhat bewildered, started to nod to indicate that I recognized that there were, indeed, spices in the bowl, he dipped the pineapple in the spice mixture and handed it to me before he hurried away to find new customers.

At the foot of the beautiful hilly slopes of Durban lies the bustling city center, one of the most fascinating, enchanting, and frustrating places in South Africa. A multicolored metropolis by the Indian Ocean, it is a place that for centuries has been a meeting point for African, European, and Asian cultures — and, since the end of apartheid, also a city that embraces its own diversity.

The spicy pineapple was a reflection of the city and its spirit: an explosion of flavor, a party in my mouth where everyone was invited. It was fiery hot, a testament to a generous dose of chili powder, and the round aromas indicated the presence of fennel and cumin and coriander. There was probably a hint of saffron somewhere, and certainly a whole lot of turmeric, both spices responsible for the intense color of the spice mixture — and a stain on my shirt that will never, ever, come off. The spice mixture was salty too, with small salt crystals biting into the palate.

All these dry and intense flavors contrasted wonderfully with the sweetness and moisture of the pineapple, not more than a day away from being harvested at the height of ripeness.

The more I have thought about the spicy pineapple I had that day in Durban, the more it has manifested itself as the perfect example of the food from the coastal areas around the Indian Ocean: In the fertile tropical and subtropical climate, anything will grow. The ingredients you find here are among the finest in the world. Even had I eaten the pineapple "without," I would probably have described it as one of the most perfect fruits I had ever sampled. But this one was something more than just perfect — giving me all the sweetness and moisture I was expecting and longing for, and then an additional explosion of flavor. It was all done so simply and effortlessly, yet it was so surprising and refreshing that it was instantly recognizable as a classic that could be appreciated anywhere in the world. It is sometimes said of spices that they are used to freshen up food that is slightly off. This is exactly the opposite of my experience with the cooking of the Indian Ocean, where I have so often experienced that very good ingredients, through the simple alchemy of spices, can be transformed into something magical.

On hot summer days, wherever I am in the world, I cut my pineapple into large chunks, thread it onto wooden sticks, and, just like a street vendor in Durban, offer it to my guests "with or without." But I don't really give them a choice.

SPICY PINEAPPLE SKEWERS

A GREAT SNACK THAT IS REFRESHING and thirst-making at the same time.

The spice mixture that I have found works best with the intense sweetness of the pineapple is a tandoori-style masala that is quite salty, hot, and bright red. I wouldn't bother to make my own spice mixture just in order to make this snack — I would much rather adjust and personalize a store-bought masala by adding more salt, saffron, and aniseed.

This can also be made with other fruits, such as mangoes.

Makes 6 to 8 skewers

1	large pineapple, peeled, cored, and cut into ⅔-inch chunks
2 to 3	tablespoons tandoori-style masala spice mix
	Salt to taste (optional)
	Chili powder to taste (optional)

1 Thread the pineapple chunks onto wooden skewers.

2 Place the spice mixture on a wide plate. Roll the pineapple skewers in the spice mixture so it covers most of the pineapple. Sprinkle with salt and/or chili powder, if desired.

PINEAPPLE
WITH MINCED SHRIMP AND PEANUT TOPPING

THIS IS A GREAT STARTER, OR PERFECT FOOD JUST TO NIBBLE AT. It can also be made with only pork, or with chicken. I strongly encourage you to chop the pork and shrimp by hand; using a food processor or ground meat just isn't the same.

Makes 12 mouthfuls

1 Combine the shrimp, pork, peanuts, ginger, coriander seeds, turmeric, cream of coconut, and salt to taste in a small pot and cook over medium heat for 5 to 7 minutes, stirring constantly to prevent burning. Allow to cool.

2 Place a spoonful of the shrimp mixture on top of each piece of pineapple. Garnish with cashews, cilantro, and chiles and serve.

4	ounces peeled shrimp, finely chopped
4	ounces boneless pork, finely chopped
3 to 4	tablespoons raw peanuts, finely chopped
1 to 2	teaspoons finely chopped fresh ginger
1	teaspoon coriander seeds, crushed
1	teaspoon finely chopped fresh turmeric or ½ teaspoon powdered turmeric
2	tablespoons unsweetened coconut cream (see page 139)
	Salt
12	pineapple chunks
	Cashews for garnish
	Chopped cilantro (fresh coriander) for garnish
	Sliced seeded chiles for garnish

A TANDOOR IS A CLAY OVEN, but as Indian cooking has become increasingly popular around the world, the word "tandoori" is also used to indicate food that is made with the traditional tandoori spice mixture.

This is a great and simple way to make your own highly flavorful potato chips. I often make these while I am preparing other food and serve them as an appetizer. Unlike commercial potato chips, these homemade chips will not stay crisp for very long, and they are in no way health food, so I never make much at a time. If you slice the potatoes in advance, they tend to brown when exposed to air; but if you place the slices in water to prevent browning, they lose some of the starch on their surfaces and consequently they will probably not be as crisp and sweet.

I use a store-bought tandoori mix that has a bright red color and is quite hot. I sometimes add more paprika to enhance the color and red pepper flakes for even more heat.

Makes a light snack for 4

Vegetable oil for deep-frying

2 medium potatoes

1 tablespoon coarsely ground black pepper

1 tablespoon tandoori spice mix,
   or more to taste

Salt

Crushed red pepper flakes (optional)

1 Pour about 2 inches of vegetable oil into a large deep pot. Heat over medium-high heat.

2 Meanwhile, peel the potatoes, and use the peeler to slice the potatoes into a small bowl. (Heaping the slices on top of each other will slow down the browning process.) Season with the pepper and tandoori spice mix, adding the spices a little at a time while tossing the potato slices, so that all are covered with the spices.

3 Add a potato slice to the oil and turn the heat to high. When the oil starts bubbling enthusiastically around the potato slice, add half or one-third of the potato slices, moving the slices around and separating them with a wooden spatula or spoon. When the bubbling subsides, it means that the moisture has been forced out of the potatoes. Remove them with a slotted spoon and drain on paper towels. Repeat with the rest of the potato slices.

4 Season with salt, and with more tandoori spice and red pepper flakes, if desired. Serve at once.

SPICY HONEY BREAD

ETHIOPIA HAS A LONG HISTORY OF SPICE TRADING. It is believed that the kingdom of Sheba stretched from Yemen to what is now Ethiopia, and both the Old Testament and the Koran tell similar stories of the Queen of Sheba bringing spices and other valuables to King Solomon. She was rewarded with wisdom, gifts, and "everything she desired." The Ethiopian imperial family, which was deposed in 1974, puts a special emphasis on that desire and claims its origin in this meeting between the wise king and the beautiful queen.

Ethiopia lost its coastline and link to the Red Sea in 1993, when the province of Eritrea became an independent country, but the ancient spice traditions remain an important part of Ethiopian cooking, something this sweet and spicy bread attests to. I like to think of this bread, a free interpretation of the traditional *ambasha*, as an extended Indian Ocean version of focaccia. It can be served as a snack or at the beginning of a meal, or together with the main course to sop up the juices and add an additional aromatic spiciness to the meal; it can even be served as dessert. Whether you would like it as a savory or sweet bread is up to you. When I intend it to accompany a main dish, I sprinkle it with sea salt and paprika or chili powder. When I serve it as a dessert, I use more honey, and I shape it into small cakes and brush the dough with egg, milk, melted butter, or just water, before baking, to give it a shiny surface.

Serves 6 to 8 as a side dish

1	tablespoon coriander seeds
1	cinnamon stick
2	cloves
1 to 2	teaspoons fenugreek seeds
3½	cups all-purpose flour
Scant 1½	teaspoons active dry yeast or ⅛ ounce fresh yeast
2	teaspoons salt
⅔	cup lukewarm water
⅔	cup full-fat milk or yogurt, heated just until lukewarm
1 to 3	tablespoons honey (see headnote)
3	tablespoons butter, melted
½	teaspoon ground ginger
1	large egg, lightly beaten
	A little coarse sea salt (optional)
	A little paprika or chili powder (optional)

1 Dry-roast the coriander seeds, cinnamon, cloves, and fenugreek in a small skillet over high heat, stirring freqently, for 2 minutes, or until fragrant. Crush the spices using a mortar and pestle.

2 In a large bowl, combine 2 cups of the flour, the dry yeast (if using), and the salt. (If using fresh yeast, do not add it yet.) Add three-quarters of the crushed spices. Combine the water (the water temperature needs to be about 110 degrees F in order to get the yeast started, but less than 120 degrees F or so, or you risk killing the yeast), yogurt, honey, and fresh yeast (if using) in a bowl, then stir into the flour using a wooden spoon until you have a smooth, sticky, and loose dough. The best technique is to mix the dough in several turns, stopping to allow it to rest after each several minutes of kneading, for at least 20 minutes. You can also mix and knead the dough in a food processor fitted with the dough blade, then transfer to a large bowl.

3 Cover the dough and let rise in a warm, draft-free place for 1 hour, or until bubbles appear in the dough. (Dry yeast is harder to get started than fresh yeast; if the dough seems "dead," unmoving, place in a somewhat warmer environment, such as an oven warmed to 90 to 100 degrees F, or on top of a radiator for 10 to 20 minutes or so, watching carefully.)

4 Grease a baking sheet with some of the melted butter. Add the ginger, egg, and the remaining butter to the dough and mix well. Knead in up to 1½ cups more flour little by little until you have a soft dough – it is better that it is rather on the soft side. Or use a food processor to mix the ginger, egg, melted butter, and then the flour, into the dough.

5 Spread the dough on the baking sheet with your hands, or shape it into several small "cakes." Cover and let rise for 45 minutes.

6 Preheat the oven to 350 degrees F.

7 Brush the dough with a little butter, milk, egg, or water if you want a shiny surface and sprinkle with the rest of the spice mixture. For a savory bread, sprinkle with a little coarse sea salt and a light dusting of paprika or chili powder. Bake on the lower oven rack, 25 to 30 minutes for a large loaf, 20 to 25 for smaller loaves. Transfer to a rack to cool.

SPICE-DUSTED AVOCADO
WITH MANGO AND CRAB

THE AVOCADO IS ONE OF THE MOST NUTRITIOUS FRUITS THERE IS, and it grows willingly in tropical climates. Still, it is often viewed with suspicion in eastern Africa, where it is sometimes referred to as "fat dog fruit" — after the surprisingly chubby dogs living under the avocado trees. Recent publicity campaigns in local newspapers have started to have an impact, though, and avocados are now displayed in most food markets as a valuable commodity, not something to be left for the dogs to enjoy.

The mangrove crabs that can be found along the Swahili Coast of the Indian Ocean are delicious, vicious, and totally capable of living life on land. They see captivity as just another obstacle, often cutting their way out of the grocery bag or box with their powerful claws — occasionally escaping as you carry them home from the market. In Mozambique, I had one break free inside the car just as I was maneuvering through the congested and frantic afternoon traffic.

This is a great, fresh-tasting starter. The fatty avocado integrates the spices nicely while still respecting the fresh sweetness of the mango and the fragile flavors of the crabmeat.

1 Dry-roast the cumin seeds, cardamom, and clove in a small skillet over medium-high heat, stirring frequently, for 1 minute to release the flavors. Combine with paprika, chili powder, and the salt in a mortar and crush to a fine powder using the pestle. Discard the husks from the cardamom.

2 Halve the avocados and remove the pits. Brush with lime juice to prevent browning. Sprinkle the avocados with the spice mixture, and arrange on plates.

3 Combine the mango, crabmeat, scallions, and mint (if desired) and mound in the avocados. Serve immediately.

Serves 4 as a starter

2	teaspoons cumin seeds
1	cardamom pod, slightly bruised
1	clove
1	teaspoon paprika
1	teaspoon chili powder
2	teaspoons coarse sea salt
2	large ripe avocados
	Fresh lime juice for brushing the avocados
½	cup mango chunks
½	cup cooked crabmeat
2	tablespoons finely chopped scallions
2	teaspoons finely chopped mint (optional)

MELON WITH PEPPER

A PERFECTLY RIPE TRUE MELON (that is, any melon but watermelon) tastes fabulous with a sprinkle of pepper. Pepper stimulates the taste buds and the production of saliva, so this simple dish is great as a starter or as a palate cleanser between courses in a long meal.

The type of pepper is of great importance here. I normally use Malabar or Tellicherry, both high-quality black peppers from south India, for a clean, pure black pepper taste.

This recipe also works well with peaches.

Serves 4 as a starter or palate cleanser

4 slices ripe melon, such as honeydew

1 tablespoon freshly ground black pepper, or more to taste

Sprinkle the melon with the pepper.

VARIATION *Adding a little cubeb pepper will impart a slightly pinelike smoky flavor; Szechuan pepper will give the black pepper a frizzy hotness.*

OYSTERS
WITH MALAY MASALA AND CUCUMBER RELISH

SOUTH AFRICA

Makes 12 mouthfuls

1	teaspoon coriander seeds
1	teaspoon black peppercorns
1	teaspoon cumin seeds
½	teaspoon powdered turmeric
½	teaspoon paprika
½	teaspoon chili powder, or more to taste
¼	teaspoon ground cinnamon, preferably freshly ground
1	teaspoon coarse sea salt
12	cucumber slices
12	small pickled onions
12	mint leaves
12	large oysters on the halfshell
	Crushed ice

THE INDIAN OCEAN IS WARM — in my opinion, too warm to produce top-quality oysters. Around Cape Town, though, the Indian Ocean meets the Atlantic Ocean, which brings cold currents from Antarctica, and the water is too cold for swimming — but just right for oysters and other mollusks.

One could be excused for thinking that lots of spices will easily overpower the fragile flavor of the oysters, but in reality spices can serve as flavor enhancers — and in this dish, the taste of the oysters and even the thin slices of cucumber is more acute and pronounced than you would think.

Oysters are really the perfect canapé, and when I serve them, I like to serve several different varieties with different garnishes; see the variations below.

1 Using a mortar and pestle, crush the coriander seeds, peppercorns, and cumin seeds. Combine all the spices and the salt, and pour the mixture into a deep plate.

2 Thread 1 cucumber slice, 1 pearl onion, and 1 mint leaf onto each of 12 toothpicks.

3 Place the oysters on a bed of crushed ice. Carefully lift out 1 oyster at a time, roll it in the spice mixture, and return it to the shell. (A simpler way would be just to sprinkle the oysters with the spice mixture.) Insert a cucumber and onion toothpick in each of the oysters and serve immediately.

VARIATIONS

Oysters with Ginger and Sweet Chili Sauce
Scatter ¼ teaspoon grated fresh ginger over each oyster and garnish with bottled sweet chili sauce and cilantro (fresh coriander) leaves.

Oysters with Spinach and Nutmeg
Sauté chopped spinach and finely chopped shallots in oil. Season with freshly grated nutmeg to taste, and then top each oyster with a little spinach.

Oysters with Piri Piri and Mango
Top each oyster with Piri Piri Sauce (page 105) and finely chopped mango.

Oysters with Cubeb Pepper and Lemongrass Vinaigrette
Combine 2 tablespoons white vinegar, 1 tablespoon finely chopped crushed lemongrass, and 1 tablespoon finely chopped shallot. Add ½ teaspoon of this vinaigrette to each oyster. Season with freshly ground cubeb pepper (or black pepper) and garnish with lemon balm leaves.

GRILLED TUNA
WITH ZANZIBAR SPICES

THE FIRST TIME I TASTED FRESH TUNA was in a small bamboo shack on the east coast of Zanzibar. The shack served as a restaurant, the only one for miles. There was no electricity and no running water on the coast at that time, so all the cooking was done over an open fire at the back of the house.

What I did not know was that the budding hospitality business on the island was still trying to figure out what a restaurant really meant, and it was a shock to the owners whenever someone, like me, just walked in and asked for food. I should have ordered several hours in advance, the woman who ran the restaurant told me. I looked at the food the other guests were eating — soggy spaghetti with meat sauce and vegetables, hard-to-define stews — and realized how that might be hard to prepare over an open fire. But then the woman took pity on me. The only thing she could offer me, she said apologetically, was fish, like the locals were having. No sauce, she explained. Would I still be interested? A few minutes later, she came back with a thick tuna steak, a bowl of rice, and a slice of lemon. It was the most delicious thing I had ever tasted. The fish was grilled, and it had a mild spice crust. A few drops of lime juice on top, and that was it.

Fresh tuna begs you to do as little as possible with it. This is a recipe that, because of its simplicity, demands precision and restraint from the cook. The fish should most certainly not be almost raw, as has become the fashion with tuna, but, conversely, if you overcook the fish, it is not much fun either. It's best to grill the fish over charcoal, but you could also use a stove-top grill pan. This recipe works well with salmon, too.

Serve with rice, possibly Rice Pilau (page 243).

Serves 2 as a main course

2	8-ounce tuna steaks
2	teaspoons coriander seeds
2 to 3	teaspoons cumin seeds
4	cloves
2	teaspoons black peppercorns
1	teaspoon powdered turmeric
1 to 3	teaspoons chili powder (optional)
	Salt
	Oil for brushing the tuna, such as canola
	Lime wedges for serving

1 Rinse and pat dry the tuna steaks. Let stand at room temperature for at least 15 minutes before cooking.

2 Light a grill or preheat a grill pan over high heat.

3 Dry-roast the coriander seeds, cumin seeds, cloves, and peppercorns in a small skillet over high heat for 1 minute to release the flavors, stirring energetically with a wooden spatula or spoon to prevent burning. Crush the toasted spices to a powder using a mortar and pestle. Add the rest of the spices and salt to taste and mix well.

4 Brush the tuna steaks with oil, then rub with two-thirds of the spice mixture.

5 Place the tuna on the grill or in the grill pan and cook over high heat for 2 minutes on each side. Remove from the grill or pan and let rest for 2 minutes. Then, if grilling over charcoal, place the tuna on a cooler part of the grill, away from direct heat, and grill for 2 to 3 minutes longer on each side. If using a grill pan, turn down the heat and cook for 2 to 3 minutes longer on each side. Dust the tuna steaks with the rest of the spice mixture, and serve with lime wedges on the side.

SPICY DEEP-FRIED VEGETABLES

PAKORA, VEGETABLES COATED IN A SPICY BATTER AND FRIED, is one of my favorite Indian-Pakistani snacks. One of the great things about it is that there is no one fixed recipe — both the spices and the vegetables vary with the seasons and the temperament of the cook.

I once had such a crush on pakora that I ate it for 150 days in a row. Then I moved away from my favorite pakora purveyor and that frequency declined rapidly, but even so, I have come to think of myself as somewhat of a pakora expert. The only reason I can claim this position is that with pakora, there is no right or wrong, no fixed recipe; the vegetables and the spices used in the batter are somewhat different every time. So I could eat pakora for lunch every day for half a year because it was different every time — I never knew what I was getting.

I have experimented with other kinds of flour when making pakora, but although all-purpose flour works acceptably, it tends to leave the deep-fried vegetables too crispy. Note that chickpea flour does not contain gluten. Chickpea flour can be found in health food shops and Asian markets, especially Indian ones (see Sources, page 272).

Serve with Coriander and Mint Sauce (page 155).

Serves 4 as a starter, 6 to 8 as a snack

1 to 2	teaspoons cumin seeds
1	teaspoon coriander seeds
2	teaspoons coarse sea salt
1	tablespoon chili powder
1 to 2	teaspoons powdered turmeric
½	cup chickpea flour
½	cup water
1	tablespoon finely chopped cilantro (fresh coriander)
1 to 3	green chiles, finely chopped (optional)
2 to 3	quarts vegetable oil, such as canola, for deep-frying
3	boiled potatoes, sliced
10	cauliflower florets
2	small onions, sliced
10 to 15	spinach leaves

1 Using a mortar and pestle, coarsely crush the cumin seeds, coriander seeds, and salt. Transfer to a large bowl and add the chili powder, turmeric, and flour. Add the water and mix until you have a thick, smooth batter. Let stand for 20 minutes.

2 Add the cilantro and chiles (if desired) to the batter and mix well.

3 Heat the oil in a deep-fryer, or heat at least 2 inches of oil (the more oil you use, the more stable the temperature of the oil) in a large, deep pot. Working in batches, add the vegetables to the batter, coating them thoroughly, then lift out, letting the excess drip off, and fry until brown and crispy. Transfer to paper towels to drain.

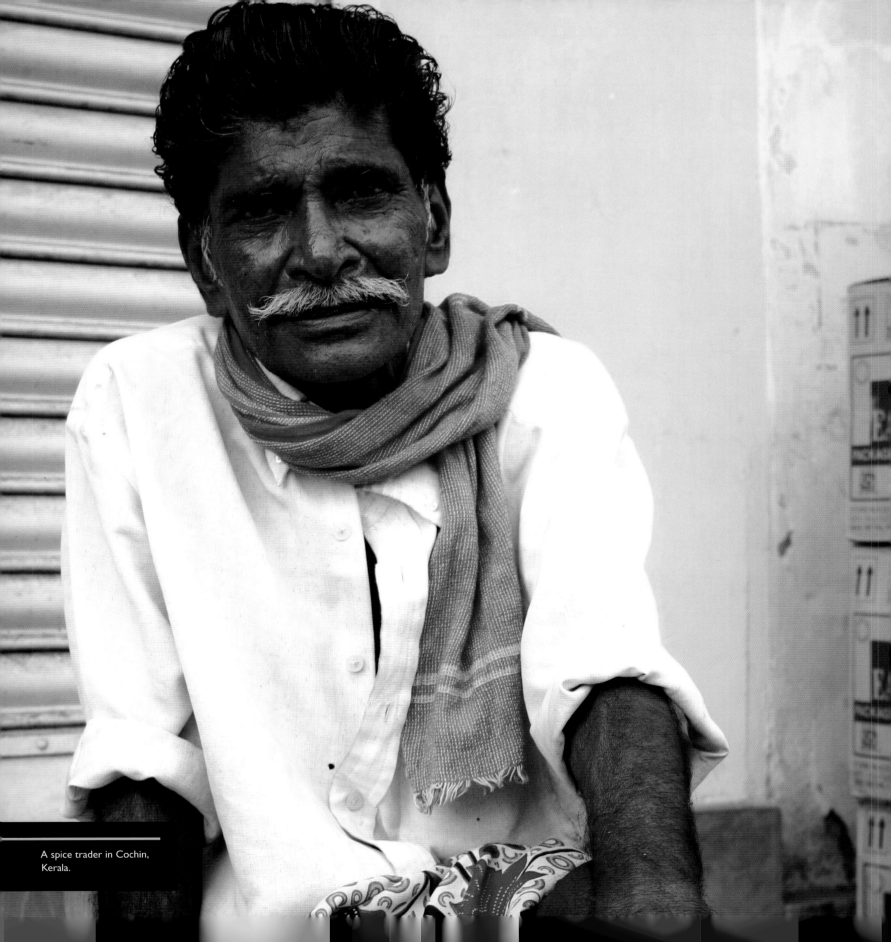

A spice trader in Cochin, Kerala.

SPICE MARKET
JEW TOWN

SPICE MARKET

The old Jewish quarter in Cochin, India, is still the seat of the important spice trade – mainly pepper and cardamom, which both originated in the area, and ginger, used for both culinary and medicinal purposes.

A young Hindu girl with offerings.

LEFT TO RIGHT: A wise old man in Kerala, India; various spice mixtures at a market in Zanzibar; a tea trader in Thekkady, one of the main tea-producing areas in Kerala.

Mangosteens at a market in Ubud, Bali. Mangosteens are sweet and exquisite tropical fruits, but they don't travel well, so they are not often found outside the tropics.

A vendor enjoying the fruit of her labors.

PEPPER

"AS WITH SO MANY OF LIFE'S GOOD THINGS, PEPPER IS MISSED WHEN IT IS LACKING BUT TAKEN FOR GRANTED WHEN IT IS THERE."

WHERE EVERY TRADE IS GOOD

I awake with a gigantic sneeze. It is one of those ear-shattering explosions that leaves a quivering echo and keeps reverberating for a long time in the austere room. And this, the first sneeze of the day, induced by the cool morning breeze coming down from the mountains, is by no means the last. But the next time my nose is tickled to this violent expulsion of air, the reason is anything but cool breezes.

I have traveled thousands of miles to the south of the Indian subcontinent for a very good reason. I am on my own small pilgrimage to the land of spices, in the mountains of Kerala, where pepper grows, and a fine pepper dust hangs in the air like a fine, dry fog.

It is about time I came here. Pepper has given me so much, and it continues to do so. I use pepper every day, with almost every dish I make or eat. I know that pepper is good with almost everything and that it makes almost everything taste better. But apart from that, I seldom allow myself time to reflect on the magic capacity of the most ubiquitous of spices. As with so many of life's good things, pepper is missed when it is lacking but taken for granted when it is there.

Although the nights up here in the mountains can be chilly, the sun has only to look up from behind the hills and all of life is enveloped in soft, tropical warmth. In this part of India, it is summer year-round. And by nine in the morning I feel an "Indian summer" in my whole body.

I was intending to visit a pepper plantation, but I soon find out that will not be necessary; or perhaps it is that my idea of a plantation — vast fields of crops — does not correspond with reality. Because here pepper grows everywhere. The palm trees that line the road are overgrown with pepper vines, neatly tied up to take full advantage of the shady area beneath the trees. I have only to stop the car and stretch out my arm to pick a small cluster of green, still-soft pepper berries.

Here in Kerala, where some of the best pepper comes from, pepper is first and foremost a small-scale family business. One family can grow a hundred pounds a year. The big guys can send off as much as a ton. Kerala is one of the most intensely utilized agricultural areas in the world, and with so many small-scale farmers, there is enough pepper to fill oversized pepper mills at Italian restaurants and season steaks on the other side of the world.

Pepper is not only visible out in the bush. Outside almost all the houses in the villages I drive through, there are straw mats covered with pepper drying in the sun. With only the help of the sun and the air, the green berries go through a complicated fermentation process that transforms them into the hard, black, and super-durable sales commodity that not only changed the way we eat but also changed world history.

Pepper originated here in the mountains of southern India. Through intricate trade routes, sometimes changing hands as many as a hundred times, doubling in price each time, it found its way to the Arab world and then to Europe more than two thousand years ago. It became the first global commodity. It was the spice trade — when pepper was the most important spice — that made cities like Istanbul, Venice, and Genoa, and later Salem, Massachusetts, achieve their greatness. It was in search of the pepper of India that Columbus went westward, and in a combination of hope and despair, he named the allspice he found "Jamaica pepper" and the islands he landed on the "West Indies." Vasco da Gama also risked his life going over the edge of the world — remember, it was still "flat" at that time — in search of pepper. Even though his first visit to India was a great failure — he was chased away after having offended his hosts with a combination

Pepper originated in Kerala, India, and it is still an important commodity there. In the mountain region around Thekkady, the vines grow everywhere, and outside most houses there are mats with drying peppercorns.

of clumsiness and heavy-handedness — he returned with enough pepper to give his financiers a handy 5,000-percent profit. The lure of the spices enticed him to return, and he ended his days in Kerala.

Not far from the St. Francis Church in Cochin, where da Gama was buried, is the spice district of Mattancherry. Hundreds of small- and medium-sized spice wholesalers line the narrow streets. They all meet me with the same bobbing of the head. In India, a soft bobbing of your head from one side to the other — a movement that tense Western necks have great difficulties in mastering — can mean anything: It is the Indian equivalent of shaking your head to say no, and nodding it to say yes, and the indifferent shrug of the shoulders. But today the bobbing means yes wherever I go. I am let in everywhere, and I spend the rest of the day between sacks, heaps, cases, and mountains of pepper.

It is a hard job, working with pepper, I can now say with certainty. At one point, when there is a gap in the line of men carrying hundred-pound bags of pepper, I volunteer to help out, only to find out that they make fun of my clumsiness, and that I feel exhausted after three rounds, not even a hundredth of a day's work.

It is like a dream world, a glimpse into a world that has not changed much over the last five hundred years. At some places, the pepper dust is so dense that the men loading and unloading the spices have to cover their faces. In one room, there is a group of women who are sorting the peppercorns one by one. There are some places where I have to climb over huge heaps of pepper to be able to pass, and so I have to take off my shoes. When I am walking through these mountains of pepper, the millions of small peppercorns keep tickling and massaging the soles of my feet and all the way up to my ankles, and I am not quite sure whether to sneeze or laugh.

The pepper traders are highly specialized, and there is something here to cater for every taste. One sells whole garbled black pepper — "garbled" means that stems, stones, leaves, and all other alien objects, as well as light-colored berries, have been removed. Another stocks uncleaned grade B pepper. One has only white pepper, which is made from the same but riper berries, with the outer husks removed, and has a drier, more intense flavor. There are even those who have specialized in customers who lack taste: one wholesaler has his entire warehouse filled with the black husks, the leftovers from the making of white pepper. After the rough decortication process in which the outer husks are removed, the husks lose most of their flavor. You do not need to have tasted more than one of those ridiculous packets that are served with hospital and airline food to know where this pepper is being sold.

Most peppercorns are harvested when still green and unripe, and left to dry out in the sun. During that time, they go through a fermentation process where the skin turns black and the flavor develops. White peppercorns are made by removing the red husks of ripe red berries.

Never-ending streams of trucks, hand-drawn carts, and men with huge bags of pepper on their heads fill the streets of Mattancherry. It all seems chaotic in a Third World way. But it is not. The pepper trade is no longer as lucrative as it used to be, and it is not as flashy as the oil industry, but it is almost as well regulated. And in the heart of Mattancherry is the Cochin Pepper Exchange — from where the market takes its lead. As on Wall Street, the trades that happen here have extended economic consequences, down to what people have to put on their table for dinner. But the pepper stock exchange is not like other stock exchanges. There are no men in smart suits and not much frenetic chasing after fast money. The stock exchange was originally a socialist project, established by the state government in 1957 to help the small farmers in the remote mountain areas get fairer prices. When the price of pepper was listed in the paper and announced on the radio every day, it became more difficult for greedy middlemen to offer two hundred rupees for something worth a thousand, and through trade with futures, the prices leveled out — and the small farmers who had to sell the moment the harvesting and drying period was over were also ensured an acceptable price.

It is in all probability the most boring stock exchange in the world, yet the one that gives most pleasure to the highest amount of people. While other stock exchanges are ever fearing a crash, this one's sole purpose is the anticipation of crushing and grinding. On the floor, there is a low buzz of chattering from the dozen or so traders. Ranged along the walls, there are slightly dated computers. It is all very informal, like a teachers' lounge. From time to time a phone rings, and someone takes down notes and punches some numbers into a computer.

Apart from a period in 2001 and 2002 when poor harvests in other parts of the world brought prices up, there usually is not much happening, one of the longtime traders, Vijay Vidalia, tells me. He seems totally content that he can go to work every day knowing that it will be more or less like the previous day. That is a sentiment that is also reflected when I talk to the secretary of the India Pepper and Spice Trade Association, which runs the stock exchange: "We like stable prices, and the farmers get what they deserve. If there is too much variation, there is bound to be someone losing."

"Does it ever get boring to just trade with one commodity, particularly when it is not even particularly exciting," I ask.

"No, not really. Here every trade is a good trade."

Spices on a truck in Kerala, India. The tiger is not just painted on the back because it looks cool. Much of the best pepper and cardamom is grown near a tiger sanctuary. Now tigers are endangered, but in earlier times they posed a threat to farmers.

INDIAN PEPPER CHICKEN

INDIA

THE FLAVOR OF PEPPER is not often appreciated as more than half of the ubiquitous salt-and-pepper duo that performs in the background of most savory dishes. This is a dish that takes pepper seriously, as it should be taken, for its unique flavor. It is based on a meal I had at Brunton Boatyard in Cochin, close to the source of the finest pepper on earth.

I have several different types of black pepper at home, and when making this dish, I use a combination of two or three different types, and sometimes also a little Indonesian cubeb pepper. Although that is an interesting way to experience the variation and complexity of the flavor of black pepper, it is by no means necessary, but I do think that it is vital to use freshly bought black peppercorns. And it is absolutely crucial to use whole peppercorns that you crush yourself.

The addition of chicken livers gives the dish more body. If you do not like the texture of liver, you can chop them, and they will more or less disintegrate, making a thick gravy.

Serve with rice and possibly also nan bread (such as one of the variations on page 48) or Yellow Rice (page 189). I like to have a small bowl of yogurt with a little bit of finely chopped onion and a sprinkle of freshly ground cloves as a soothing accompaniment to the fiery pepper. A simple tomato salad is also nice, or a few chunks of mango, with or without a sprinkle of chili powder or red pepper flakes and chives.

If you do not have a mortar and pestle, you can crush the pepper on a cutting board using a heavy skillet.

Serves 4 as a main course

4	large boneless chicken breasts, preferably with skin
2	tablespoons coarsely crushed black peppercorns, or more to taste, plus 1 tablespoon whole peppercorns
½	cup chicken stock or bouillon
	Oil for panfrying, such as canola
4 to 6	onions, chopped
2 to 4	cloves garlic, chopped
8	ounces chicken livers, or more if desired, cleaned and chopped
	Salt
2	teaspoons fresh green peppercorns or dried green peppercorns, reconstituted in 3 tablespoons hot water for 10 minutes, drained, and coarsely crushed
2 to 4	tablespoons butter or ghee (optional)
2	teaspoons finely chopped fresh ginger

1 Cut several ½- to 1-inch-long slashes in each chicken breast, and rub the breasts with half of the crushed black peppercorns.

2 In a small pot, combine the chicken stock and whole peppercorns and bring to a boil. Reduce the heat, cover, and keep at a simmer.

3 Heat a tablespoon or so of oil in a large, deep skillet over high heat. Sauté the onions and garlic with the rest of the crushed black pepper for 3 to 5 minutes, until starting to lightly brown. Transfer to a bowl or plate.

4 Season the chicken breasts and livers with salt. Add the breasts to the pan and cook for 3 to 4 minutes over high heat. Reduce the heat to medium-high, add the livers, onions and garlic, green peppercorns, and chicken stock (with or without the whole peppercorns left in), and cook for 10 to 12 minutes, until the chicken breasts are cooked through.

5 Just before serving, stir in the butter (if desired) and the ginger. If desired, season with more crushed pepper to taste.

WHERE FLAVOR WAS BORN

SPICY BEEF SALAD
WITH GREEN PEPPERCORNS

THE THAI ARE SPECIALISTS AT USING BEEF IN LIGHT-TASTING DISHES, like this salad.

Green peppercorns have a fresher, more earthy flavor than black peppercorns. Here both are used – but what you notice are the green peppercorns.

1 Pat the meat dry with a paper towel. Combine the oyster sauce, soy sauce, 1 teaspoon fish sauce, sugar, and black pepper in a deep plate and add the meat, turning to coat both sides of the steak. Set aside to marinate for a couple of minutes.

2 Heat a little oil in a large skillet over high heat. Sear the meat for 2 minutes on each side, then return it to the marinade (set the skillet aside). Let rest for 2 to 4 minutes, turning twice.

3 Set the skillet over medium heat, add the steak, and cook for 3 minutes on each side for medium-rare. Transfer to a cutting board and let rest for 3 to 5 minutes.

4 Meanwhile, in a large bowl, combine the tomatoes, scallions, onion, cucumber, and mild chiles.

5 Crush the green peppercorns gently with the side of a knife. In a small bowl, combine the lime juice, 2 teaspoons fish sauce, sugar, bird's-eye chiles, and green peppercorns.

6 Cut the meat diagonally across the grain into ¼-inch slices. Add to the salad. Add the dressing and toss well. Sprinkle with the crispy dried onions (if desired) and serve immediately.

NOTE *Fresh green peppercorns can be found in Thai food shops. If you cannot find the fresh, substitute 2 teaspoons dried green peppercorns reconstituted in 3 tablespoons hot water for 30 minutes. The resulting green pepper water also tastes good and can be used in the dressing.*

**Serves 2 as a light meal,
4 as a starter**

1	8-ounce boneless sirloin steak
2	teaspoons oyster sauce
2	teaspoons soy sauce
3	teaspoons fish sauce (*nam pla*)
1	teaspoon sugar
2	teaspoons freshly ground black pepper
	Oil for panfrying, such as canola
2	tomatoes, cut into 6 wedges each and seeded
2	scallions, chopped
1	small onion, sliced
1	2-inch chunk of cucumber, peeled, seeded, and cut into sticks
2	mild chiles, seeded and sliced
2	tablespoons fresh green peppercorns or reconstituted dried peppercorns (see note)
2	tablespoons fresh lime juice
1	teaspoon sugar
1 to 4	small bird's-eye chiles, bruised
1	tablespoon crispy dried onions or deep-fried scallions for garnish (optional)

PEPPER-CRUSTED FISH
WITH WATERCRESS AND SPRING ONION SAUCE

Serves 4 as a main course

2	tablespoons black peppercorns, coarsely crushed
2	tablespoons white peppercorns, coarsely crushed
2	tablespoons Szechuan peppercorns, coarsely crushed
	Salt
4	8-ounce skinless line-caught fish fillets, such as yellowtail snapper
2	cups dry white wine, preferably unoaked
2	cups fish stock
⅓	cup heavy cream
½ to 1	teaspoon ground ginger
¼	cup small watercress sprigs
3 to 4	spring onions or scallions, blanched in boiling water for 3 to 4 minutes, drained, and chopped
	Vegetable oil for drizzling
1	pound cherry tomatoes (optional)
	Croutons for garnish (optional)

THIS RECIPE IS BASED ON A DISH SERVED BY CHEF PETER PANKHURST at the Cape Town restaurant Savoy Cabbage. The restaurant is situated in the historical center of town, in a building previously inhabited by a representative from the Dutch East India Company, so the spices are more than just ingredients — they are in the walls and in the soul of the place.

Peter uses a combination of black and white peppercorns, along with Szechuan pepper, for a hot, almost frizzy, aftertaste.

The smooth spring onion sauce forms a nice contrast to the spiciness of the fish. If you would like more vegetables, leeks sautéed in fish stock and some lightly broiled baby tomatoes would be very appropriate.

1 Combine the peppercorns in a small bowl, season with a modest amount of salt, and spread on a plate. Roll the fillets in the pepper so that they are covered on all sides. and place on a plate. Cover and refrigerate while you make the sauce.

2 Preheat the broiler. Combine the wine and fish stock in a small pot and bring to a boil. Boil until reduced to about 1 cup. Add the cream and continue cooking until the sauce is reduced to about ⅔ cup and is thick enough to coat the back of a spoon. Transfer to a blender or food processor, add the ginger, watercress, and spring onions, and puree until smooth. For an extra-smooth sauce, pass the sauce through a fine-mesh sieve.

3 Arrange the fish fillets on the broiler pan, drizzle with a little oil, and broil for 8 to 10 minutes, turning once; keep an eye on them so they do not burn. Meanwhile, if you are serving the tomatoes, place them in a small baking dish and broil them next to the fish.

4 Reheat the sauce just before serving. Garnish with croutons, if desired.

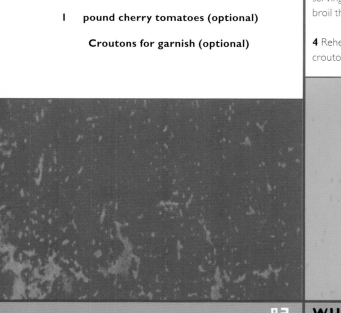

BLACK PEPPER CRABS

I HAD THIS DISH FOR THE FIRST TIME IN THE MALAYSIAN CITY OF MELAKA, and it seems to me that the harmonious fusion of flavors from various parts of the region sums up the many influences that have helped form the city. Ever since it was established in the fifteenth century, Melaka has been one of the most important spice trading cities in Southeast Asia, where the East meets the West, with strong Chinese, Arab, Indian, and European influences. It was through Melaka that chiles were introduced to Southeast Asia.

The combination of sweet crabmeat and the rich full flavors of soy sauce and oyster sauce in this dish is a sign of Chinese influences on Malay cooking. At the same time, however, the amount of pepper used, the curry leaves, the fresh coriander, and the hot bird's-eye chiles establish it as closely related to Indian and Thai cooking as well.

For the best results, use uncooked crab claws; crabmeat that is already cooked can get dry when reheated, especially when for a prolonged period. If you can only find cooked crab claws, I recommend cutting down the cooking time for the crab to a minimum; just add them towards the end of the cooking process.

The crabs should be served at room temperature or warm rather than hot. Serve with rice.

Serves 4 as a main course

3	pounds uncooked crab claws
3	tablespoons vegetable oil
2 to 4	bird's-eye chiles
2	tablespoons butter
3	shallots, finely chopped
4	cloves garlic, crushed
I	tablespoon dried small shrimp, chopped
2	tablespoons black peppercorns, coarsely crushed
8	curry leaves
2	tablespoons soy sauce
I	tablespoon oyster sauce
¼	cup boiling water
2	teaspoons coriander seeds, coarsely crushed (optional)
	Chopped cilantro (fresh coriander) for garnish

1 Crack the crab shells: The best way is to use a hammer and to hit the shells lightly several times at the same point until a small crack is evident, then continue until the crack opens. If you hit it with all your force, you are more likely to crush it, leaving the meat damaged. Leave the crab claws in the shells.

2 In a large pot, heat the oil over high heat. Add the crabs and chiles, cover, and cook for 10 minutes, turning and rearranging the claws once.

3 Add the rest of the ingredients except the cilantro, toss well, and cook for another 10 minutes over medium-high heat. Toss the ingredients a couple of times, making sure to keep the crab claws covered. Add a little more boiling water if the sauce is drying up. Conversely, if the sauce is still very thin, remove the crabs and boil the sauce until it thickens.

4 Arrange the crabs on a platter, pour the sauce over them, garnish with cilantro, and serve.

CUBEB PEPPER FIGS
COOKED IN RED WINE

ONE OF THE MORE DRAMATIC EXPERIENCES I HAD WRITING THIS BOOK was staying at a friend's vineyard just outside of Cape Town. The area around Wedgewood Farm was so peaceful, just vines and grassland, that it seem as if nothing bad could happen. Then, suddenly one afternoon, the entire farm was covered in thick, dark smoke. A ferocious bushfire was spreading rapidly, a dangerous combination of dry grass and wind. For hours we fought to control the fire, having no other means than buckets of water and wet towels, until neighbors came to the rescue with portable water tanks. Miraculously, even though a couple of acres of grassland were affected, very little harm was done; the fire was stopped before it reached the vines.

In the evening, as I inspected the damage among the fig and oak trees, I found some nearly baked figs behind a cover of wilted fig leaves. They were intensely sweet and slightly smoky, and with a deep feeling of gratitude, I cooked the figs in red wine from the merlot grapes that had just been saved, with some cubeb pepper to accentuate the smoky flavor.

Cubeb pepper is also called tailed pepper. It is an Indonesian relative of black pepper that originated in India, but it has a pungent, smoky, almost pinelike flavor and it does not have the white core of *Piper nigrum*. If you cannot find cubeb pepper, you can use black pepper, with a sprinkle of Szechuan pepper.

Serve with crème fraîche, yogurt, or ice cream, such as Bourbon Vanilla Ice Cream (page 257), or, for a low-fat alternative, some cottage cheese or ricotta mixed with a little freshly grated nutmeg and orange zest.

Serves 4

8 to 12	ripe figs
2	teaspoons coarsely crushed cubeb peppercorns or 2 teaspoons crushed black peppercorns mixed with Szechuan pepper, or more to taste
½	cup red wine, preferably Merlot
2 to 3	tablespoons sugar
3	tablespoons finely chopped dried figs (optional)

1 Cut a small slit in each fig and place a small amount of pepper inside each one.

2 In a medium pot, combine the red wine, sugar, dried figs (if desired), and the rest of the pepper and bring to a boil. Cook for 10 minutes, or until the wine is reduced and it is starting to get syrupy.

3 Add the figs and cook for 10 minutes over low heat, turning a couple of times. (The dessert can be made up to 4 hours in advance and simply reheated before serving.) Sprinkle with a little freshly ground pepper just before serving.

LEMON PEPPER CHICKEN

Serves 4 as a main course

I	**3-pound chicken, preferably free-range**
2	**tablespoons black peppercorns**
I	**tablespoon fennel seeds**
I	**cinnamon stick**
2	**cloves garlic, crushed**
2	**organic lemons**
4	**tablespoons (½ stick) butter, at room temperature**

THE SOUTH AFRICANS ARE SUCKERS FOR GRILLED FOOD, and it is common to have a *braii* — a wood-fired grill — even indoors. This fresh-tasting, peppery marinated chicken is at its best when marinated for 24 hours or more. It can also be cooked under the broiler.

Serve with green beans and salad.

I Using a butcher's knife or poultry shears, cut the chicken open down the back, and open it out flat. Place in a baking dish.

2 Using a mortar and pestle, coarsely crush the black peppercorns, fennel seeds, and cinnamon. Rub the chicken with the spices and garlic.

3 Rinse the lemons well in warm water, and cut into chunks. Using your hands, squeeze most of the lemon juice over the chicken (use rubber gloves if you have sensitive skin), making sure to bruise the lemon peel to release some of the essential oils. Scatter the lemon chunks over and underneath the chicken. Cover, refrigerate, and let marinate for 24 hours, turning the chicken twice.

4 Light a grill or preheat the broiler.

5 Rub the chicken with the butter. Place on the grill and grill, turning often to prevent charring, and moving the chicken away from the flames if the coals flare up, until cooked through, about 30 minutes . Or place the chicken on a rack in a roasting pan and broil for 15 minutes, or until browned. Reduce the temperature to 400 degrees F, move the chicken to the middle of the oven, and bake for about 30 minutes. Test for doneness by poking a sharp knife or fork into the thickest part of a thigh. If the juice runs clear, the chicken is done.

VARIATION *If you are baking the chicken in the oven, place the chicken on a roasting rack over a roasting pan with potatoes. The potatoes will sop up the juices and serve as a nice side dish. Season the potatoes with crushed fennel seeds.*

CHOCOLATE PEPPER COOKIES

I GREW ADDICTED TO CHOCOLATE PEPPER COOKIES when I was staying in Cape Town while writing this book. The addition of a generous amount of coarsely ground black pepper gives the cookies real attitude and a nice peppery flavor; at the same time, the pepper also works as a flavor enhancer, so the cookies actually taste more chocolaty.

The secret is to find the right balance between sweet chocolate and pungent pepper. I like the cookies rather on the peppery side. Start by adding a little pepper and make one small batch to sample, then add more pepper to taste.

I use an imported dark chocolate, such as Vahlrona, with a cocoa content of 58 to 65 percent.

If you cannot find finely ground brown sugar, you can pulse regular brown sugar in a blender until you have a fine powder.

Makes about 20 cookies

1	pound bittersweet or semisweet chocolate, chopped
12	tablespoons (1½ sticks) butter, at room temperature
⅔	cup fine brown sugar (see headnote)
2	large eggs
2	cups all-purpose flour
⅔	teaspoon baking soda
1	tablespoon coarsely ground black pepper

1 In a small heavy pot, melt half the chocolate over low heat. Remove from the heat and allow to cool to about 100 to 110 degrees F.

2 In a large bowl, beat the butter until light and airy. Add the sugar and beat until completely incorporated into the butter. Beat in the eggs one by one. Combine the flour and baking soda and sift into the butter mixture, little by little, beating until completely incorporated.

3 Check to make sure the chocolate is not too hot, or it will melt the butter in the dough. Slowly beat in the melted chocolate. Stir in the remaining chopped chocolate and the pepper. Cover and refrigerate until the dough is cool and firm.

4 Preheat the oven to 350 degrees F. Generously grease two baking sheets.

5 Place tablespoonfuls of batter on the greased baking sheets, leaving about 1½ inches between them. Bake on the bottom oven rack for 10 to 12 minutes, until crisp and crunchy on the outside but still somewhat chewy inside. Cool the cookies on a wire rack.

GINGER

"IN THE KORAN IT SAYS THAT THOSE VIRTUOUS ENOUGH TO REACH PARADISE WILL BE ABLE TO DRINK FROM THE FOUNTAIN OF GINGER."

Ginger is perhaps the most successful of all spices, and by many accounts it is the oldest spice, too. While pepper is still, after more than two thousand years, associated with its place of origin, India, and the Indonesian Spice Islands and Zanzibar claim joint custody over cloves, no one knows where ginger originated.

In fact, wild ginger, as it was once found by a lucky human being and transplanted to her garden, no longer exists. It has grown under human control for so long that it has lost its ability to propagate by seeds; only by splitting the root can it be propagated. This is why it is the one spice people do not write home about. Ginger needs us to exist and knows no home apart from its adopted homes — which are everywhere around the Indian Ocean, and in other tropical and subtropical regions of the world.

Six thousand years ago, the Austronesians — a people from what is today southern China — started their slow migration westward, a great trek that would take them all the way across the Malay Archipelago and eventually across the sea to what is now Madagascar, at the extreme opposite part of the Indian Ocean. There are no written records of this migration, and not much oral history either. What the Austronesians left behind was not the remains of great palaces or cities but a language group with hundreds of different tongues. Through what the eminent food historian Andrew Dalby calls "linguistic detective work," we know that this migration took place. We also know that when these people migrated, one of the things they took with them, all that time ago, was ginger; the word for ginger is more or less the same on both sides of the ocean.

While much of the attraction of other spices is that they are rare and exclusive, bragging about their virtues and claiming their weight in gold, ginger moves about the world so gingerly. While the bellies of the spice merchants' ships were packed full of pepper and cloves, on the deck there would be ginger growing in wooden troughs, as the fourteenth-century Arab explorer and travel writer Ibn Baṭṭūṭah noted in his journals. Ginger was eaten by the crew to aid indigestion, to help circulation, to prevent scurvy, and just for the lovely taste, considered sublime or sacred in the Muslim world. And when the ships reached their destinations, there would still be ginger left. Like Salsabil, the eternal fountain of ginger-flavored water promised by the Koran to those virtuous enough to reach Paradise, true ginger would keep growing as it was transported across the sea.

Ginger grows willingly in almost all conditions as long as the soil is well-drained. If you cut away a part of the rhizome, it will soon grow back.

GROUPER
WITH GINGER AND SPRING ONIONS

THAILAND | ZANZIBAR | INDIA | SOUTH AFRICA | MAURITIUS

I HAVE HAD VARIATIONS OF THIS DISH ALL OVER THE INDIAN OCEAN, and it is really no wonder that what is basically the same combination has popped up so many different places. The fresh clean flavor is not only perfect with fish, but the ginger also serves a purpose: it helps neutralize the "fishy" smell from the odorant triethylamine, which is released when fish fat oxidizes, and it prevents bacterial growth, an especially important quality in warm climates.

The best version of the dish is the one I had at Lanta Sea Food in the Krabi region of southern Thailand, a spectacularly unfashionable restaurant–cum–seafood wholesaler with heavenly food and more than questionable service – not the kind of place where you would take anyone for the style and glamor. But the shabby surroundings were of no importance once the fish was served. It came in a translucent seafood broth, covered with a blanket of ginger and finely chopped spring onion, and it made the longboats racing past the restaurant terrace at suicidal speeds, and the proprietor and his gang watching the climax of an action movie a few feet away, just disappear.

I have made this dish with other fish too, and it works well with salmon and trout as well as sea bass and snapper. I have tried to find out how the broth at Lanta Sea Food was made and have learned that it was probably prepared with a combination of stock and local seaweed. The simplest way to get some of the same rich complexity of flavor is simply to use instant miso soup with a few extra vegetables and a hint of ginger. To simplify the dish even more, use chicken stock or bouillon, or a combination of fish and chicken stocks, instead.

The best way to preserve the flavor of the fish and the freshness of the ginger is to steam the fish. This can be done either by using a steamer or by baking the fish, covered with foil, in the oven, as described below. If you would like the skin to be somewhat crisp, remove the foil for the last couple of minutes. If you are baking the fish in a heavy ovenproof dish, it is advisable to preheat the dish in the oven, as it will otherwise absorb a lot of heat and make the cooking time longer and more difficult to predict.

The ginger should be very fresh and juicy. If you can only find slightly wrinkled fresh ginger, reduce the amount by half. The best way to peel fresh ginger is to use a teaspoon and just scrape off the skin.

Serves 2 as a main course

1	1½- to 2-pound grouper or other white-fleshed fish, cleaned, scaled, rinsed, and patted dry
	Dark soy sauce for brushing
1	teaspoon ground ginger
1	2-inch piece of fresh ginger
1	tablespoon candied ginger or homemade ginger syrup (see note)
2	cloves garlic, finely chopped
1	teaspoon coriander seeds, crushed (optional)

For the broth (optional)

1	cup water
1	tablespoon instant miso soup or paste (or amount directed on packet)
½	kaffir lime leaf (optional)
½	teaspoon ground ginger
1	1-inch piece of fresh ginger
¼	cup finely chopped carrots
½	cup finely chopped spring onions
2	large red chiles, seeded and cut into matchsticks

1 Preheat the oven to 400 degrees F.

2 Cut several ¼-inch-deep slashes in the skin on both sides of the fish. Brush the fish with dark soy sauce and sprinkle with the ground ginger. Finely chop enough of the fresh ginger to make 1 tablespoon, then cut the remaining ginger into matchsticks; set the ginger matchsticks aside. Mix the chopped fresh ginger with the candied ginger, garlic, and coriander seeds, if using. Fill the slashes with the ginger mixture.

3 If serving the fish with the broth, combine the water, miso soup powder, kaffir lime leaf (if using), and ground and fresh gingers in a small pot and bring to a boil. Keep hot.

4 Place the fish in a baking dish. Add ½ cup of the boiling stock (or water, if not serving with the broth), and cover tightly with foil. Make a small hole in the foil for the steam

to escape, and bake for approximately 20 minutes. Make sure the hole in the foil is close to the oven door so that you can see the steam escaping: there should be a steady stream of steam for at least the last 7 minutes. Check for doneness by poking the flesh with a fork near the neck part, where the flesh is thickest. It should come away from the bone easily.

5 To serve, add the carrots to the hot broth, if you have it, and pour the broth over the fish. Place the ginger matchsticks on top of the fish and the spring onions and chiles on top of the ginger. There is a whole lot of ginger in this dish, and you are not meant to eat it all.

NOTE *If you cannot find candied ginger, you can make a simple ginger syrup by combining 1 tablespoon chopped fresh ginger, 1 tablespoon sugar, and ½ teaspoon ground ginger with ¼ cup water and boiling until reduced and syrupy.*

GOAN FISH CAKES

THIS IS A GREAT EXAMPLE OF THE CONFLUENCE OF INDIAN AND PORTUGUESE COOKING THAT MAKES THE COOKING OF GOA, ON THE SOUTHWESTERN COAST OF INDIA, SO SPECIAL. These fish cakes are great as party food, leaving people thirsty and fired up. And once cooked, they freeze well, so make a generous amount.

Serves 4 as a main course

1 Combine the fish and potatoes and grind in a meat grinder. If you do not have a meat grinder, the second-best option is to grate the potatoes and finely chop the fish and then combine them, but this takes some time. You could also use a food processor and pulse to a coarse mixture, but this tends to leave some of the mixture quite unnecessarily mushy.

2 In a large bowl, combine the fish mixture, onions, garlic, ginger, chiles, turmeric, crushed coriander seeds, garam masala, cilantro, and salt. Cover and refrigerate for at least 30 minutes, or up to 24 hours.

3 Place the flour on a plate, the beaten eggs in a deep plate, and the bread crumbs in a separate deep plate. Using your hands and a spoon, mold some of the fish mixture into a small ball, then roll it in the flour, dip it in the egg mixture, and roll in the bread crumbs. Set on a plate, and continue until you have used up all the fish mixture.

4 Heat a couple of tablespoons of oil in a large nonstick skillet over medium-high heat. Add the fish cakes and fry for 4 to 6 minutes, rolling them around in the skillet to make sure they are browned on all sides. You might have to do this in several batches in order not to crowd the skillet. Drain briefly on paper towels before serving.

VARIATION *If you want a milder, more aromatic flavor, sauté the onions and garlic with the spices for 3 to 4 minutes before adding them to the fish mixture.*

2	pounds white-fleshed fish fillets, chopped
1	pound waxy potatoes, peeled and chopped
2	small onions, finely chopped
6 to 10	cloves garlic, finely chopped
2	tablespoons finely chopped fresh ginger
1 to 3	green chiles, finely chopped
1 to 2	tablespoons finely chopped fresh turmeric or 1 to 2 teaspoons ground turmeric
1	tablespoon coriander seeds, coarsely crushed
2	teaspoons garam masala, or more to taste
⅓	cup cilantro (fresh coriander) leaves, finely chopped
2	teaspoons salt
3 to 4	tablespoons all-purpose flour
2 to 3	eggs, lightly beaten
1½	cups bread crumbs
	Oil for shallow frying, such as canola

STUFFED ONIONS
WITH GINGER AND LAMB

SWEET AND AROMATIC STUFFED ONIONS HAVE A WARMING GENEROSITY that is typical of the cooking of the Persian Gulf. The onions are also great appetizers, served on a piece of nan bread (such as one of the variations on page 48).

Serve with rice, or with Rice Pilau (page 243).

Serves 4 as a main course

8	onions
1	tablespoon powdered turmeric
2 to 3	tablespoons butter or ghee
2	cloves garlic, chopped
2	pounds ground lamb
2	red bell peppers, roasted, peeled, seeded, and chopped
2	dried apricots, chopped
2	tablespoons chopped almonds
1	tablespoon grated fresh ginger
1	teaspoon ground ginger
2	teaspoons cumin seeds
	Salt
2	teaspoons paprika for garnish
About 1	tablespoon chopped parsley for garnish

1 Peel the onions and, using a sharp knife, cut out the root ends, leaving the onions intact.

2 Boil the onions in lightly salted water seasoned with the turmeric for 15 minutes, or until soft on the outside. Drain and let cool slightly.

3 Preheat the oven to 300 degrees F.

4 Cut a slit in the bottom of each onion and press out the inner layers, leaving a shell of 2 or 3 outer layers. Chop the inner parts of the onions.

5 Heat 1 tablespoon of the butter in a large skillet. Sauté the chopped onions and garlic for 3 minutes, or until softened. Combine the onion mixture, ground meat, bell peppers, apricots, almonds, ginger, and cumin in a bowl. Season with salt. Stuff the onions with the meat mixture, as gently as you can. If the onion casings split open, they can still be used; wrap them around the meat mixture and close with a toothpick.

6 Place the onions in a baking dish, and add the remaining 1 to 2 tablespoons butter and a little water. Bake for 25 minutes. Cover with foil and bake for another 20 minutes, or until the filling is cooked through. If the onions are packed close together, make sure that the one in the middle is cooked through.

7 Sprinkle with the paprika and parsley before serving.

VARIATION *For a fresh, slightly sour tang, add 1 tablespoon tamarind pulp mixed with 1/3 cup water to the baking dish along with the butter.*

NOTE *If using a heavy ovenproof dish, it will take some time to heat the dish itself, so it may be a good idea to preheat it.*

CARROTS
WITH GINGER AND SOY SAUCE

SLIGHTLY CARAMELIZED CARROTS HAVE A VERY NICE BALANCE between sweetness and fresh crispness. This recipe was inspired by Phillippa Cheifitz's wonderful book *Cape Town Food*. Seeking out both the cool flavors of fresh ginger and the intense lemony flavors that come out after drying, I use a combination of fresh and ground ginger.

This is a great side dish with fish or grilled meats, and it also makes a nice snack.

1 Melt the butter in a large nonstick skillet over medium-high heat. Sauté the carrots and shallots for 2 minutes. Add the fresh and ground gingers, the coriander seeds (if desired), and the honey, reduce the heat to medium, and cook for 2 minutes, stirring constantly to prevent burning, or until the carrots are slightly caramelized. Add the tangerine juice and soy sauce and cook for 3 to 4 minutes, reducing the liquid to a syrupy glaze.

2 Transfer the carrots to a serving plate, pour over the glaze, and sprinkle with cilantro and the garlic, if using.

Serves 4 as a side dish

1	tablespoon butter
1	pound baby carrots, or regular carrots cut into ⅓-inch-thick sticks
	2 tablespoons finely chopped shallots
1	tablespoon finely chopped fresh ginger
1	teaspoon ground ginger
1 to 2	teaspoons coriander seeds, crushed (optional)
1	teaspoon honey
⅓	cup fresh tangerine juice or orange juice
1	tablespoon soy sauce
	Chopped cilantro (fresh coriander) or chives for garnish
1	clove garlic, finely chopped, for garnish (optional)

POTATO CROQUETTES
WITH GINGER AND HONEY

Serves 4 as a starter or side dish

2	pounds russet (baking) potatoes
2	large eggs, lightly beaten
2	tablespoons finely chopped shallots
2	tablespoons honey
1	tablespoon grated fresh ginger
1	teaspoon ground ginger
2	teaspoons freshly ground white pepper
	Vegetable oil for deep-frying
1	cup bread crumbs

POTATOES ARE RELATIVELY NEW TO INDIA, and they have never become the staple food there that they are in the West. But perhaps because of this, Indian cuisine seems to be much more inventive and appreciative in its relation to the modest tuber. These crispy ginger-and-honey-flavored potato croquettes are sensationally fresh-tasting, and they can be served as a small starter dish or as a side dish with hot spicy food, such as Chicken Piri Piri (page 103) or sweetly fragrant dishes like Curried Duck with Vanilla (page 255).

1 Cook the potatoes in boiling water until tender, about 25 minutes. Drain and let stand until cool enough to handle.

2 Peel the potatoes and mash well, either with a masher or a potato ricer or by pressing them through a sieve using the back of a spoon. (Do not use a blender, or the potatoes will become gluey.) Mix in the eggs, shallots, honey, fresh and ground gingers, and white pepper.

3 Pour the vegetable oil into a deep-fryer, or pour at least 2 inches of oil into a large, deep pot. Heat over medium-high heat. Once the oil starts getting hot, add a small teaspoon of the potato mixture. When the oil starts bubbling enthusiastically around the potato, start preparing the croquettes: Place the bread crumbs in a small bowl. Using a spoon dipped in water, make a small ball out of the potato mixture, then roll the potato ball in the bread crumbs and place in the oil. Continue with 3 to 5 more balls, making sure not to crowd the pot. Fry for 3 to 5 minutes, until attractively brown and crispy. Lift the croquettes out with a slotted spoon and place on a paper towel to drain. Continue frying, in batches, until all the potato mixture has been used.

VARIATION *This recipe also works well as flavored mashed potatoes. In that case, use only half the honey, no eggs, and perhaps a sprinkle of parsley.*

NOTE *The croquettes can be made up to 12 hours in advance and reheated in the oven just before serving.*

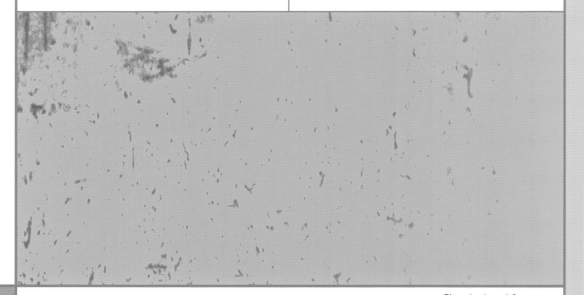

Clove buds and flowers on Zanzibar. Cloves are unripe flower buds, and they need to be picked continuously. Once left to bloom, they lose much of their characteristic taste.

CHILES

"THE WORLD OF CHILES IS A WORLD OF ITS OWN, HUNDREDS OF DIFFERENT VARIETIES WITH DIFFERENT FLAVORS AND VASTLY DIFFERENT LEVELS OF PUNGENCY AND HOTNESS. THE MILDEST VARIETIES ARE SWEETER THAN THEY ARE HOT; THE HOTTEST CAN BE ALMOST AS HOT AS TEAR GAS. BUT THERE IS NO SHAME IN CRYING."

STEP OUTSIDE, SIR

It isn't until I have started poisoning the other customers that the headwaiter comes over to my table and asks me to step outside. "Excuse me, sir, may I ask you to move outdoors? I have a nice table on the veranda for you. Otherwise, I suggest you add the piri piri after grilling the meat."

Some like it hotter: It is hard to judge chiles by the color of their skin, or even their shape – although, in general, smaller chiles tend to be hotter. These fiery red chiles at a Balinese market are surprisingly mild. The same chiles grown elsewhere in less fertile soil may be hot enough to take your breath away.

It is about time. At the table next to mine, the guests are getting ready to leave in a hurry. Most of the waiters have sought refuge on the veranda or in the kitchen. The headwaiter himself has covered his mouth with a handkerchief. I am crying, as is the rest of my party. It is, all in all — thanks largely to me — not a very good evening at the venerable Manjar dos Deuses in Maputo's restaurant district.

Fine dining in Maputo, the capital of Mozambique, in southern Africa, is never quite like other places I know. First of all, there are no smoking restrictions, and even parents with small children are puffing away like old steam engines without anyone lifting an eyebrow. The service is slow and unpredictable, and what finally ends up on your table, after often excruciatingly long waits, is frequently not what you have ordered. The food is often grilled, but that does by no means indicate that the cooks are particularly skillful at it. Food may be grilled to perfection one day, charred beyond recognition the next. Meals are nonetheless always eaten and enjoyed with the same devil-may-care nonchalance and lust for life. During the country's long civil war, the classy colonial-style beachfront restaurant Costa do Sol on the outskirts of town never closed down. Even when the front line was less than a mile away, the drinks kept flowing and whatever food was available kept being ordered and consumed with the same greedy energy.

The Mozambican kitchen is limited, and much of it is Portuguese-inspired, though perhaps lacking some of the variation of its former colonial power's cuisine. But there is one set of home-grown Mozambican dishes, and it can be found everywhere. Every place from fancy restaurants to roadside stands proudly offers their customers the same thing, the culinary export commodity that is responsible for Mozambique's singular contribution to world cuisine: piri piri – a sauce so hot and nice that they named it twice, the first time gasping for air, the second to confirm that you can still talk.

No one really knows the true story of the piri piri chile. *Piri piri*, or *pil-pil*, means "pepper-pepper" in the local language of the eastern African Swahili Coast. Legend has it that these small, incredibly hot bird's-eye chiles are indigenous to the African bush, but that is highly improbable, as all capsicums originated in the Americas. What is more likely is that the chiles were brought to what is today Mozambique by the Portuguese explorers and spice traders in the fifteenth or sixteenth century, and that they have since become indigenized up to the point where they now form the axis around which Mozambican food seems to have evolved. From the destitute Tete Province in the northwest to booming Maputo in the south, I have been fascinated by the Mozambicans' passion for piri piri. You see it everywhere: *frango piri piri* is grilled in every courtyard and can be bought on almost every street corner, the chicken most often cooked on ramshackle scrap-metal grills.

You won't find ramshackle scrap metal in stylish and expensive Manjar dos Deuses. But there is a small grill on every table so you can grill your meat and prawns to your own liking — a fine way of making you pay to *not* have anyone cook, and possibly ruin, your food. And there is, of course, piri piri sauce. It would not be possible to run a restaurant in Maputo without piri piri, since their definition of a restaurant is a place where you can get your fix of flaming-hot sauce to flavor your food.

And that is where I went wrong. As I had seen the street vendors do, I dipped my prawns in piri piri sauce and placed them on the grill. Immediately the fumes were almost unbearable. I should have known: The capsaicin in chiles is the same volatile crystalline substance that is found in pepper spray, and in early types of tear gas. When eaten, it will give you that tingling or burning sensation that can be ever so pleasantly painful. But when burned over an open fire, the smoke is just terribly unpleasant.

Windows and doors are opened; fans are set in motion. I apologize to the others, cough and cry some more, drink lots of water, and after a few minutes all is more or less normal again at the Manjar dos Deuses. And, to the extent that I am able to taste anything, apart from the feeling of my own embarrassment and slightly sore respiratory system, I have a very good dinner. But I somehow get the feeling that something is lacking, that it is not quite as good as the food served on the street. Suddenly it dawns on me: The reason nearly all piri piri dishes are made outside, in gardens or on street corners, is not only poverty, of which Mozambique has had more than its fair share. In order to get the right balance between smoky and hot, it is in fact best if the meat or fish is basted or rubbed with piri piri before it is grilled. That way, some of it will burn, and the fumes that will make us cry and choke if we inhale them, flavor the meat nicely with a deep smoky flavor that hints of hotness without burning. But this has to be done outside. The stylishness of Manjar dos Deuses is agreeable, and the small individual indoor grills are quaint. But it is not the right place to make a good piri piri, unless you don't mind poisoning yourself and the people around you. If you want the right kind of heat, get out of the kitchen, or better, out of the house altogether.

Peanuts, chiles, and garlic, longing to become an Indonesian satay sauce.

CHICKEN PIRI PIRI

CHICKEN PIRI PIRI SHOULD AND MUST BE QUITE HOT, but it does not have to be unbearably hot. In general, one can say that how much piri piri is used before grilling will determine the flavor, the amount put on afterward will give it the last extra punch. That said, this is not a dish for those who normally order dishes less than medium-hot.

Grilling a whole chicken can be tricky: the lean meat of the breast tends to be overdone before the collagen-rich meat of the thighs is cooked. But when a chicken is butterflied by cutting it open along the back, the thighs, which need more heat to be cooked through, are pushed forward into a position where they are more exposed to heat, while the breast is pushed back and isolated.

This is a dish that should be made outside. It can be made inside in your kitchen only if you have an exceptionally good kitchen fan. And an exit strategy.

You can either rub the chicken with dried chiles or red pepper flakes, lemon, oregano, and garlic, as in the recipe, or use a homemade or commercially made piri piri sauce — in which case, that is really all you need, apart from the oil for basting. (Use 3 to 6 tablespoons piri piri sauce for marinating the chicken.)

Serve with a simple salad, such as Tomato and Cucumber Salad with Cumin Salt (page 41), rice, and piri piri sauce or a milder ketchup-style chili sauce. I also think that it is nice to have a small bowl of plain yogurt sprinkled with freshly ground cloves on top (see recipe on page 104); it is soothing if the chicken is too hot for you and nice even if it is not.

Serves 2 as a main course

1	2- to 3-pound chicken, preferably free-range
2	tablespoons crushed dried piri piri or bird's-eye chiles
	Salt
2	teaspoons oregano
3 to 4	cloves garlic, crushed (optional)
1	lemon, halved
	Vegetable oil for brushing
	Piri piri sauce, homemade (page 105) or store-bought, for basting (optional)

1 Using a butcher's knife or poultry shears, cut the chicken open down the back and flatten it out. Rub the chicken with the dried chiles, salt to taste, oregano, crushed garlic (if desired), and the juice from half the lemon; reserve the lemon shell for later. (You should wear rubber gloves when rubbing the chicken.) Leave to marinate for a few minutes to 1 hour, depending on how chile-hot you would like the chicken to be.

2 Light a grill.

3 Brush the chicken with a thin film of oil to prevent sticking. Grill over high heat for 15 minutes, turning frequently. Then move the chicken away from the coals, or, if using a gas grill, turn down the heat to medium, and grill for 25 to 30 minutes longer, until the juice runs clear when you pierce a thigh at its thickest part. Continue to turn the chicken every couple of minutes to prevent burning, and baste with oil and piri piri, if desired. If the chicken is showing a tendency to burn, squeeze over some lemon juice. You can also insulate parts of the meat that you fear are being overdone by placing some of the squeezed-out lemon shell under it. The lemon will also flavor the meat nicely.

VARIATION *You may prefer to finish the chicken off in the oven. In that case, preheat the oven to 400 degrees F and roast the chicken on a baking sheet for 20 to 25 minutes.*

SOOTHING CLOVE
AND YOGURT DIP

Makes about ½ cup

½	cup plain yogurt
1	tablespoon finely chopped shallot
1	teaspoon sugar (optional)
½ to 1	teaspoon freshly ground cloves

YOGURT HAS A COOL MOUTHFEEL that can be nice for countering an overdose of chiles. Freshly ground cloves not only add flavor; although intensely pungent, they are also soothing. In fact, clove oil used to be prescribed for toothache. THIS SIMPLE MIXTURE OF YOGURT AND CLOVES WORKS WELL WITH MOST REALLY HOT DISHES.

In a small bowl, mix the yogurt, shallot, and sugar, if desired. Sprinkle with the cloves.

PIRI PIRI SAUCE

PIRI PIRI SAUCE IS SIMPLE TO MAKE and can be used whenever you want a really hot condiment, not only when making chicken or shrimp piri piri; and it keeps well. That said, although the sauce itself is such a simple affair, I do not always bother making my own — a commercially made piri piri sauce works just as well.

This is a relatively acidic piri piri sauce. There are also ketchupy versions that are quite nice, too. If you would like to try that variation, add one 14½-ounce can chopped tomatoes and 1 to 3 tablespoons sugar, and boil gently for 1 hour.

It is advisable to add the chiles a little at a time. It is easier to adjust the sauce up a few notches than down.

Heat 3 tablespoons of the oil in a pot or large skillet over medium heat. Add half the chiles and the onion, garlic, and ginger and sauté for 5 minutes. Transfer to a blender and add the remaining 5 tablespoons oil and the rest of the ingredients. Process until almost smooth. Adjust the seasoning with more piri piri, salt, vinegar, and/or sugar to taste.

Makes 1 to 1½ cups

½	cup vegetable oil
3	tablespoons crushed dried piri piri or bird's-eye chiles, or crushed red pepper flakes, or more to taste
1	onion, finely chopped
3 to 6	cloves garlic, minced
1	tablespoon finely chopped fresh ginger
1	tablespoon paprika
2	tablespoons tomato paste
1 to 2	teaspoons salt
3	tablespoons white vinegar, or more to taste
1 to 2	tablespoons sugar (optional)

SHRIMP PIRI PIRI

PRAWNS THAT ARE FOUND IN THE WATERS OFF THE COAST OF MOZAMBIQUE are among the best in the world — and some of the largest, too. Like chicken, they are typically butterflied, then rubbed with piri piri sauce and grilled.

You can also cook these shrimp in a skillet over high heat. I dust the flesh with ground ginger and turmeric for flavor and color, and perhaps some lime, cilantro, and finely chopped ginger for freshness.

For a main course, I would serve this with a simple Rice Pilau (page 243).

**Serves 4 to 6 as a starter,
2 as a main course**

12 to 16	large shrimp in the shell
1	teaspoon powdered turmeric
1	teaspoon ground ginger
1	tablespoon piri piri sauce, homemade (page 105) or store-bought, or more to taste, or 1 tablespoon finely minced chiles
	Vegetable oil for brushing
	Salt
1	tablespoon finely chopped fresh ginger
1	tablespoon finely chopped parsley or cilantro (fresh coriander)
1	lime, quartered

1 If grilling, light the grill.

2 Using kitchen shears or a sharp knife, split the shrimp open lengthwise to butterfly them (cut down the "belly," not the back, of the shrimp), then remove the dark intestinal tract that runs down the back. Mix the turmeric and ground ginger, and season the flesh side of the shrimp with this mixture. Rub with the piri piri sauce (or chiles) and oil and season with salt.

3 Place the shrimp flesh-side down on the grill over high heat and cook for 2 minutes, then turn and cook for 2 to 4 minutes longer, depending on the size. Or, if cooking inside, heat a film of oil in a large nonstick skillet over high heat. Turn your kitchen fan on max. Sauté the shrimp for 2 to 3 minutes, then turn and cook for 3 to 5 minutes longer, depending on size. You may have to cook the shrimp in two or more batches in order not to crowd the pan.

4 Sprinkle the shrimp with the fresh ginger and parsley, squeeze the lime juice over them, and serve.

VARIATION *For a distinctly Thai flavor, add 1 tablespoon coarsely ground coriander seeds and use the cilantro rather than parsley. You may also want to use fish sauce rather than salt.*

NOTE *If you do not have an efficient kitchen fan, add the piri piri sauce after cooking.*

CHILES
WITH HOT TUNA STUFFING

CHILES, ESPECIALLY LARGER ONES, are perfect containers for different types of stuffing. This recipe was inspired by Sri Lankan chef Channa Dassabayaka. I normally serve this as an appetizer — one that always leaves my guests very thirsty — but if you want to serve it as a main course, you can use regular bell peppers or, preferably, long pointed peppers such as banana peppers.

Putting a whole chile in your mouth may seem frightening, but if you use a relatively mild variety and scoop out the seeds and the white fleshy material that connects the seeds to the fruit, the level of pungency is drastically reduced. The heat level can also be adjusted up by adding more chiles to the stuffing, if desired. But do test one scraped-out chile yourself before using, and check out the chart of Scoville units measuring the heat level of different chiles on page 284. I have found that this dish works best with canned tuna in oil, but it can also be made with leftover poached fish.

Makes 20 small mouthfuls

20	large chiles, preferably a relatively mild variety
	Oil for panfrying, such as canola
2	onions, finely chopped
8	curry leaves
½ to 1	teaspoon cumin seeds
1	teaspoon mustard seeds
1 to 3	small green chiles, finely chopped
1	16-ounce can tuna packed in oil
2	boiled potatoes, mashed
1	tablespoon finely chopped mint
2	tablespoons fresh lime juice
	Salt and freshly ground black pepper

1 Preheat the oven to 400 degrees F.

2 Wearing gloves, use a sharp knife to cut open the wider end of each chile, without cutting it off. Scrape out the seeds using a knife or a small spoon. You can also slit the chiles lengthwise to get better access to the seeds, but I find that much of the pleasure of the dish is that the chiles are still (almost) whole.

3 Heat a couple of tablespoons oil in a large skillet over medium-high heat. Add the onions, curry leaves, cumin seeds, mustard seeds, and chopped green chiles and sauté for 3 to 5 minutes, until the onions are soft.

4 Transfer the onion mixture to a bowl, add the tuna, mashed potatoes, mint, and lime juice, and mix well. Season with salt and pepper.

5 Put a small amount of stuffing into each chile and close up. Place in a baking dish and bake for 15 to 20 minutes, until the stuffing is steaming hot and the chiles are slightly wrinkled. Allow to cool for at least 5 minutes before serving.

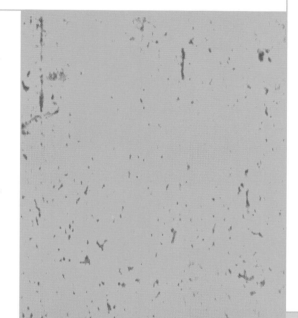

CHILI POTATOES

Serves 4 to 6 as a side dish

2½	pounds russet (baking) potatoes, scrubbed and quartered
1 to 3	teaspoons chili powder
1 to 3	teaspoons paprika
1 to 2	teaspoons powdered turmeric
2 to 4	tablespoons vegetable oil
1	lime or lemon, quartered

WHO SAYS THAT SIDE DISHES MUST BE BLAND? These beautifully turmeric-yellow and chili-red hot potatoes are wonderful as a side dish to accompany mild and aromatic curries. Although Indian cuisine is unique within the region in its love of *aloo* – potatoes – I find that this also goes well with Middle Eastern dishes.

1 Preheat the oven to 350 degrees F.

2 Place the potatoes in a baking dish. Sprinkle with about half of the chili powder, paprika, and turmeric and toss well, then sprinkle with the rest of the spices. Add the oil and toss well.

3 Bake for 45 minutes, or until tender. Serve with the lime wedges.

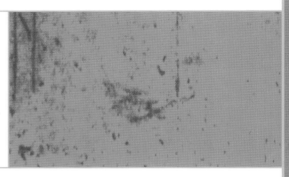

GREEN PAPAYA SALAD

THE MOST IMPORTANT ELEMENT IN MASTERING THE ART OF THAI COOKING is to find the perfect balance between hot, sweet, sour, and salty, and the traditional green papaya salad — *som tam* — is a fine place to start. It is a recipe where no exact measurements can be given, and a successful result depends not only on your ability to re-create an "authentic" Thai flavor but also on your personal taste.

In Thailand, this is a dish that is normally sold by street vendors, and it is always made to order. It is a fine example of true craftsmanship and strong tradition that still allows for individual preferences. Although the papaya salad makers do nothing but make papaya salad, you would have to look hard to find a cook more willing to make adjustments to please the palate of his or her customers.

The ceremony starts with the vendor asking how hot you would like the salad to be — one or two small chiles for the careful, five or six for the brave. Then the ingredients are mixed. While the customer watches, the chiles, garlic, and dried shrimp are pounded; the tomatoes, papaya, and beans are gently bruised; the peanuts are added; and, finally, the lime juice, fish sauce, and palm sugar are added and carefully mixed together. At this point, the vendor will taste the final result with his or her spoon, and the balance will be adjusted. Once the vendor is satisfied that this is the best he or she can offer, the customer is asked to taste and encouraged to provide input as to whether it should be a tad more salty, or perhaps brightened with even more of the fresh acidity from the lime. Only when vendor and customer have agreed that this is as good as it gets is the salad served. And by that time it is one of the best things that can be served. It is also a stark contrast to most European and American salads, where much of the point seems to be to dress up the greens in fatty dressings. This contains no fat whatsoever.

The papayas should be green and unripe. A ripe papaya will result in a mushy salad that will look more like a sauce. If you cannot find hard green papayas, you can increase the amount of finely shredded carrots and mix them with a little ripe papaya. It surprised me to learn that this is something even Thai people do when no green papayas can be found. If you cannot find dried shrimp, you can use a small amount of shrimp paste. As shrimp paste is often very salty, you should reduce the amount of fish sauce in the dressing. Palm sugar has a special flavor that cannot be copied, but if you cannot find it, you can substitute brown sugar.

It's best to make this salad using a mortar and pestle, preferably wooden, large enough to hold the salad. If your mortar is too small, transfer the crushed ingredients to a bowl, then mix and bruise the rest of the ingredients in the bowl using the pestle.

You can shred the papaya and carrot using a regular box grater, but as the salad is much more interesting to eat when the strands of papaya and carrot are long and spaghetti-like, I prefer to cut them with a sharp knife or use a julienne peeler or mandoline.

Serves 4 as a starter

3 to 4	cloves garlic, peeled
2 to 6	small chiles
2 to 3	tablespoons dried shrimp or 1 to 2 teaspoons shrimp paste
6	long beans or ¼ pound green beans, trimmed and cut into 1-inch pieces
2 to 3	tomatoes, cut into 8 wedges each
1	large green papaya (1 to 1 ½ pounds), peeled, halved, seeded, and shredded
1	medium carrot, peeled and shredded
3 to 4	tablespoons fish sauce (*nam pla*)
4 to 6	tablespoons fresh lime juice
3	tablespoons palm sugar or brown sugar
1	kaffir lime leaf, stemmed and finely chopped (optional)
3	tablespoons finely chopped cilantro (fresh coriander) or holy basil (optional)
¼	cup peanuts, toasted and coarsely chopped

Using a mortar and pestle, crush the garlic, chiles, and dried shrimp. Add the beans and tomatoes and crush somewhat more gently. Add the papaya and carrot and bruise. The idea is to bruise the cell walls of the papaya enough to make it susceptible to the flavors of the dressing but not enough to make it mushy. Add the fish sauce, lime juice, and sugar. Mix everything well. Adjust the seasoning to taste. Add the lime leaf and cilantro (if desired) and the peanuts, mix well, and serve.

LEFT: Men with rice bags on Bali. RIGHT: Rice and pulses at the food market in Stone Town, Zanzibar.

LEFT TO RIGHT: A funeral procession in Kuta, Bali; a woman bringing offerings to the temple in Tabanan, Bali; a whole family on the road.

A woman (RIGHT) working in the rice fields on Bali while her kids (LEFT) watch. Rice is the staple food in almost all of Southeast Asia.

CARDAMOM

"CARDAMOM IS AN INVALUABLE COMPONENT IN EVERYTHING FROM INDIAN AND ARABIAN MASALAS TO SCANDINAVIAN CHRISTMAS CAKES AND INDONESIAN SATAYS. AND FOR THE PEOPLE OF KERALA, CARDAMOM HAS BEEN AN ALMOST INEXHAUSTIBLE SOURCE OF WEALTH—OR AT THE VERY LEAST, OF SURVIVAL IN

Third World motoring is seldom just a drive, and going out of town for a couple of days has a different meaning in India. What in other places may be taken for granted and enjoyed as a quiet outing can here offer more excitement than you may have bargained for.

The first hour on the road afforded me with the near possibility of being crushed to pieces by three different buses that, at certain particularly hard-to-maneuver places along the road, came chasing against me at a phenomenal speed, oblivious of the dangers of driving without brakes on narrow and winding roads. And if my heart was in my throat at the sight of a family of five passing me on mopeds just as a huge cement truck was approaching in the other direction, it found a constant supply of good reasons to remain there. The last time was as I started the ascent to Cardamom Hills, when the car nearly hit an elephant that came marching along the road accompanied by his two helpers. The elephant seemed unaffected by the situation; it kept walking at its slow, steady speed. I could not help wonder who would suffer most in a collision — the medium-sized car or the four-and-half-ton elephant? — but I was quite comfortable not learning the answer.

However, at Shalimar Garden Resort in Cardamom Hills, a hundred fifty miles north of Kerala's hectic and tongue-twistingly named capital Thiruvananthapuram, it is as peaceful as can be. A cool breeze plays in the leaves, and life slowly moves along with a carefree inefficiency that makes you forget time. And everything smells of cardamom.

At first I think it is the tea. It could have been, but it is not. I eat a chicken curry, and while it definitely contains cardamom, the smell remains after I have eaten and the plate has been taken away.

It is the air that carries the camphorous aromas of cardamom; the entire valley is perfumed.

I have finished my meal and am about to move on when I hear the singing. In the beginning, it does not really sound like singing — to ears that are accustomed to other scales and different melodies, the sounds are strange: high-pitched and exotic, but captivating nonetheless. Then, gradually, I begin to recognize the singing as melodies, with parts that seem like refrains. And with every verse, new voices start singing. And suddenly the entire valley is filled with song. From my vantage point on a wooden terrace on top of a steep hill, it seems as if the green bushes and trees themselves are singing, as if the rustle of the lazy breeze through their leaves is transformed into frail female voices.

Enchanted, as if hearing the song of the Sirens for the first time and having no mast to tie myself to, I leave the secluded terrace and climb down into the valley. And there, under the bushes, I find the singing women, and the reason why the highlands here in eastern Kerala are called Cardamom Hills.

The valley is covered with green bushes of about human height. And under almost each of these bushes, at the base of the pointy, lance-shaped leaves, sits a singing woman picking cardamom. Cardamom grows in small crowns near the ground. At first they are tiny white flowers, and after pollination they become the highly fragrant cardamom pods that are used in

Cardamom fresh from the pod. The pod becomes papery when dried, but the seeds are best when still somewhat sticky.

cooking. They are in season almost all year. New beautiful orchidlike flowers are blooming at the same time as pods are ready to be picked — that is, just before maturity, when they will open up and spread their seeds on the ground.

It is here cardamom originated, and it is still grown much the same way as when the plant's unique qualities were discovered millennia ago. The hands of the cardamom ladies follow the peduncles from the base and outward with a certainty and speed that transcends routine; before them, generations upon generations of women have been sitting in the same place doing the same thing, finding the pods and picking just those that have reached the right stage.

I converse with the cardamom ladies without any of us understanding all that much. Never have the women seen anything as ridiculous as this big, pale man. They smile and laugh and allow me to taste the green cardamom pods. The skin, normally papery and hard, is soft. The seeds are sticky, and they have not yet achieved the pungency that will come with aging.

Still, once I have tasted the cardamom of three or four of the women, I am, it seems, obliged to taste the cardamom of all the women. Soon my mouth grows slightly numb. At the same time, I feel that my breathing — up to that point still a little congested by city air, highway dust, and my own nervousness — is flowing more freely, as if I had inhaled mentholatum. And my whole world tastes of cardamom. The women are chewing betel nuts and pepper leaves; along with the singing, this helps them through long days. As a result of the constant chewing, most of their teeth have fallen out, and those that are left are colored orange or red.

I try to ask them why they do not chew cardamom. From ancient times up until the advent of modern dentistry and hygiene, cardamom was universally known as a remedy for bad breath, an aid for cleaning your teeth, and a tool to help circulation and release energy. And for the ladies here, cardamom is readily available to the extreme. But my attempt to communicate this stalls miserably; it is merely seen as a plea for more. I am laughed at, sung for, and stuffed so full of cardamom that I have to start spitting it out while all the time smiling and praising it, as not to seem ungrateful.

"That must be that madman," they seem to say to each other in between the bursts of laughter.

"That foreigner who eats all the cardamom we pick and send off to faraway places."

"Yes, it must be him. Let us stuff him full of even more cardamom."

In these parts of India cardamom is known as the "queen of spices," pepper being the king. It is used in many dishes and, despite the singing cardamom ladies' preference for betel nuts, it is also often used in local traditional medicine. Elsewhere cardamom is an invaluable component in everything from Indian and Arabian masalas to Scandinavian Christmas cakes and Indonesian satays. And for the people of Kerala, cardamom has been an almost inexhaustible source of wealth — or, at the very least, of survival in dignity without poverty. A couple of times a month, the small, fragrant bushes growing down in the shady part of the valley could be harvested and the pods then traded for all kinds of necessities, even those from faraway places.

This was considered such a fortunate situation that no one bothered to grow cardamom — people were content with picking what was growing wild. And only when the English arrived with their ideas of rationalization were the first cardamom plantations established.

Back to the roots: A woman picking cardamom in its place of origin, Cardamom Hills in the Kerala state of southern India.

CARDAMOM MANGOES

JUST OUTSIDE THE MAIN MARKET IN ZANZIBAR'S STONE TOWN there is a mango seller who has set up shop under a great mango tree. It is a simple business model if there ever was one. Every time a mango falls down to the ground, if it is not too badly bruised by the fall, he adds it to his pyramid of fruits for sale.

This is a simple and delicious dessert where you get the maximum out of the fresh, sweet cardamom flavor. You should use whole cardamom pods, not ground cardamom, and you can decide for yourself how strong you want the cardamom flavor to be. I normally crush two or three pods to a fine powder, and the rest I just bruise with my hands.

It is often difficult to find perfectly ripe mangoes, but in this case that is not a problem; here it is actually an advantage to use firm fruits, as perfectly ripe fruits will turn mushy when they are cooked. I got the idea for this from Ian Hemphill's wonderful encyclopedia on spices, *The Spice and Herb Bible*. This recipe also works well using other fruits, such as apples and bananas.

Serve with ice cream: mango, coconut, or Bourbon Vanilla Ice Cream (page 257).

Serves 4

2	large mangoes
½	teaspoon freshly ground cardamom, plus 8 cardamom pods, preferably green, slightly bruised
2	tablespoons butter
2	tablespoons brown sugar

1 Wash the mangoes thoroughly in warm water. Cut each mango in half: This can best be done by locating the sharp edge of the fruit with your finger, then inserting the knife there and slicing off half the mango by cutting alongside the flat side of the pit. Repeat on the other side. Cut a crisscross pattern in the flesh of each mango half so the flavors can penetrate the fruit, and season with the ground cardamom. Cut off and finely chop whatever mango flesh is left on the pits.

2 Melt the butter in a large skillet over medium heat. Add the sugar and bruised cardamom pods and cook, stirring, until the sugar has melted and the kitchen starts smelling of cardamom. Add the halved mangoes, flesh-side down, and the finely chopped mango flesh and cook for 5 to 7 minutes. (This may have to be done in two batches in order not to crowd the skillet.)

3 Serve the mangoes with the cardamom pods as garnish. The pods can be eaten, if desired, but be warned that they have a quite overpowering taste.

CHICKEN CARDAMOM MASALA
WITH CASHEWS

Serves 4 as a main course

½	cup plain full-fat yogurt
2	tablespoons garam masala
6 to 10	cardamom pods, lightly bruised
1	1-inch piece of cinnamon stick
2	teaspoons chili powder, or more to taste
2	teaspoons chopped fresh ginger
2	teaspoons salt
1	chicken, cut into 8 pieces, or 4 chicken thighs, halved
1	teaspoon powdered turmeric
	Oil for panfrying, such as canola
4	onions, chopped
3 to 5	cloves garlic, chopped
4 to 6	tablespoons cashews
1 to 2	tablespoons tomato paste or ketchup
¼	cup heavy cream (optional)
	Chopped cilantro (fresh coriander) or parsley for garnish

THE COOKING OF KERALA IS VARIED AND OPEN TO OUTSIDE INFLUENCE. This is a not unusual combination of north and south Indian cooking. The recipe is based on a dish I had at Preethi Restaurant in Thripunithura. The easiest way to make it at home is to take a garam masala spice mix, homemade or store-bought, and jazz it up a bit with more spices, most of all fresh-tasting cardamom, but also sweet cinnamon and strong chiles.

Yogurt has a tendency to separate when cooked; if it does, you may add a few tablespoons of heavy cream just before serving. In any case, do not use low-fat yogurt.

1 In a large bowl, combine the yogurt, garam masala, cardamom, cinnamon stick, chili powder, ginger, and salt. Add the chicken, turning to coat. Let marinate for as long as you have time – if more than an hour, place the bowl in the refrigerator.

2 Using a rubber spatula, scrape off as much of the yogurt marinade from the chicken as possible; reserve the marinade. Pat the chicken dry using paper towels, and sprinkle with the turmeric.

3 Heat a tablespoon or so of oil in a wide pot over high heat. Add the chicken and cook, turning occasionally, for 10 minutes, or until the skin is nicely browned. You may have to do this in two batches in order not to crowd the pot.

4 Remove the chicken, reduce the heat, and sauté the onions and garlic for 4 to 5 minutes, until starting to soften. Add the chicken, the reserved marinade, the cashews, and tomato paste, cover, and cook for 25 to 30 minutes, until the chicken is cooked through.

5 Stir in the cream (if desired) and cook for 2 more minutes. Garnish with cilantro.

VARIATION *If you would like to make a thick sauce without adding a lot of calories, add another ½ cup of yogurt along with the marinade and chicken.*

NOTE *This is not a dish that demands any purity of flavor – the more flavors, the merrier. You may want to add more vegetables: for example, cauliflower and carrots. A sprinkle of crushed fennel seeds and ground coriander would not go amiss.*

BANANAS
WITH COCONUT AND CARDAMOM

WHEN I VISIT ZANZIBAR, I ALWAYS MAKE SURE TO HAVE THIS SIMPLE DESERT. Unlike most Zanzibari cooks, I prefer not to add more than the minimum amount of sugar, feeling that some of the freshness of the cardamom gets lost if the coconut milk is so sweet that it gets syrupy. In accordance with Zanzibari tradition, though, I use whole cardamom pods that I gently crush between my hands, and I appreciate the fact that you can actually see the spice that is responsible for the transformation of the dish. If you pound or crush the cardamom, you should reduce the amount significantly. I normally use green or light brown cardamom; the larger black cardamom often seems to have less of the sweet aromas and is in my opinion better suited to savory dishes.

The number of different banana varieties that can be found in the market in Zanzibar's Stone Town is absolutely impressive, and this dish is often made with relatively small firm, sweet bananas. If you have only a limited choice, I have found that I get the best results with bananas that are ever so slightly unripe, still light green at the ends. Completely ripe bananas tend to fall apart when cooked for more than a couple of minutes.

Serve with ice cream.

Serves 2

4 to 8   **cardamom pods**

1   **cup unsweetened coconut milk or a combination of coconut milk and unsweetened coconut cream (see page 139)**

1   **clove**

4   **small slightly underripe bananas**

1 to 3   **tablespoons brown sugar**

1 Bruise the cardamom pods gently between your hands, making small cracks in the hard pods but stopping short of breaking them open. The more you crush them, the stronger the cardamom flavor.

2 Combine the coconut milk, cardamom, and clove in a pot large enough to hold the bananas. Bring to a boil, reduce the heat, and simmer for 3 to 5 minutes to release the flavor of the cardamom. Sample the coconut milk and adjust the flavor if necessary by crushing or bruising one or more of the cardamom pods with a wooden spatula or spoon.

3 Peel the bananas and add to the coconut milk. Boil gently for 5 minutes, turning once. Add sugar to taste and allow it to dissolve before gently transferring the bananas to serving plates. Spoon over the coconut milk and serve.

VARIATION *When the bananas are cooked, take them out of the coconut milk and transfer to a baking pan, sprinkle with the brown sugar and a small dusting of ground cardamom, and place under the broiler until the sugar is caramelized.*

COCONUT PANCAKES
WITH CARDAMOM

Serves 4

2	cups all-purpose flour
3	large eggs
1	cup unsweetened coconut milk, or as necessary
1	teaspoon salt
2 to 3	tablespoons palm sugar or brown sugar
	Whole milk if necessary
½	cup grated fresh coconut or packaged shredded coconut
5 to 6	white cardamom pods, crushed to a fine powder and husks removed
2	tablespoons melted butter or ghee, plus more for cooking the pancakes

THIS RECIPE IS BASED ON A DISH SERVED BY THE CHRISTIAN MINORITY IN KERALA, in southern India, where it is called *madakusan*. It also has some similarities to the traditional *appam* — rice and coconut pancakes that are often served with savory dishes. The boundary between savory and sweet dishes is often blurred in Indian cuisine, but this is a more pronounced dessert. It is very good with fruits, such as Cardamom Mangoes (page 121).

It should preferably be made with white cardamom.

1 Sift the flour into a medium bowl. Whisk in the eggs, coconut milk, salt, and 1 tablespoon of the sugar. The batter should be fairly thick but still runny. If it needs more liquid, whisk in some whole milk or more coconut milk. Let stand for 20 minutes.

2 Combine the rest of the sugar, the grated coconut, and cardamom in a small bowl. Whisk the melted butter into the pancake batter.

3 Heat a small amount of butter in a large nonstick skillet over medium-high heat. Add some of the pancake batter and spread it more or less evenly in the pan. Sprinkle the top of the pancake with some of the coconut mixture. When the top of the pancake is almost set, flip it over and cook until it is cooked through and the coconut is a nice golden color. Transfer to a plate, and continue until all the batter is used up.

AROMATIC CARDAMOM LAMB
WITH SAFFRON CARROTS

I WOULDN'T KNOW EXACTLY WHERE THIS DISH COMES FROM. I first tasted it in Oman, served by an Egyptian chef who had previously worked in Iran and Pakistan. Like much of the cooking of the region, it sports characteristics of all these different but closely related cuisines. It is also a nice example of how Middle Eastern cooking often makes use of all the spices we know from Indian cooking, but without the heat.

Do try to use cheap stewing meat, as it is more flavorful and contains lots of collagen that is transformed to juicy gelatin upon cooking. If you can find mutton, it would be even better, but in that case I would increase the cooking time by 45 minutes.

Serve with rice or Nan with Cumin, Raisins, and Onions (page 48).

Serves 4 as a main course

8 to 12	cardamom pods, lightly bruised
2	teaspoons cumin seeds, or more to taste
	Oil for panfrying, such as canola
1½	pounds lamb stewing meat
3	onions, chopped
1	2-inch piece of cinnamon stick
4	tomatoes, quartered
2	red bell peppers, roasted, peeled, cored, seeded, and sliced
2	cups lamb stock or vegetable stock
1	tablespoon butter
1	pound carrots, sliced
3	tablespoons raisins
4	cloves garlic, finely chopped
1	tablespoon white vinegar
	A small pinch of saffron threads (approximately ½ gram)
2	tablespoons honey
	Salt

1 Dry-roast the cardamom and cumin seeds in a wide pot over high heat, stirring frequently, until fragrant. Add a little oil, then add the lamb and onions and sauté until the meat is browned. You may have to do this in two batches in order not to crowd the pot.

2 Add the cinnamon stick, tomatoes, bell peppers, and stock, bring to a simmer, and let simmer uncovered for 1½ to 2 hours, until the meat is very tender. Check to make sure that the pot does not boil dry, and add more stock or water if necessary.

3 Just before the stew is done, combine the butter, carrots, raisins, and garlic in a small pot and sauté the carrots for 5 minutes. Add the vinegar and saffron and allow to simmer for 5 minutes.

4 Add the honey and the carrot mixture to the lamb stew. Cook for 3 to 5 minutes, then season with salt and serve.

NOTE *If you are unable to monitor the stew as it simmers, you can simmer it covered for 1½ hours and then reduce the liquid by boiling for 10 to 20 minutes — but the result is more likely to get mushy.*

CURRIES

"CURRIES ARE THE THERMOMETERS OF CULTURES. HOW A SOCIETY COMBINES THEIR FLAVOR SAYS MORE THAN HOW THEY DRESS OR WHAT MUSIC THEY LISTEN TO."

IT IS ALL IN THE MIX

"And then you need an authentic masala, not the imitation they give you many places these days," she said, quite sternly. "If not, your curry will not taste right. So it has to be the one they make here, at Atlas."

I was standing in Atlas Trading, the old-fashioned spice shop in Cape Town's Bo Kaap district, getting advice on how to make some of the local specialties, and we had come to the part about the seasonings, a subject on which my helpful teacher was most insistent. In order to underline her point and make sure that I did not leave without the right spice mixture, she went behind the counter and got a small bag of the freshly made spice mix.

"Take this," she said. "Only this is the right one. Made with the original recipe, right here. With lots of cardamom and cumin, just as it should be."

I thanked her and took the bag to the cashier along with what I had already got. My helpful friend watched me all the time until I got into my car, as if she wanted to make sure that I did not leave the masala behind, that what she had just taught me would not go to waste because I took the wrong spice mixture, what she would consider an imitation.

What I did not say was that what she so derogatorily referred to as "imitations" are just what people at the other end of the Indian Ocean actually prefer. And that they have just as strong opinions on what is authentic as she has. I have heard the same warning in every place I have visited in the region. From the market in Muscat to a home on Mauritius, masala is at the center of the cooking, and the composition of the masala is what gives it its individual character.

Masala is, gastronomically, what makes the world go 'round. For most curries, curried dishes, and a majority of all food containing spices, a masala of some kind is used. The word *masala*, writes Alan Davidson, was originally Arabic for "interests," and today it is used to refer to a wide variety of spice mixtures. "Masala can be ground or whole spices; mild or strong; bland or sharp; 'dry' or 'wet,'" he says. The masalas of the region around the Indian Ocean, I have come to realize, are good examples of how the cuisines of the different cultures living there relate to each other, emphasizing different flavors, all having their own distinctive features. And, just as other dialects of your own language can seem like mispronunciations, the unseasoned traveler may think that there is something wrong, lacking, or inauthentic in a spice mixture that is somewhat different from his own. Yet for me, these differences are what make cooking and eating so interesting. It is not about looking for the right answer, but more like experiencing the orchestra of flavors playing different songs with a wide variety of instruments.

I've got a crush on you: Spices are being combined to make a Thai curry.

THE BEST CONFUSION I EVER HAD

Zanzibar's Stone Town is a place of secrets. For centuries, people from all over the world have been living together in this small city on a tropical island off the coast of East Africa. Here different cultures and religions that have been in conflict in other parts of the world, sometimes engaging in bloody battles of hegemony and power, have found ways to live together side by side.

And the diversity that seems overwhelming at first is even more impressive when studied closely: Muslims here are not just Shias or Sunnis but also Ishnashiris, Ishmailis, Ibadis, and Bahoras. There are Anglican Christians from mainland Tanzania and from India. There are Catholics, Hindus, and even Zarathustran Parsis.

And it is all about secrets and semi-secrets, about what is hidden and what lies in the open, about lies that serve noble causes and truths that can hurt. There are rumors and gossip, more so than other places, one should think. A recent research report showed that the average male here spent between three and four hours gossiping every day; no figures were given for women. In the space between truths and lies, between what is public and what is secret, everything happens.

There are signs that are impossible for strangers to understand. The sight of a beautiful henna tattoo visible on the arm of a young woman otherwise veiled and dressed in black from top to toe might or might not signify something more than just the latest Shia fashion. The shopkeeper closing his door for a few minutes in the middle of the day during the holy month of Ramadan, and then suddenly looking more content and less tired, may or may not be an indication of a small transgression of the rules of fasting. Whatever you do or say or however you behave, it is destined to be discussed and interpreted and whispered

around town until nearly everyone has heard, reinterpreted, and retold the stories, with ever-so-fine nuances added or subtracted. But no one will admit that they know anything.

The boundaries between the different religions and groups are maintained through tight social control, and frustrations and disagreements both within and between groups are expressed through gossip and steady creation of myths. Sometimes the austere Muslim Bahoras will be referred to as the Bahorribles; the Muslim Ishmailis, who pray only three times a day, are often seen as somewhat less pious by other Muslims. The Hindus are often suspicious of each other; as it happened, almost all the Hindus who arrived on the island claimed to belong to the Brahmin caste, the highest caste. Some of them must be lying, so it is better not to be too closely associated with that guy on the other side of town, lest you be taken for a mere merchant or farmer parvenu. Even the two small groups of Indian Christians, who are on relatively friendly terms, do not socialize — it is telling that their church bells go off a few minutes apart, the Anglicans at two to six, the Catholics at ten past. This is part of what creates the mystique of Zanzibar, and also Zanzibari cooking.

What food needs sometimes is secrets, something that somehow obstructs our view, making us incapable of seeing what is really there,

On top of the world: My favorite place on Zanzibar is the teahouse on the roof of Babu Emerson's house in Stone Town.

and thereby making it seem magical, impossible to decipher or fully comprehend. True, some food is better when it is simple and unfussy, when you can follow the tomato from the vine to the table and are able to taste last week's sunshine on your plate. That can give you a revelation of pure taste and clarity. In other cases, though, your appetite is whetted by a veil of uncertainty and the aura of magic that surrounds it.

"You know, there is a story behind the sor patel," Babu Emerson says, chuckling, in a low, conspiratorial voice. The wildly aromatic pork stew is nearly ready. For hours the smell of meat and spices has been driving us almost mad. Even here, in the small teahouse on the roof of Babu Emerson's house on Sokomohogo Street in Stone Town, where the evening breeze caresses us, the smell is almost too much to bear. To make things worse, or perhaps because it is impossible to think of anything but the sor patel, Babu has been describing the dish, how it is made and how it tastes, with its unique combination of pork meat and liver, pepper, turmeric, chiles, cinnamon, and apple cider.

I don't know how Babu Emerson got hold of pork. It is never sold in the open on Zanzibar, where more than 90 percent of the population is Muslim. But it can be found, if you just know the right people, and if anyone knows how to get hold of it, it must be my landlord Babu Emerson, who knows everyone.

When you, every once in a blue moon, get hold of something as rare as pork, it is not just cooked any old way, so Babu Emerson has summoned Maria Barretto and her daughter, Lesley Lobo, to cook the meat and serve it to us in his beautifully ornamented teahouse, where we, from our secluded pavilion, have a lovely view over all of Stone Town. Maria is part of the small Indian Christian minority. Her family is originally from Goa, and she used to run one of the best restaurants in town.

Babu, not a stranger to gossip and storytelling himself, is dying to tell me the story behind the sor patel. Even though it is not a typical Zanzibari dish, it is a good example both of the island's rich and open food traditions and of how religion is ever present in daily life — and, as it turns out, how rumor and fact are often the same thing on Zanzibar. The name, Babu tells me, is of Indian origin. *Sor* means something like "friar" or "brother" and *Patel* is one of the most common Indian names, like Smith in England or Dupont in France. And this "Brother Patel" is one of the new converts to Christianity. But even though he is a pious member of the congregation, there is still a whole lot of the Hindu left in him. And, still fearing the consequences were he to break that ultimate Hindu taboo, he will not eat beef — therefore, the dish must be made with pork.

"You see, that's how it works," Babu says, and giggles.

I remember a previous trip to Kizimkazi on the south side of the island, where I was kept awake all night by what reminded me of a traditional African religious sermon, with loud drumming and wild shouting that did not end until fifteen minutes before the call to morning prayer from the muezzin. Perhaps that was also an example of how the conversion to a new religion did not necessarily mean that the old one was completely tossed aside.

The sor patel seems to take an eternity, and Maria and Lesley come up to us to talk about the food. I remember Maria's restaurant fondly — when I came to the island for the first time in 1992, the hospitality sector was in shambles and Chit Chat restaurant was the only place you

A woman in Stone Town, Zanzibar. The majority of Zanzibaris are Muslims, but they belong to different sects, each with its own customs and traditions.

could be guaranteed a good meal. On subsequent visits, the restaurant was still popular. I ask why she closed the place down, and a cloud passes over her face. It was impossible to continue, she says. The restaurant manager, she explains, was suddenly born-again and insisted on not serving alcohol, which made it even harder to face the stiff competition from all the fresh upstarts, and she lets it be understood that the conflict level had taken its toll.

"I'll go and look after the food," Lesley says, and leaves in a hurry.

"If the restaurant manager was so impossible, why didn't you just get rid of him?" I ask naively. Lesley arrives with freshly made poori bread, fish cakes, and chutney. Maria is suddenly reminded of something that needs her attention in the kitchen and leaves before she answers the question.

"Did you notice the tension when Maria started talking about the restaurant manager?" Babu asks. "Well, there is something more to that story, too. Not only are the born-agains and the traditionalists two almost separate groups within the Indian Catholic community — the traditionalists are not always happy about guitar-playing born-agains and would rather stick to how it has always been. What makes this so — what should I say? — *piquant* is that the restaurant manager is Maria's son-in-law. He is Lesley's husband. You see? That's Zanzibar for you."

Shortly after that, the food arrives, a sumptuous meal with at least ten dishes with all the flavors of the Indian-Portuguese Goan kitchen, fused with that of Zanzibar. And the centerpiece of this meal is, of course, the sor patel. I do not know how much of my impression is colored by the fact that I have been looking forward to it for so long, have almost been driven mad by the smell of it filling the house, have heard the story of its origin and met the people who made it, and then, finally, am eating it at the top of the world, surrounded by secretive and magical Stone Town. I only know that the sor patel is one of the best dishes I have had, the mother of all stews, a showcase of the possibilities of spices to blend so that they create one majestic, wonderfully nuanced whole where it is all but impossible to distinguish the individual spices or components.

I leave Zanzibar with yet another story, yet another great dish. But then, a few months later, on the other side of the Indian Ocean, in India, I come across a dish with almost the same name. It must be. It must. It tastes almost the same — perhaps not quite matching Maria's masterful way with spices — and the name is almost the same, *sarapatel*. But the story behind the dish is different, and leaves me thinking yet again about Zanzibar — the stories, the confusion and secrets, and the way that all adds to the magic of the place and the cooking.

The word *sarapatel*, as it turns out, has nothing to do with newly converted Indians and their unwillingness to break Hindu taboos. The Goan *sarapatel* is the spicy offspring of the original *sarapatel* from Alentejo, Portugal. And in Portuguese, *sarapatel* simply means "confusion" or "mishmash." That may, in fact, be a quite accurate albeit somewhat crude way to describe what makes the Zanzibari sor patel, and Stone Town itself, so special.

LEFT: A steaming hot poori bread. RIGHT: Lesley and Maria are two of Zanzibar's best cooks. Like most things on Zanzibar, their cooking is a combination of different influences — local ingredients mixed with Goan influences.

SOR PATEL

THE ZANZIBARI *SOR PATEL* AND THE ORIGINAL GOAN *SARAPATEL* HAVE MANY SIMILARITIES BUT I PREFER THE VERSION THAT MARIA BARETTI, the proprietor of the now-defunct Chit Chat restaurant in Zanzibar's Stone Town, made for us. Maria does not pound the spices to powder using a mortar and pestle; she simply crushes them lightly with a rolling pin. This is somewhat more difficult and is preferred but not crucial.

This is a dish that takes a lot of time to make from start to finish, but once all the ingredients are in the pot, it tends itself and all you have to do is wait. It tastes better on the second day, or even the third or fourth, so you can make it in advance and simply reheat it before serving. The dish can also be frozen for one or two months, if kept in an airtight container.

Even if you are normally not a big fan of liver and kidneys, you will do well to use them here — perhaps in smaller quantities than given in the recipe. They almost disintegrate but help give body and fullness to the dish. I stop well short of the Portuguese, who use lungs, heart, blood, and tripe as well.

If you would like to reduce the active kitchen time, you can skip pre-cooking of the meat. Just make sure to allow enough cooking time when simmering the dish.

Serves 6 to 8 as a main course

8	cups water
3	pounds boneless pork, shank or shoulder, cut into 1-inch chunks
2	teaspoons coarse sea salt, plus more to taste
1	tablespoon black peppercorns, plus more to taste
2	teaspoons powdered turmeric, or more for a brighter color
2 to 3	dried chiles
2	teaspoons ground ginger, or to taste
5 to 6	cloves
1 to 2	tablespoons cumin seeds
3	tablespoons paprika, or to taste
	A small pinch of saffron threads (optional)
3 to 4	tablespoons vinegar, preferably apple cider vinegar, or to taste
	Butter or ghee
1	pound pork liver, cleaned and cut into 1-inch chunks
11	ounces pork kidney (optional)
2	onions, chopped
2	large red bell peppers, cored, seeded, and sliced, or jarred pimentos
	Oil for panfrying, such as canola
1	tablespoon chopped fresh ginger

1 In a large pot, bring the water to a boil. Add the pork and simmer for 1 hour. Remove from the heat.

2 Remove the meat and pat dry or allow to drain in a colander. Strain the cooking liquid through a sieve lined with cheesecloth or a clean (not soapy-tasting) kitchen towel and reserve for later.

3 Combine the salt and dry spices on a cutting board and crush them lightly using a rolling pin. Or crush them using a mortar and pestle. (The salt helps grind the spices.) Transfer to a small bowl if necessary, add the vinegar, and mix until you have a wet spice paste with a coarse but fairly consistent texture.

4 In a large skillet, melt a little butter over medium-high heat and brown the meat, liver, and kidneys (if using). You will need to do this in several batches in order not to crowd the skillet; 3 to 5 minutes for each batch should be enough. Set aside.

5 In a large pot, sauté the onions and bell peppers in a little oil (if using pimentos, they do not need to be sautéed). Add the meat, the pimentos (if using), the spice mixture, fresh ginger, and the reserved cooking liquid and bring to a simmer. Simmer for an hour or longer. (The dish can be made ahead and reheated; it will just keep getting better.)

6 Just before serving, season with more vinegar, paprika, ginger, salt, and/or pepper to taste and with a little more turmeric if you want a brighter color.

FISH IN COCONUT CURRY

Serves 2 as a main course

I	**pound mackerel or other white-fleshed fish**
I	**teaspoon finely grated fresh ginger**
I	**teaspoon finely grated fresh turmeric or ½ teaspoon powdered turmeric**
2	**cardamom pods**
2	**teaspoons cumin seeds**
2 to 3	**cloves**
I	**¼-inch piece of cinnamon stick, or ¼ teaspoon ground cinnamon**
½	**teaspoon chili powder**
¼	**teaspoon freshly ground black pepper**
I to 2	**tablespoons vegetable oil**
I	**red onion, finely chopped**
I	**tomato, chopped**
	juice of I lime
⅔	**cup fresh coconut milk (see facing page) or canned unsweetened coconut milk**
½	**red chile, seeded and chopped**
⅔	**cup fresh coconut cream (see facing page) or canned unsweetened coconut cream**

I GOT THIS RECIPE FROM NAILA GIDAWI, a Zanzibari restaurateur who runs Palm Beach Villa, a small, charming hotel on the east coast of Zanzibar, where I have been a regular guest for the last fifteen years. Outside her kitchen, Naila has a row of coconut palms, so when she wants to use coconut milk in her cooking — as she does all the time — she commands Abdullah, an elderly, slightly frail-looking man, to climb up to the top of the palm. Hanging there, thirty feet above the ground, Abdullah points at several coconuts before Naila finally nods approvingly and he is allowed to cut it down. She then makes her own coconut cream by mixing the coconut with hot water and extracting the cream. This process is repeated, and each time the extracted liquid is thinner and less fatty. The thinner liquid — referred to as coconut milk — and the liquid inside the coconut are used for cooking rice. Only the coconut cream is used in the curry dish itself.

If you do not have your own coconut palm with someone to climb it, you can use unsweetened commercial coconut cream and milk.

In Zanzibar, this dish is made with a local mackerel-like fish that is, to my puzzlement, just called samaki, which literally means "fish." I have come across variations of this dish in several places in Zanzibar, occasionally with other fish like red snapper or barracuda as well. You can use any white fish, preferably a whole one-pound fish. You can also use a swordfish steak, preferably with the skin on to prevent it falling apart.

I have not found many cooks who can match Naila's thoughtful blend of spices, and I have always found it an impressive act of self-restraint not to use more than two or three cloves when the spice is so abundant. But one time at home, when I added a good tablespoon in the hope of bringing the Zanzibari feeling into my kitchen, I got a stark reminder that the strong, almost overpowering taste of cloves is best used in moderation.

In a Zanzibari curry, the whole spices are roasted in a pan, not ground to a fine powder as in an Indian curry. As a result, the flavors are milder and subtler. The recipe calls for a small quantity of chili powder and fresh chile, but here, as elsewhere in Zanzibari cooking, chile is used as a flavor enhancer, much as Western cuisines use pepper; the dish should not be hot like Indian or Thai curries. Therefore, it's best to add the chile a little at the time.

1 Wash the fish thoroughly under cold running water. Remove the gills, or cut off the head. Make sure there are no traces of blood or intestines in the cavity. Scale the fish if necessary. Pat dry with a paper towel.

2 With a sharp knife, cut four slashes in each side of the fish. Rub the grated ginger and the turmeric into the slashes. (Turmeric is a terrible stain maker, so it might be a good idea to wear rubber gloves when doing this.)

3 Open the cardamom pods and discard the pods; keep the small seeds. Crush the cumin gently between your hands. Cut 2 cloves lengthwise into 4 pieces if possible; if they are too dry to cut, use 3 whole cloves. Crush the cinnamon stick (if using) between your hands, or using the flat side of a knife.

4 Dry-roast the cumin, cloves, and cinnamon in a small skillet over medium heat, stirring frequently, for 2 minutes to release the flavors. Remove from the heat and add half the chili powder and the black pepper.

5 Heat the oil in a nonstick skillet with a lid — the skillet should be wide enough to hold the fish. Add the onion, tomato, and lime juice and cook over medium-low heat for 5 minutes

6 Add the coconut milk, roasted spices, and half of the chile pepper and let simmer gently for 10 minutes. Make sure the pan does not boil dry; if necessary, add a little water.

7 Add the fish and coconut cream, then add more of the chile to taste. Let simmer, covered, for 8 to 10 minutes, until the fish is cooked and the flesh comes away from the bone when poked with a knife.

HOW TO CRACK A COCONUT

TO OPEN A COCONUT CAN BE DIFFICULT, occasionally even dangerous. The hard brown nut can seem absolutely unbreakable, and when it bounces around in the kitchen, it has an ability to bump into anything breakable. This is seldom a problem in the tropics, however, where most coconuts are eaten before they have time to harden. The coconut vendors on Zanzibar simply cut the nuts open with a sharp knife or machete.

If you cannot find green, softer coconuts, the best method is to bake the coconut in the oven until the shell becomes more porous. The liquid inside the coconut can be drunk as a refreshment with ice and a twist of lime. It can also be used for cooking rice.

1 fresh brown coconut

1 Preheat oven to 425 degrees.

2 Pierce two of the eyes of the coconut using a skewer, small screwdriver, or corkscrew. Pour the liquid into a bowl. Sample the liquid. It should taste fresh and slightly sweet. If it tastes oily or at all fermented, the coconut is rancid and should be discarded.

3 Place the coconut in a small baking pan and bake on the highest oven rack for 10 minutes. There is a good likelihood the nut will crack. If not, let cool, wrap in a kitchen towel, and crack with a hammer.

4 Remove the white flesh with your hands and discard the hard shell. If you are using the flesh in itself, not just for making coconut cream, you will probably want to remove the brown skin from the flesh, using a vegetable peeler.

HOW TO MAKE COCONUT CREAM AND MILK

THE FIRST PRESSING is called the coconut cream. With each pressing, the fat content drops and there is less flavor. The first two pressings are suitable for using in a curry, while subsequent pressings can be used for boiling rice.

1 coconut, cracked

Boiling water

1 Finely grate the coconut flesh into a bowl, or process it in a food processor. Add ⅔ cup boiling water. If using a food processor, pulse to mix. Let stand for 1 to 2 minutes.

2 Line a sieve with a cheesecloth or a thin kitchen towel. Add the grated coconut and press out the liquid, using a large spoon or a spatula to extract as much of the fatty liquid as possible.

3 Return the grated coconut to the bowl or food processor and repeat the extraction process two or three times, straining each pressing into a separate container.

THE MANY FACTIONS OF MUSLIMS ON ZANZIBAR — FROM THE ISHMAILIS, WHO ARE RELATIVELY LIBERAL, TO THE PIOUS AND STRICT IBADIS AND BAHORAS — disagree passionately about most things: food, clothing, the role of women. During the holy month of Ramadan, the differences are bridged, in part by the emphasis on Muslim brotherhood, but also, to a large extent, by a family of enterprising and not particularly religious Chinese-Zanzibaris of Buddhist origin. The Shum family, owners of several noodle factories and the Pagoda restaurant in Stone Town, have, through genius marketing, managed to convince most of the island's Muslims to eat noodles when breaking the fast in the evening. During the holy month, they serve more than three hundred thousand portions of freshly made noodles a day, amounting to more than one serving per household, one for every three people.

This is a recipe I got from George Shum for a dish served in the restaurant — it consists of a combination of typical Chinese and Zanzibari flavors. Being the owner of several noodle factories, he makes wonderful dry noodle baskets that he serves the dish in. But apart from aesthetics, the noodle basket does not contribute much to the dish and may well be skipped if you do not have a noodle factory. The dish can also be made using only one of the three main ingredients.

Serves 4 to 6 as a main course

8	ounces rice noodles
2 to 3	tablespoons vegetable oil, such as canola
8	ounces boneless, skinless chicken breasts, sliced
5	ounces peeled raw shrimp
2	teaspoons finely chopped fresh ginger
1	small chile, chopped or crushed
2 to 3	cloves, coarsely crushed
1	½-inch piece of cinnamon stick, coarsely crushed
8	ounces cleaned squid or octopus, sliced and cooked in boiling salted water until tender, approximately 30 minutes
2	tablespoons soy sauce
2	teaspoons brown sugar
1	head broccoli, cut into small florets (main stalks discarded) and blanched in boiling water for 5 minutes
2	teaspoons cornstarch (optional)
⅓	cup finely chopped spring onions or scallions
1 to 2	tablespoons light sesame oil
1 to 2	tablespoons sesame seeds

1 Bring a large pot of water to a boil. Cook the noodles according to the package instructions (usually no more than 3 to 5 minutes). Drain, toss with a little oil, and set aside.

2 Combine the chicken and shrimp with the spices and mix well. Heat oil in a wok or large skillet until hot, and stir-fry the chicken and shrimp over high heat for 4 to 6 minutes, stirring energetically. Add the squid, soy sauce, brown sugar, a couple of tablespoons water, and the broccoli, reduce the heat to medium, and cook for 2 to 3 minutes. If you would like the sauce to be a little thicker, add the cornstarch and bring to a boil, stirring until thickened. Add the noodles, spring onions, sesame oil, and sesame seeds and mix well.

MUSSAMAN CURRY
PASTE

**Makes approximately ½ cup,
enough for about 8 servings**

I	star anise
I	tablespoon black peppercorns
5	cloves
I	teaspoon fennel seeds
I	tablespoon cumin seeds
I	tablespoon coriander seeds
I	1-inch piece of cinnamon stick
6 to 8	cardamom pods
½ to I	teaspoon freshly grated nutmeg
I	tablespoon coarse sea salt
I	2-inch piece of galangal
I	stalk lemongrass, green tops and tough outer layers removed, finely chopped
5	small shallots, chopped
4	cloves garlic, chopped
8	large dried red chiles, seeded and soaked in water for 30 minutes, or 4 large mild chiles, seeded and chopped, plus I tablespoon chili powder
I	teaspoon shrimp paste
2	tablespoons vegetable oil, or more as needed, if using a blender

THIS SWEET AND AROMATIC CURRY PASTE — *KRUANG GAENG MUSSAMAN* – IS THE ESSENTIAL ADDITION TO THE RELATIVELY MILD CURRIES OF THE MUSLIM POPULATION OF SOUTHERN THAILAND. I first tasted this at the Time for Lime Cooking School on the island of Ko Lanta, in the Krabi region, and I still find this the best mix ever.

The traditional way to make this and most other curry pastes is to use a mortar and pestle. When Noum and Junie at Time for Lime make it, they assign one person to the pounding of the spices — a laborious process that takes nearly half an hour and perfumes the air. If you cannot be bothered to pound and pound until you have a smooth paste, then at least start off by pounding the spices for a couple of minutes before you transfer them to a blender, or, even better, a meat grinder.

The curry paste can be frozen for up to 3 months if kept in an airtight container.

I *Dry-roast the star anise, black peppercorns, cloves, fennel, cumin, coriander, cinnamon, and cardamom in a large skillet over medium-high heat, stirring frequently, for 2 to 3 minutes, until fragrant. Transfer to a large mortar, along with the grated nutmeg and sea salt. Pound the spices, using a pestle, until you have a fine powder. Use short movements and make sure not to strain your shoulder; the weight of the pestle should be enough to crush the spices.*
2 *Add the rest of the ingredients one by one and pound and crush until you have a fine, smooth paste. If you do not have time to make the curry paste by hand from beginning to end, coarsely pound all the ingredients and transfer to a blender, along with the oil, and process until you have a smooth paste; or grind the mixture through a meat grinder.*

SLOW-COOKED LEG OF LAMB

ONE OF THE MOST IMPORTANT DISHES IN OMANI COOKING IS THE *SHUWA*, A SPICY MEAT DISH WRAPPED IN LEAVES AND BAKED IN A HOLE IN THE GROUND, or baked in a specially made clay oven. *Shuwa* is only served on special occasions, such as the third day of Eid, the festival at the end of the holy month of Ramadan. A traditional *shuwa* is an incredibly laborious process, taking more than twenty-four hours to prepare. How the dish is made varies hugely within the long-stretched and traditionally tribally divided country. Some versions are made with lamb only, others with lamb and goat, yet others with camel meat. I have also heard talk of versions made with donkey meat, but this was vehemently denied by most people I talked to. The meat is baked for twelve hours or up to two days — which is an appropriate length of time only if you have a very old and tough camel or donkey.

In many ways, *shuwa* resembles Southern barbecue; the meat is spicy and aromatic, flavored not only by the spice mixture but also by the smoke and coals in the underground oven, and, as if almost by magic, it manages to be nearly dried out but still quite juicy. This is a version adapted for home cooking. I like to reproduce some of the smokiness by wrapping the meat in leaves and broiling it until there is some smoke; I have tried both banana leaves and birch leaves still on their branches, with good results. You can also wrap the meat in parchment paper, preferably along with some slightly bitter herbs or nettles.

I cook the meat for 8 hours, but if you are in a hurry, the time can be reduced by half; just cook at slightly higher temperatures.

Serve with rice, grilled or roasted peppers, and salad.

Serves 6 to 8 as a main course

1	bone-in leg of lamb (5 to 7 pounds)
1	tablespoon cumin seeds
6	cardamom pods
1	tablespoon coriander seeds
1	tablespoon paprika
1 to 2	teaspoons crushed red pepper flakes or strong chili powder, or more to taste
1	teaspoon powdered turmeric
1	tablespoon coarse sea salt
3	tablespoons white vinegar
2	cloves garlic, or more to taste
2	tablespoons finely chopped fresh ginger (optional)
	Banana leaves or other (unsprayed, nontoxic) leaves or parchment paper

1 Let the leg of lamb stand at room temperature for at least 2 hours before you start cooking.

2 Dry-roast the cumin, cardamom, and coriander seeds in a small skillet over high heat, stirring frequently, until they start to smoke — at which point you must immediately remove the spices from the skillet. Coarsely crush the toasted spices using a mortar and pestle. Add the paprika, red pepper flakes, turmeric, salt, vinegar, garlic, and ginger (if using) and crush until you have a more or less smooth paste.

3 Preheat the broiler. Trim off as much of the excess fat from the meat as possible. Rub the lamb thoroughly with the spice mixture. Wrap the meat tightly in banana leaves (or parchment) and tie it up with string or wire.

4 Place the meat in a roasting pan. Broil 25 minutes, or until the leaves are slightly charred, turning several times. (If using parchment paper, place the roasting pan on the lowest oven rack, and check occasionally to make sure the paper does not scorch or burn.)

5 Reduce the oven temperature to 275 degrees F and bake the roast for 3 hours. (If your oven has a fan, turn it off, as the air will cause the meat to dry out.) Turn the meat a couple of times along the way.

6 Reduce the oven temperature to 225 degrees F, cover the roast loosely with foil, and continue baking for 4 to 5 hours. If you wish to cook the meat even longer, cover it more tightly to prevent it from drying out and reduce the temperature to 200 degrees F.

NOTES You can add ½ teaspoon liquid smoke to the spice mixture to help create the smoky flavor of a traditional *shuwa*.

This recipe also works well for shoulder of lamb, in which case you should use 2 shoulder roasts. Shoulder of lamb is tougher than leg, but because it contains higher levels of collagen, it will become even moister and more tender when baked for a long time.

KERALA SPICY BEEF
CURRY

THE IDEA OF AN INDIAN BEEF DISH SEEMS SELF-CONTRADICTORY, or at least incredibly far-fetched: one of the few things almost everyone knows about India is that cows are sacred. When looking closer, however, one finds that there are modifications and exceptions. The southern Indian state of Kerala is one of the more secular states, and it is the only one that allows the slaughter of cows for human consumption. The explanation given to me was that in Kerala cows are considered sacred but not divine. The difference eludes me, but the consequence is that beef can be eaten by non-Hindus without giving offense, and it is even occasionally eaten by Hindus — but never in public. This particular dish, *mattirachi peralen*, is of Christian origin.

It's best to use a cheap cut of meat, such as brisket, that is tough at first but with prolonged cooking, as required here, becomes wonderfully moist, tender, and flavorful. More expensive and tender cuts are leaner and have a tendency to become dry.

The dish is fresh-tasting and aromatic, and it should be quite hot. I normally use large, relatively mild green chiles without the seeds, and I use quite a few of them. One or two super-hot small green chiles — like Thai chiles or bird's-eye chiles — on top will give the dish quite a kick. You should adjust the heat to your taste by adding the chiles a little at a time.

Serve with rice, preferably a colorful special rice such as Yellow Rice (page 189) or Red Coconut Rice (page 162).

Serves 6 as a main course

	Oil for panfrying, such as canola
2 to 3	pounds beef brisket, cut into 1-inch chunks
2	teaspoons salt, or more to taste
3 to 4	tablespoons finely chopped fresh ginger
2	teaspoons powdered turmeric or mild yellow curry powder
1	tablespoon coriander seeds, lightly crushed
1	cup beer, preferably lager, or water
1	tablespoon mustard seeds or strong English mustard
2	tablespoons apple cider vinegar or white vinegar, or more to taste
3	cloves (optional)
1	teaspoon cumin seeds (optional)
2	teaspoons freshly ground black pepper, or more to taste
3	medium onions, chopped
4 to 6	cloves garlic, chopped
2 to 8	green chiles, seeded and chopped
6 to 8	curry leaves (optional)
1	tablespoon all-purpose flour
	Honey or sugar to taste (optional)
	Chopped cilantro (fresh coriander) or parsley for garnish

1 Heat a couple of tablespoons of oil in a large pot over high heat. Add the meat and season with the salt and half of the ginger, turmeric, and coriander. Sear the meat for 10 minutes, stirring occasionally, so that most of it is at least somewhat browned.

2 Add the beer, mustard seeds, and 2 tablespoons vinegar and bring to a boil. Reduce the heat and simmer for 1½ hours.

3 Meanwhile, dry-roast the cloves and cumin (if using), the remaining coriander, and the pepper in a medium skillet over medium heat, stirring frequently, for 2 to 4 minutes, until the spices start giving off a nice smell. Add enough oil to coat the skillet, the onions, garlic, chiles, remaining turmeric, curry leaves (if using), and the remaining ginger and cook for 3 to 5 minutes, until the onions are somewhat softened. Sprinkle with the flour, stir well, and remove from the heat.

4 Add the onion mixture to the meat and cook for 15 minutes. Season with salt, honey (if using), and/or more vinegar to taste, and garnish with cilantro.

LAMB KORMA

Serves 4 as a main course

1	teaspoon cumin seeds
2	cloves
2 to 3	cardamom pods
1	teaspoon black peppercorns
1 to 2	teaspoons coriander seeds
1	½- to 1-inch piece of cinnamon stick
½	teaspoon freshly ground mace or grated nutmeg
2	teaspoons finely chopped fresh ginger
1 to 3	green chiles, finely chopped
2	cloves garlic, minced
2	teaspoons coarse sea salt
3	tablespoons boiling water
1½	pounds boneless shoulder of lamb, cut into 1½-inch cubes
	A small pinch of saffron threads (approximately ½ gram)
2	tablespoons ghee or butter
1	onion, chopped
10	blanched whole almonds, chopped
1	tablespoon poppy seeds, plus more for garnish
1	cup full-fat Greek-style yogurt, plus more for garnish
	Chopped cilantro (fresh coriander) or parsley for garnish
About 1	tablespoon slivered almonds for garnish

ACCORDING TO TRADITION, this is one of the dishes brought to the country by the Muslim Moghuls, who, during the sixteenth and seventeenth centuries, ruled much of what today is Afghanistan, Pakistan, and all but the southern tip of India. Many of the dishes that we consider Indian might just as well be classified as Pakistani, or, more accurately, as belonging to several countries around the subcontinent.

Moghul cooking is said to have originated in the palaces of the empire, and, just like the palaces, the rich dishes are meant to express abundance and opulence. This korma uses expensive saffron and mace, and the yogurt sauce is thickened with almonds and poppy seeds; some versions also contain cream, sour cream, or coconut cream.

This recipe can also be made with chicken, in which case I would use chicken legs. Serve with rice and nan (such as one of the variations on page 48).

1 Using a mortar and pestle, crush the cumin seeds, cloves, cardamom, peppercorns, coriander seeds, and cinnamon. Remove the papery husks of the cardamom. Add the mace, ginger, chiles, garlic, salt, and boiling water and pound until you have a fine paste.

2 Place the meat in a bowl, add the spice mixture and most of the saffron, and mix well. Cover and refrigerate for 24 hours. Or, if you do not have time for this, let marinate for 30 minutes to 1 hour at room temperature.

3 Melt the ghee in a large pot over medium-high heat and sauté the onion for 3 to 5 minutes, until soft and light brown. Scrape most of the marinade off the meat, reserving the marinade, and sauté the meat for 5 to 7 minutes.

4 Add the reserved marinade, the almonds, 1 tablespoon poppy seeds, and 1 cup yogurt. Bring to a boil, then cover, reduce the heat to low, and let simmer for 1½ to 2 hours, until the meat is so tender that it almost falls apart.

5 Transfer to a serving bowl. Garnish the stew with a spoonful of yogurt and a sprinkling of saffron, and sprinkle the cilantro, almonds, and reserved poppy seeds around it.

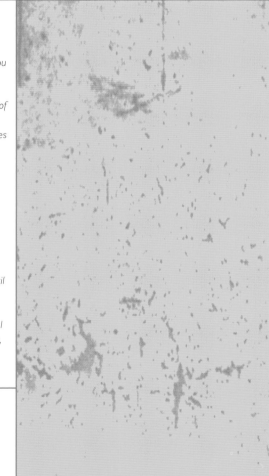

COCONUT CURRY CAKE

To use a curry mixture in a dessert may seem odd, but when you stop to consider it, this is mainly psychological: the same spices are all common in desserts, from cinnamon rolls to gingerbread. This is a mildly spicy cake, inspired by a recipe by the British spice enthusiast Gavin McArdell, and to me it has a distinctly Indian feel. Serve with whipped cream and passion fruit or Bourbon Vanilla Ice Cream (page 257).

Serves 4 to 6

1 *Preheat the oven to 350 degrees F. Generously grease a 10-inch baking pan.*

2 *In a food processor, combine the butter and sugar and pulse until well mixed. Add the eggs one at a time, pulsing so that each egg is incorporated before adding the next.*

3 *Combine the flour, spices, and grated coconut, and add to the butter mixture a little at a time. The consistency should be that of a thick batter. If you fear that it is getting too dry or dense, add a little milk or coconut cream.*

4 *Transfer the batter to the greased cake pan. Bake on the lower oven rack for 20 to 25 minutes, until golden brown. Cool in the pan for 10 minutes, then turn out onto a wire rack to cool completely.*

8	tablespoons (1 stick) butter, at room temperature
⅓ to ½	cup sugar
3	large eggs
1½	cups self-rising flour
1	teaspoon freshly ground cinnamon
¼	teaspoon freshly ground cloves
½	teaspoon freshly ground cardamom
¼	teaspoon freshly ground star anise or aniseed
¼	teaspoon freshly grated nutmeg
1 to 2	teaspoons finely grated fresh ginger
3	tablespoons grated or shredded coconut
	Milk or unsweetened coconut cream (see page 139), if necessary

MUSSAMAN BEEF CURRY

MOST THAI DISHES, INCLUDING CURRIES, ARE QUICKLY STIR-FRIED OR BOILED AND DEMAND MORE PRECISION THAN PATIENCE FROM THE COOK. The Muslims of southern Thailand take a different approach to their cooking, boiling their curries for a long time, often several hours. The cooking will typically be started in the morning, and the pot left simmering in the dying embers of the fire all day. Just before dinner, the dish is reheated and the last ingredients added. This tradition resembles the cooking of other Muslim areas around the Indian Ocean, such as those of the Arabian Penninsula, southern India, and Malaysia. The flavor is also similar — mild and aromatic rather than fiery and temperamental. But Mussaman curry is not merely a dish that has crossed over from the other side of the ocean; the inclusion of such typical Thai ingredients as shrimp paste and lemongrass and the use of galangal as well as ginger make this a dish that is firmly rooted in both Muslim and Thai traditions.

This recipe is best if you use a cheaper cut of beef, like brisket. Not only are the tough and well-used muscles better suited to prolonged cooking, they are also much more flavorful and contain larger amounts of collagen, which is transformed into gelatin when cooked. If you would like to make this dish with lamb or mutton, it is best to use shoulder.

Since this dish contains sweet potatoes and onion I find that rice is not strictly necessary. When making it at home, I often serve it with a simple salad, like Tomato and Cucumber Salad with Cumin Salt (page 41), and nan (such as one of the variations on page 48).

Serves 4 as a main course

2	tablespoons vegetable oil
3	cloves garlic, chopped
1	tablespoon chopped fresh ginger
2	shallots, chopped
1½	pounds beef brisket, cut into 1-inch dice
3	tablespoons Mussaman Curry Paste (page 142)
2½	cups unsweetened coconut milk
1	pound sweet potatoes, peeled and cut into 1-inch dice
2	medium onions, quartered
3	tablespoons grated or shredded coconut
2	tablespoons fish sauce (*nam pla*), or more to taste
1	tablespoon sugar, or more to taste
3	tablespoons bottled tamarind sauce or 1½ tablespoons tamarind paste
3	tablespoons chopped roasted peanuts
	Salt

1 In a large pot, heat the oil over medium heat and sauté the garlic, ginger, and shallots for about 3 minutes, until soft. Add the meat and sear over medium-high heat for 5 to 7 minutes, until lightly browned.

2 Add the curry paste and fry for 2 to 3 minutes, then add the coconut milk. Reduce the heat, cover, and let simmer for 1 to 1½ hours, until the meat is almost falling-apart tender. (The dish can be made up to this point the day before; it only gets better if reheated.)

3 Bring the curry to a boil, add the sweet potatoes and onions, and boil gently for 20 minutes.

4 Meanwhile, toast the grated coconut in a small, dry skillet until lightly browned. Add to the pot.

5 Check the potatoes for doneness. They should be soft but not falling apart. Add the fish sauce, sugar, tamarind, and roasted peanuts. Season with more fish sauce or salt to taste.

VARIATION If you do not have time to make your own curry paste, you can use a smaller amount, about 2 tablespoons, of a commercially made Thai or Indian curry paste and add 2 teaspoons minced galangal, 1 teaspoon shrimp paste, and 1 crushed lemongrass stalk. The result is not the same but delicious nonetheless.

CORIANDER

"IF YOU THINK OF CORIANDER, YOU HAVE THREE VERY DIFFERENT THINGS: A SOAPY HERB, A MILD YET PEPPERY ROOT, AND A SEED THAT IS AROMATIC AND ENIGMATIC AT THE SAME TIME. AND IF YOU COMBINE THE THREE, YOU HAVE MAGIC."

That cannot be! Or can it? Yes, it can. I just forgot for a minute that here, in India, everything is possible. I sit down on the pavement, still shaken. But it is okay. It is all in perfectly good taste – there is no harm meant. Kerala is probably the only place on earth where the swastika and the word "Jew" can coexist without people raising an eyebrow.

And here, on the sign outside one of the many spice traders in Cochin, is the proof: "Swastik Spices – Synagogue Lane, Jew Town."

This south Indian state has for the last two millennia been an important part of the global spice trade and a meeting point for people from all over the world. Like most of India, the majority of the population is Hindu, with a significant Muslim minority, but in addition, Kerala is home to one of the first Christian communities, established (according to legend) by the apostle Thomas, and also to a small Jewish community.

The Jews of Kerala have, despite their small numbers, played a pivotal role in both trade and matters of state, excelling in trade and involved in intellectual exchange with Europe, the Middle East, and China. At certain periods, the rajah's favorite soldiers were Jewish, and occasionally fighting was postponed to allow them to observe the Sabbath. And the center of Cochin is still referred to as Jew Town.

A stark contrast to the Jewish part of Cochin's spice-trading European cousin, Venice, Jew Town is certainly no ghetto – rather, it is a stately part of town close to the rajah's palace, bustling with trade, with beautifully ornamented buildings and a synagogue sporting decorative elements from both the East and the West. And the swastika, the symbol that was adopted by Hitler and inverted both in form and meaning, was originally a sun wheel, an ancient Hindu symbol of prosperity and well-being. It is often seen in decorative patterns in India, and also used on the covers of account books – all in all, a very fitting sign to be bestowed on the trade that for as long as man can remember has ensured the livelihood of Hindu farmers, Jewish merchants, and Muslim rajahs alike.

In India everything is possible. Ancient Hindu symbols like the swastika can be seen everywhere, even in the old Jewish part of town.

KERALA JEWISH FISH
WITH GREEN HERBS AND SPICES

THIS IS AN ANCIENT KERALA JEWISH DISH — *chuttulli meen* — that is still being served even though most of the Jewish population emigrated after India's independence and the formation of the State of Israel. This recipe was inspired by a dish I had at Brunton Boatyard in Cochin, Kerala, where chef Joy Mathew is a great upholder of tradition. It is easy to recognize a few of the typical Indian flavors, like cardamom, coriander, and ginger, but this dish is also lighter and more fresh-tasting than many typical Indian dishes.

Ordinarily it is made with small pearl onions, but you can substitute shallots.

At the Brunton Boatyard, you have a wonderful view over the bustling port of Cochin, and of the Chinese fishing nets that are constantly being lowered and hoisted — not only one of the most beautiful backdrops for a good meal, but also something that ensures a constant supply of fresh fish. This dish is often made with mullet, but it can also be made with sea bass or trout. Have your fishmonger butterfly the fish for you, if possible, and bone it, if you like. If you cannot find a whole fish of the right size, you can use a 1-pound fillet — it just will not look as impressive.

It's best to grill the fish over charcoal. If that is not an option, you can use the broiler. In that case, if possible, sprinkle the fish with cubeb pepper to get that nice smoky pinelike flavor.

Serve with Pearl Onions with Coriander and Mint (page 154), rice, and possibly a simple yogurt dip.

1 Light a grill or preheat the broiler.

2 Cut the fish open, cutting from the stomach cavity down almost to the dorsal fin, so it opens flat. No need to remove the bones, although that will make the eating a little easier.

3 Crush the cardamom pods, coriander seeds, cumin, pepper, mint, cilantro and cilantro roots (if using), the chiles, pearl onions, ginger, lemon zest, lemon juice, and cubeb pepper (if desired) using a mortar and pestle, or coarsely grind in a food processor.

4 Rub the fish with the spice mixture, season with salt, and drizzle with oil.

5 Place skin-side down on the grill and grill for 5 minutes, or until just cooked through; make sure the fish does not burn. Or place it skin-side down on a rack in a roasting pan and broil for 6 to 8 minutes, until just cooked through.

Serves 2 as a main course

1	1½-pound firm fish, such as mullet, sea bass, or trout, cleaned, scaled, rinsed, and patted dry
2 to 4	cardamom pods
1 to 2	teaspoons coriander seeds
1 to 2	teaspoons cumin seeds
1	teaspoon freshly ground black pepper
1	tablespoon finely chopped mint
1	tablespoon finely chopped cilantro (fresh coriander), plus (optional) 4 to 5 cilantro roots, crushed
1 to 3	small green chiles, finely chopped
3 to 4	pearl onions
1 to 2	teaspoons finely chopped fresh ginger
1	teaspoon grated lemon zest
3 to 6	tablespoons fresh lemon juice
1	teaspoon freshly ground cubeb pepper (optional)
	Salt
	Oil for drizzling, such as canola

PEARL ONIONS
WITH CORIANDER AND MINT

Makes 1¼ pounds

1 pound pearl onions, small shallots, or small red onions

3 to 5 tablespoons oil

1 tablespoon finely chopped fresh ginger

1 to 3 cardamom pods, lightly bruised

2 teaspoons coriander seeds, lightly crushed

2 to 3 tablespoons Coriander and Mint Sauce (facing page), store-bought mint sauce, or 2 tablespoons finely chopped mint plus 2 teaspoons sugar

2 tablespoons fresh lemon juice

Salt

SOME DISHES NEED SOMETHING sweet and fresh-tasting as an accompaniment to balance against the heavy spiciness; others, like the Kerala Jewish Fish with Green Herbs and Spice (page 153), do well in the company of a side dish with similar temperament.

In a small pot, combine all the ingredients except the lemon juice and salt and cook over medium-low heat for 10 minutes, or until the onions are tender. Add the lemon juice and season with salt to taste.

THE FRESH AND COOL FLAVORS OF THE MINT AND CORIANDER SAUCE ARE FABULOUS WITH FISH AND LAMB, but they are also nice and soothing with hot dishes. You might want to try to stir a little of this sauce into plain cooked rice for a fresh-tasting aromatic side dish to grilled meats and fish or spicy stews.

I have had mixed results freezing the sauce, as there is some discoloration, but if you add some fresh herbs after thawing and process one more time, it works well.

Makes about ½ cup

½	cup water
1	cup mint leaves, finely chopped
2	tablespoons sugar
1	tablespoon coriander seeds, coarsely crushed
3	tablespoons finely chopped cilantro (fresh coriander), or more to taste

1 Bring the water to a boil in a small saucepan. Add half the mint and cook for 3 to 4 minutes. Strain the liquid through a sieve into a small bowl, making sure to press out as much of the liquid from the mint as possible.

2 Add the sugar and coriander seeds and stir until the sugar dissolves. Transfer to a food processor, add the rest of the mint and the cilantro, and process until smooth. If desired, add more cilantro to taste.

CORIANDER LAMB SKEWERS
WITH GRILLED PEPPERS

Serves 4 as a main course

2	pounds lean lamb, cut into 1½-inch cubes and excess fat removed
2	tablespoons coriander seeds
1	teaspoon cumin seeds
1	tablespoon paprika
	A small pinch of saffron threads (optional)
2 to 4	cloves garlic, crushed, plus 2 cloves garlic, finely chopped
2	teaspoons salt
2	tablespoons fresh lemon juice
8	red bell peppers
⅓	cup vegetable oil, plus more for brushing
2	tablespoons finely chopped almonds or pistachios
3 to 5	dried apricots, chopped
	Freshly ground black pepper
⅓	cup olive oil
2	lemons, cut into 8 wedges each
	Finely chopped cilantro (fresh coriander) for garnish

I HAD THIS DISH IN MUSCAT, the capital of Oman, after a long day in the desert, and the explosion of flavors and colors seemed unlikely after all the sand and dust. Omani cooks often prefer slow-cooked stews, one reason being that the meat is often taken from recently slaughtered animals and has not had time to go through natural tenderizing processes that occur during aging. Store-bought lamb is much more tender, so here only ten minutes or less will suffice.

This is a dish that uses both the sweet and spicy flavor of coriander seeds and the slightly soapy flavor of cilantro, fresh coriander.

Serve with plain rice or with Rice Pilau (page 243).

1 Place the lamb in a bowl. Using a mortar and pestle, crush the coriander and cumin seeds. Add the paprika, saffron (if desired), crushed garlic, salt, and lemon juice and mix until you have a semi-dry paste. Rub the meat with this paste and let marinate for 30 minutes to 1 hour at room temperature, or up to 24 hours in the refrigerator.

2 Light a grill or preheat the broiler.

3 Brush the bell peppers with vegetable oil. Grill or broil, turning frequently, until the skin is charred black and slightly puffed and the bell peppers are starting to collapse. Place the bell peppers in a large bowl, cover tightly, and leave to cook and steam in their own heat for 10 minutes. By this time, the skin should come off easily.

4 Halve, core, and seed the bell peppers. Slice and place in a bowl. Add the finely chopped garlic, the almonds, apricots, black pepper to taste, and the olive oil. Mix well.

5 Add ⅓ cup olive oil to the meat and mix well. Thread the meat onto eight wooden skewers, with a lemon wedge on each end.

6 Grill over high heat or broil for 7 to 8 minutes, turning several times, until nicely browned or possibly even slightly charred on the outside and still juicy and pinkish inside.

7 Meanwhile, just before serving, add the cilantro to the grilled peppers. Serve with the lamb skewers.

NOTE *The flavor is best when the meat and bell peppers are grilled, but if you broil them, you can get that slightly smoky flavor by adding about ¼ teaspoon of liquid smoke to the marinade for the lamb. It is cheating, but it works.*

THIS DISH IS A TESTAMENT TO PERSIAN CUISINE'S ABILITY to mix the subtle flavors of mild spices with the sweet flavors of mint and apricots in a savory dish. In Iran, as in so many other places in the Middle East, many families have their own pigeon houses on the roof. The pigeons are fed some leftovers but are otherwise capable of finding their own food.

If you cannot get squab, this dish can be made with baby chickens (poussins) or Cornish hen.

Serve with rice or couscous and a fresh-tasting yogurt sauce.

Serves 2 as a main course

1 Combine the garlic, cumin and coriander seeds, mint, orange zest, turmeric, cardamom, salt, peppercorns, and parsley in a mortar or a food processor and crush with a pestle or process until you have a coarse mixture. Add the butter and honey and mix well.

2 Rub the squabs with the spice mixture. Let marinate for 15 minutes to 1 hour at room temperature or up to 24 hours in the refrigerator – the longer, the better.

3 Heat the oil over medium-high heat in a pot just big enough to hold the squabs. Sauté the onion until it is soft.

Remove the onion, and sear the squabs over medium-high heat for 5 minutes, turning to brown on all sides.

4 Turn the squabs breast-side up in the pot, add the onion, lemon wedges, pistachios, apricots, and water, and bring to a boil. Reduce the heat to medium-low and let simmer, covered, for 1 hour, or until the squabs are tender.

5 Remove the lid and transfer the squabs to serving plates. Simmer the cooking juices over medium-high heat for 5 minutes, or until somewhat thickened. Serve with the squabs.

2	cloves garlic
2	teaspoons cumin seeds
1	teaspoon coriander seeds
1	teaspoon dried mint or 1 tablespoon finely chopped fresh mint
2	teaspoons finely grated orange zest
1	teaspoon grated fresh turmeric or ½ teaspoon powdered turmeric
1	cardamom pod
1	teaspoon salt
1	teaspoon black peppercorns
1	tablespoon chopped parsley
1	tablespoon butter, at room temperature
2	teaspoons honey or sugar
2	squabs or spring chickens
1 to 2	tablespoons vegetable oil
1	onion, finely chopped
½	lemon, cut into 4 wedges
⅔	cup shelled pistachios
4 to 5	dried apricots, coarsely chopped
2	cups water

GRILLED GREEN FISH
WITH RED RICE

I LOVE THE SIMPLE, COLORFUL PLAYFULNESS OF THIS DISH, which combines two dishes from different countries in the Indian Ocean, using green curry paste from Thailand to flavor the fish and serving it together with the aromatic red coconut rice of Sri Lanka. When I don't want a traditional curry, I construct a recipe like this.

If you want to thread vegetables such as bell peppers or onions on the same skewers as the fish, I strongly suggest partially baking or grilling them in advance, so they will finish cooking in the same time as the fish.

I like to use an assortment of different firm fish, such as yellowfin tuna, snapper, and salmon.

Serves 4 as a main course

2	pounds firm white-fleshed fish fillets, preferably a mix of different varieties, cut into 1½-inch pieces
4 to 6	tablespoons Green Curry Paste (page 161)
3	tablespoons fresh lime juice
1 to 3	small green chiles, chopped (optional)
	Mint leaves
	Partly cooked vegetables, such as bell peppers or onions, cut into 1½-inch pieces (optional)
	Oil for brushing, such as canola
	Lemon wedges for serving
	Red Coconut Rice (page 162) for serving

1 Light a grill or preheat the broiler.

2 Rinse the fish thoroughly under cold running water, or place it in a bowl of ice water for 10 to 15 minutes before cooking. This makes the flesh firmer. Drain and pat dry.

3 In a medium bowl, mix the green curry paste, lime juice, and green chiles, if desired. Add the fish and toss well, so that the curry paste completely covers the fish. Allow to stand for at least a few minutes, or for as long as 8 hours; refrigerate if marinating the fish for more than 15 minutes.

4 Thread the fish onto skewers, alternating with mint leaves and the partly cooked vegetables, if desired. Reserve whatever is left of the green curry paste.

5 Baste the fish skewers with oil. Place on the grill or on the broiler pan and grill or broil, turning frequently. It is difficult to give an exact cooking time, but if the heat is intense, 3 to 5 minutes should suffice. Pay close attention so the fish does not burn.

6 Serve with lemon wedges and the red rice.

VARIATION *If you have other spice pastes at hand or in your freezer, you can make many different skewers — for example, fish skewers with red curry paste, beef skewers with Mussaman Curry Paste (page 142), and chicken skewers with an Indian-style curry paste. In that case, I serve them with plain white rice, adding 2 kaffir lime leaves and chopped spring onions and holy basil for freshness.*

GREEN CURRY
WITH CHICKEN

THIS CLASSIC THAI DISH IS JUST AS GOOD WITH PORK OR FISH. There are lots of different interpretations and variations of the recipe; this one is based on one from Time for Lime Cooking School on the island of Ko Lanta, off southern Thailand.

Serve with rice.

Serves 4 as a main course

2	tablespoons vegetable oil
5	tablespoons Green Curry Paste (facing page)
2	cups unsweetened coconut milk
½	cup chicken stock or vegetable stock
4	kaffir lime leaves
1	pound boneless, skinless chicken breasts, sliced into ⅓-inch-thick slices
5	ounces small round Thai eggplants, halved
4	long beans or a small handful of green beans, trimmed and cut into 1½-inch pieces
3	tablespoons fish sauce (*nam pla*)
2	teaspoons bottled tamarind sauce, 2 teaspoons reconstituted and strained tamarind pulp, or 1 teaspoon tamarind paste
1	tablespoon sugar
2	tablespoons chopped holy basil, plus additional for garnish
2	large green chiles, sliced
1 to 3	small green Thai chiles (optional)
	Lime wedges for garnish

1 Heat the oil in a wok over high heat. Add the curry paste and cook for 1 minute, stirring energetically. Add the coconut milk and stock and bring to a boil over high heat. Add the lime leaves, chicken, eggplant, and beans and cook for 5 minutes, stirring occasionally.

2 Stir in the fish sauce, tamarind, sugar, chopped basil, sliced chiles, and Thai chiles (if using) and bring to a boil. If you want a really hot curry, bruise the Thai chiles with a wooden spatula or spoon.

3 Transfer to soup plates, garnish with basil and lime wedges, and serve.

GREEN CURRY PASTE

THE TRADITIONAL GREEN CURRY OF THAILAND — *kruang gaeng keow wan* — is a fine way to make use of the many different flavors of coriander: the sweet flavors of the spice, the peppery roots of the fresh herb, and the soapy leaves. Here they come together in a way that serves them all well. When you buy cilantro, fresh coriander, look for bunches with the roots still attached. It only needs to be cleaned before use.

Green curry paste provides the all-important flavoring for a whole range of traditional Thai dishes, like Green Curry with Chicken (facing page). I also like to use it to flavor fish, shrimp, or chicken as a wet spice rub or marinade before grilling.

Commercially made Thai curry paste is readily available and generally quite good — and for a normal Tuesday dinner I will use that, unless I have some homemade left in the freezer. But most of the ingredients in a curry paste are fragile and ephemeral and whenever you take the time and effort to make your own curry paste, you will find that it tastes a whole lot better. When making your own curry paste you are also free to adjust the flavors to your own liking, adding more or less chile, galangal, and/or herbs.

The traditional way to make a Thai curry paste is using a mortar and pestle. You can use a blender for finishing the paste, but you should at least take the time to crush the spices and herbs using a mortar and pestle, as the blender will only chop the ingredients.

The curry paste can be frozen for up to 3 months. I divide it into smaller amounts, wrap tightly in plastic, and freeze. Ideally it should be allowed to thaw before use, but I have found that, when in a hurry, it works fine to add it straight to boiling water or coconut milk.

Makes approximately ½ cup, enough for about 8 servings

1	tablespoon coriander seeds
2	teaspoons cumin seeds
1	teaspoon black peppercorns
3	stalks lemongrass, green parts removed, and chopped
2	tablespoons chopped galangal,
2	teaspoons finely chopped fresh turmeric or 1 teaspoon powdered turmeric
2	teaspoons grated kaffir lime zest (or ordinary lime zest)
3 to 4	small shallots, chopped
8	cloves garlic, chopped
6 to 8	small green bird's-eye chiles (or 2 large green chiles)
2	tablespoons cilantro (fresh coriander) leaves, plus 4 cilantro roots, chopped
1	tablespoon holy basil leaves
2	tablespoons shrimp paste
2	tablespoons canola oil (or other neutral vegetable oil), if using a blender

1 Dry-roast the coriander seeds, cumin seeds, and peppercorns in a small skillet over medium heat, stirring frequently, just long enough for the flavors to be released. This normally takes less than 1 minute; when you start smelling the spices, they are done.

2 Crush the roasted spices using a large mortar and pestle. You should not have to use the force of your arm to pound the spices — that exerts unnecessary strain on your arm and shoulder; the weight of the pestle should be enough. When the spices are finely ground, add the rest of the ingredients one at a time, making sure you crush each one before you add another. When you have added all the ingredients, either continue pounding the mixture until you have a fine paste — this may take an additional 15 to 20 minutes — or transfer the mixture to a blender, add the oil, and mix until you have a fine paste.

NOTE *There is also a middle way between the admittedly laborious process of pounding and smashing away to make your own curry paste and the easy escape of the ready-made, and that is improving on the ready-made. Mix a small amount (half a teaspoon or so) of store-bought green curry paste with a small amount of unsweetened coconut milk, and use this mixture to decide what is missing. Would you like it hotter (the commercial curry pastes, both red and green, are typically quite mild), or would you like the flavors of the cilantro and holy basil to be more predominant? Then chop the ingredients and crush them using a mortar and pestle before you mix them into the curry paste — it just takes a few minutes, but you will find that it makes a whole lot of difference.*

RED COCONUT RICE

Serves 4 as a side dish

1	cup water
2	cups unsweetened coconut milk
1½	cups red rice
2	teaspoons salt
3 to 4	cardamom pods, slightly bruised
1	tablespoon butter

ON SRI LANKA, *kiribath* (coconut rice) made with red rice has great importance. It is served at weddings and other festivities, and it is typically the first solid — or, in this case, somewhat less than solid — food served to a baby. It is mildly fragrant and sweet from the coconut and cardamom, and I like to serve it with all kinds of hot and spicy dishes — though only those that are not made with coconut.

I think the attractive pinkish color of the red rice adds something nice, but the dish can also be made with white rice.

1 Bring the water and 1 cup of the coconut milk to a boil in a medium pot. Add the rice, salt, and cardamom, reduce the heat to medium-low, cover, and let simmer for 20 minutes. Make sure it does not boil dry; add a little more water if necessary.

2 Add the remaining 1 cup coconut milk and bring to a boil. Turn off the heat and stir in the butter. Place a folded kitchen towel under the lid to absorb the steam, and allow to stand for 5 to 10 minutes.

3 This can be served hot or cold — I think it is best when temperate.

Green papayas on a tree in Thailand. The papayas are best when allowed to mature on the tree. Unripe papayas can also be used as a vegetable, as in Green Papaya Salad (page 109).

A woman at the market in Ubud, Bali.

Rambutans are sweet and tart tropical fruits. Rather than using them in cooking, they can be used as a palate cleanser or as a simple dessert.

Ingredients laid out for making a Mussaman Curry Paste (page 142) at the Time for Lime cooking school in Ko Lanta, Thailand. Clockwise from left: coriander seeds, cumin, fennel, nutmeg and mace, cinnamon, star anise, cloves, cardamom, shrimp paste, red onion, garlic, black peppercorns. In the middle: Reconstituted dry chiles (in bowl), galangal, lemongrass.

LEFT TO RIGHT: **Young Buddhist monks in Ko Lanta, Thailand; super-hot Thai chiles; a Muslim woman in southern Thailand, with traditional headscarf and not-so-traditional apron; a street vendor in a Balinese market.**

A vegetable vendor on the way to a market outside Ubud, Bali. Typical "Western" vegetables such as potato and cauliflower are also used in Southeast Asia, but they do not form the backbone of the cuisine.

A market stall in Thailand always offers something for the mouth and something for the eye, too.

"Traveling" in the Far East does not necessarily mean riding inside a car; it can mean riding on the back of pickup trucks or traditional

Shopping is a more personal experience in the small spice shops, such as this one on Bali.

Making peppercorns stay green even after drying can be difficult, and nowadays it is often done by freeze-drying. The green peppercorns in the photo are fakes, just white peppercorns colored green. When crushed or ground, the result is a pale gray-greenish powder.

TURMERIC

"NO MAN OR WOMAN IN THEIR RIGHT MIND WILL COOK A DISH CONTAINING TURMERIC WHILE WEARING THEIR BEST WHITE SHIRT OR BLOUSE –UNLESS, THAT IS, THEY

WHY GOD TAKES A BATH

A small herd of elephants is standing patiently outside the temple, waiting for dusk and the start of their workday, while the elephant herdsmen fuss around, applying makeup and jewelry — thereby transforming the gray and wrinkled old animals into shiny representatives of deities and spirits.

Meanwhile, inside the Chettikulangara Temple, in Kottayam in the southern Indian state of Kerala, the festivities are about to begin. As I enter the temple grounds, people are flocking around the small pond in the middle of the courtyard. Anticipation is thick in the air — seldom have I heard so many hundreds of people make so little noise. We are just standing next to each other, waiting for something, I know not what. Then a tremor goes through the crowd. A group of priests comes out of the small building next to the dam, wearing nothing but loincloths. They are carrying something. I catch a glimpse of what looks like a black statue on a small metal tray covered with a yellow powder of some kind.

"What is it?" I ask my neighbor in a low whisper.

He answers, without turning away from the sight, "It is Devi, consort of Shiva, daughter of the Himalayas. She is having a bath. A bath that will purify us all."

The men walk down the ramp and into the water, holding Devi between them. They pour water over her, washing and stroking her carefully. Then, on a silent cue, they submerge themselves, taking the deity with them. During the few seconds they remain there, something happens. Not only do all the people watching hold their breath, speechlessly overwhelmed with awe, but gradually the water around the point in the water where we know Devi is changes color. When the men

reemerge with the deity, the previously brownish water surrounding them is also bright yellow, the color of the sun in children's paintings.

The deity is taken back into the small house. Some people walk down to the pond and wash themselves in the yellow water, but most flock to the other side of the building. One of the young priests reappears, handing out brightly yellow paste from the tray around the deity. Now I realize that the yellow stuff that colored the water is turmeric, the yellow powder that is such an intense coloring agent that I have decided never, ever, to wear white while using it in my cooking. I also notice that the loincloth that the priest is wearing is no longer white, but now more the color of egg yolk.

Having been a part of Devi's bathing ceremony, the turmeric is now sacred, and there is some commotion as everyone fights to get their foreheads painted by the hand of the priest. There is gentle pushing and rustling, and even when an elephant comes around to drink from the pond, there is a reluctance to move, as if the danger of being stepped on is not nearly as urgent as the wish to be colored beautiful, colored pure.

Turmeric is a close relative of ginger, a rhizome that has been so long under human cultivation that it is hard to say where it came from or what it was like in its original wild state. In the West, turmeric is often seen as a kind of poor man's saffron, and in French, it occasionally goes

Power powder: Turmeric is always the brightest thing in the spice shop. Some of the best turmeric in the world is grown on the island of Réunion and the southern Indian state of Kerala.

under the name of *safran d'Inde* — Indian saffron. Elsewhere it is often passed off as saffron to those gullible enough to mistake a yellow powder or rhizome for the orange-red stigmas of a crocus flower.

But in India and most other countries around the Indian Ocean, turmeric has a long and proud history of its own, being used as a coloring agent for garments and foods alike, turning traditional customs, tablecloths, cake, and curries pleasantly yellow. In addition, turmeric serves several medicinal purposes, as a mild digestive and an antitoxin. Supposedly it is also helpful for the blood circulation, and there are currently investigations under way to test the validity of claims that it is beneficial for liver problems and preventing Alzheimer's disease. So it is perhaps not only the color that has led to its use in purifying rituals.

LEFT: Fresh turmeric has a milder flavor than dried, and it is not so overpowering. RIGHT: The author is shown with a fine specimen at a market on Bali. The rhizome grows like the knobby hand of a creature you would not like to meet.

Just another day at the office: Grilled Balinese pigs are prepared in a special house on the outskirts of the village, then carried to a market or food stall. They can weigh as much as a hundred fifty pounds; in other words, quite a headful.

WAITING FOR MY BABI

There is a long line spreading from the unpretentious fast-food joint out into the street. But there is no food.

It is ten to twelve in the town of Ubud, Bali's culinary capital, and the locals gathered under the "Ibu Oka — Babi Guling" sign are eagerly awaiting the arrival of the Man with the Pig. The place is run strictly on a first-come, first-served basis, and if you are too late, then. . . no food for you. So it is not your regular kind of fast-food place, since everyone has to wait and not all will get served.

The ladies behind the counter are sharpening their knives and cleavers. Jokes are exchanged, and a man who is trying to be circumspect as he maneuvers for a better position in front of the counter is gently asked to go back to his place. I am caught between two men smoking the powerful Indonesian *kretek* cigarettes, almost engulfed by the clove-scented smoke, and chatting with a woman about the new mortar and pestle I have just bought at the market. Then it is suddenly as if the whole world has come to a halt. The woman stops midsentence, the men drop their cigarettes on the ground, the queue disintegrates, and all eyes are on that wonderful spectacle at the end of the street. A skinny guy is coming toward us with a great big roasted pig on his head. He walks gracefully, well aware that he is the center of everyone's attention, and pretending that the weight of the hundred-pound roasted pig is nothing to him.

The Man with the Pig sets it down on the counter, unable to suppress a sigh of relief. Then begins the noonday ritual of the *babi guling*, roast suckling pig: The animal is chopped up. Rice and meat are placed in papers lined with banana leaf. One woman is responsible for overseeing that everyone gets a piece of the crunchy skin and the stuffing, consisting of spices and cassava leaves.

By a quarter past twelve, the pig is finished, and most of the late arrivals leave hungry. Some order a cup of tea and wait for the next pig to arrive — no one knows exactly when.

The island of Bali is a mostly Hindu enclave within predominantly Muslim Indonesia, and the Balinese have found thousands of big and small demonstrations of their exceptionalism, from the parades matching or even surpassing India in color and grandeur to their intense love of everything pork. The suckling pig served at the communal street market in Ubud and in dozens of other places around the island is a wonderful example of how street food can be something quite contrary to junk food. For less than a dollar, you get a taste of some of the best food Bali has to offer, a cuisine that cannot be reasonably described as less than *haute*. The yellow skin is so crisp that it cracks as you eat it, the meat is melting. And, almost as if by magic, the spice mixture that defines the dish by no means overpowers the fine meat. The sheer size of the pig leads me to doubt that it can really be a suckling pig. But the sweet, almost milky flavor and melting juiciness leave me confused: I cannot understand how it cannot be.

And I am hungry for more. I had foolishly turned down the offer of a large portion, but what I had merely whetted my appetite. Instead of waiting for the next pig to arrive from that mysterious place up the road, I ask for the address and seek it out.

The pigs, it turns out, are cooked in an old workshop that looks like an old-fashioned blacksmith's. As I arrive, four men are busy preparing the spices and vegetables for the stuffing. Another man is roasting a pig over an open fire.

He turns the pig around slowly, brushing the skin with a bright yellow turmeric-and-water mixture. Every now and then he fans the fire to make the heat more intense; or, if the heat gets too intense, he rakes away a few of the glowing coals. Even after several hours on the spit, the pig is whole, and uncannily lifelike, with a glowing yellow color and an insincere, almost mocking smile.

There is nothing in the room that could not have been from the fifteenth century, apart from the colorful T-shirts with occasional corporate logos that a couple of the men are wearing. I am allowed to taste the spices, and to the general merriment of the workers, I eat a large piece of one of the lava-hot bird's-eye chiles. I immediately start sweating like a pig. How appropriate, I think, as the men laugh at the sight of my puffing and heaving. I feel miserable, and sorry for myself — and then I see the guy manning the spit, all soaked, and realize that he has it like this every day.

There is another pig cooling on a counter, ready to be taken to its final destination. The large stake that serves as the spit is removed with brutal efficiency. The pig is placed on a large tray and lifted up onto the head of the frail-looking pig carrier, and he heads down the street to the even longer line of people waiting now. He seems to grow with confidence and strength as he walks. Heads turn, the normally frantic Balinese drivers slow down and cede passage. From my vantage point a few feet behind the Man with the Pig, I feel as if I am partaking in a victory procession of sorts, and I see the anticipation and hunger in the eyes of the people waiting.

What I hadn't allowed for was that some of these people have been waiting for more than an hour, now hungrier than ever, and that none of the people in line are particularly interested in giving up their place. Just before it is my turn, the last portion is served.

I could leave hungry, but that would be a shame. I sit down with a cup of tea, knowing that in another hour there will be a new pig. And I will still be here.

LEFT: At noon, people on Bali flock to the food stalls and markets to have a bite of juicy, whole-grilled pork. Bali is a Hindu enclave in a predominantly Muslim country, and the Balinese people love all things pork. RIGHT: The sign leaves little doubt as to what the specialty is.

BALINESE SUCKLING PIG

THE YOUNG PIGS THAT ARE TYPICALLY SERVED IN BALI ARE LARGE ENOUGH TO SERVE A WHOLE LOT OF PEOPLE, sometimes weighing as much as 150 pounds. This recipe calls for a 12- to 15-pound suckling pig, and it is adapted from a recipe I got from Heinz von Holzen, chef-proprietor of Bumbu Bali Restaurant and Cooking School and author of several inspiring cookbooks on Balinese cooking. I have also used the recipe for a pork roast, and although not nearly the same experience, it was very good nonetheless. The most important thing is that you get the skin just right, without burning it — admittedly not an easy task, but one made a whole lot easier if you have a rotisserie function on your oven, and definitely also possible with a normal household oven as well. You would get the most authentic result if you cooked the pig over a charcoal fire — but that demands constant attention for several hours and a mastery of the grill. Instead, I bake the pig in the oven at a moderate temperature (325 degrees F for 3 hours) and then finish it on the grill. Make sure that there are hot coals on only one side of the grill, so you can get the skin nice and crispy and get that nice smoky aroma without burning the skin. Adding a teaspoon of liquid smoke to the turmeric water is cheating a bit, but it will do much the same.

The stuffing should be quite hot and then eaten only in moderation.

Serves 8 to 10 as a main course

1	12- to 15-pound suckling pig
1½	tablespoons salt
6	ounces fresh turmeric, finely chopped, or 5 to 6 tablespoons powdered turmeric
½	cup water
1	tablespoon shrimp paste
1½	pounds cassava leaves, blanched and chopped, or spinach, chopped
1	pound shallots, chopped
10 to 20	plump cloves garlic, finely chopped
2	ounces galangal, peeled and finely chopped, or 3 tablespoons finely chopped fresh ginger
8 to 15	bird's-eye chiles, depending on how hot you would like your stuffing
10	stalks lemongrass, crushed and chopped
2 to 3	tablespoons coriander seeds, crushed
1	tablespoon black peppercorns, crushed
5	kaffir lime leaves, finely chopped
	Vegetable oil

1 Remove all the oven racks except the bottom one, and preheat the broiler.

2 Rub the pig inside and out with the salt. Set aside.

3 If you have fresh turmeric, combine 2 ounces of the turmeric with the water in a blender and process until smooth. Strain the liquid and reserve it. If using powdered turmeric, combine 2 tablespoons of it with the water and mix well.

4 In a small skillet, toast the shrimp paste over high heat until dry and crumbly. Make sure to use your kitchen fan – this process gives off a powerful smell. Transfer to a bowl, add the cassava leaves, shallots, garlic, galangal, chiles, lemongrass, coriander seeds, peppercorns, kaffir lime leaves, and the remaining fresh turmeric or 3 to 4 tablespoons powdered turmeric, and mix well. Stuff the pig with this mixture and close the cavity as well as you can, either sewing it with trussing string or using wire. (If you don't have steel wire at hand, you could use the wire of a paper clip.) Brush the skin of the pig with turmeric water.

5 Brush the oven rack with oil (or, better still, wrap the individual bars with foil before heating the oven and brush them with oil). This will prevent the skin of the pig from sticking to the roasting rack.

6 Place the pig on the oven rack and broil for 20 minutes. Take the pig out and brush with turmeric water. Turn the pig over and bake for another 20 minutes. All ovens have slightly different broilers — pay close attention so that it does not burn the skin.

7 Reduce the oven temperature to 350 degrees F and continue baking for 1½ hours, brushing the pig with turmeric water and turning it a couple of times. At this point, the pig should be cooked. If it will be some time before you plan to serve it, reduce the oven temperature to 250 degrees F and leave the pig there for up to 2 hours – it only gets better that way.

8 Just before serving, you might want to give the skin a final crisping. This can be done by using the broiler, or, preferably, if you have a convection oven, simply by increasing the temperature to 450 degrees F and baking for an additional 15 minutes. Pay close attention so the skin does not burn — during this process, you should not leave the kitchen, or even the immediate vicinity of the oven.

THIS IS A LOVELY TROPICAL FISH AND SHELLFISH STEW typical of the playful Mauritian cooking. That it claims to be an interpretation of the classical Marseilles fish soup is also characteristic of a cuisine that is unique and homegrown but not, in the strictest sense of the word, indigenous.

When, in the years after 1715, the French East India Company established a colony on what is now Mauritius, the island was almost uninhabited save for the remains of a Dutch trading post. The new possession was named Île de France, after the mother country, but its rapidly growing population was global rather than French: Indians, Chinese, Malagasy, and Africans as well as different European tribes.

The island was lost to Great Britain during the Napoleonic Wars, at the battle of Cape Malheureux — "Cape Unlucky" — in 1810. Today, even though it is nearly two hundred years since the French lost and left, and English has long been the official language, French is still more commonly spoken. But the language, people, and culture are highly creolized.

This is especially true when it comes to cooking — the food is hardly ever "purely" French, Indian, or Chinese, and nearly always more an image of the heterogeneous population than of its purported place of origin. In this "bouillabaisse," which has been adapted to the local temperament and taste, little more than the French name remains; I think that it is reasonable to say that a fiery yellow and spicy bouillabaisse with coconut milk would be impossible in Marseilles.

I make it a point to use both shellfish and fish. I also make a nice, quite intense shellfish stock. You can, however, make do with a store-bought stock.

Serves 6 as a main course

2	pounds assorted shellfish, such as crabs, langoustines, small lobsters, and shrimp (see Note)
1	pound assorted white-fleshed fish fillets, cut into 1-inch dice
2	teaspoons powdered turmeric
1	teaspoon ground ginger
2	cups shellfish stock, homemade (page 187) or store-bought
2	cups unsweetened coconut cream (see page 139) or full-fat coconut milk
1	stalk lemongrass, bruised
	A small pinch of saffron threads (approximately ½ gram)
1	kaffir lime leaf
2	tablespoons finely chopped fresh ginger
1	tablespoon tomato paste (optional)
	Salt
1	pound cherry tomatoes
2	red bell peppers, roasted, peeled, cored, seeded, and sliced (optional)
2	onions, chopped
1	tablespoon coriander seeds, coarsely crushed
6 to 8	curry leaves, plus extra for garnish
1 to 4	green chiles, chopped
2	teaspoons thyme leaves, plus a few sprigs for garnish

1 Remove the shells from the shellfish using your hands. If you are using live shellfish, such as lobster, kill it first by plunging into boiling water for 30 seconds.

2 Place the shellfish meat in a bowl, cover, and place in the refrigerator. Make stock from the shells or discard.

3 Place the fish in a bowl, season with the turmeric and ground ginger, and mix well using a spatula. (Your hands would be seriously discolored by the turmeric.)

4 In a large pot, bring the shellfish stock to a boil. Add the coconut cream, lemongrass, saffron, lime leaf, half of the fresh ginger, and the tomato paste, if desired. Cook for 10 to 15 minutes, until the lemongrass and lime leaf have released their flavors and the stock is reduced by about one-third. Season with salt to taste.

5 Add the fish, shellfish, tomatoes, the bell peppers (if desired), the onions, coriander seeds, curry leaves, chiles, and thyme and cook for 10 minutes, or until the fish is just cooked through. Transfer to soup plates; garnish with curry leaves, the rest of the ginger, and thyme; and serve.

NOTE *How much expensive shellfish you use is up to you. You can use only fish and a handful of shrimp and still have a wonderful dish. The shellfish should be raw. If using already cooked shellfish, add it to the dish after it has been plated, as it will get rubbery if reheated in the soup.*

WHERE FLAVOR WAS BORN

SIMPLE SHELLFISH STOCK

THIS IS A VERY SIMPLE SHELLFISH STOCK, based mainly on shrimp, which is cheaper than most other shellfish and yields a good stock in less time than the thicker shells of lobster or langoustines. If you use these thicker shells, first broil them for 10 minutes, or until dark patches appear. Most of the flavor of shellfish can be found in the shell, so there is no need to use the valuable shellfish meat to make stock.

1 Heat the oil in a large pot. Add the shells and onion and sauté over high heat for 5 to 7 minutes, stirring and crushing the shells with a wooden spatula. Add the boiling water, bay leaf, peppercorns, tomatoes, and ginger and boil over high heat for 15 minutes.

2 Strain the stock through a clean coffee filter or a sieve lined with cheesecloth or a kitchen towel. (Make sure that the kitchen towel does not smell of soap.) Allow to cool to room temperature before refrigerating. Remove any fat from the surface before using. (If you are making the stock right before making the bouillabaisse, you do not have to wait until it cools, but note that you will then have a more cloudy stock that is more prone to pick up off flavors.)

Makes approximately 2 cups

1	tablespoon vegetable oil
1	pound shells from assorted crustaceans, mostly shrimp
1	onion, chopped
2 ½	cups boiling water
1	bay leaf
5	black peppercorns
2	tomatoes, quartered
1	tablespoon chopped fresh ginger

RÉUNIONNAISE YELLOW CHICKEN
AND BANANA CURRY

Serves 4 as a main course

1	**large chicken, cut into 8 pieces, or 4 chicken thighs, halved**
2	**teaspoons powdered turmeric, or more to taste**
2	**sprigs thyme, or more to taste**
	Salt
3	**tablespoons vegetable oil**
2	**small onions, chopped**
2 to 4	**cloves garlic, chopped**
4 to 5	**tomatoes, chopped**
1	**teaspoon finely chopped fresh ginger**
1 to 2	**tablespoons butter**
3	**bananas, cut into 4 pieces each**
2	**teaspoons yellow curry powder**
½	**cup chopped spring onions**
	Finely chopped parsley for garnish

THE CREOLE CURRIES FROM THE ISLAND OF RÉUNION, in the Indian Ocean, are very different from Indian, Arab, and Zanzibari curries, or even from those of Mauritius, only a few miles away. The most important spice here is turmeric – Réunion is one of the world's leading producers of turmeric, and the spice is featured in most savory dishes on the island. The use of thyme is an example of French-Mediterrenan cooking combining well with a tropical spice-based cuisine.

Serve with rice and perhaps another vegetable dish. The Réunionnaise are crazy about all members of the cabbage family, especially the chou chou that was imported from Brazil in the 1830s and now grows wild, covering large parts of the valleys and up into the mountainous areas.

1 In a large bowl, sprinkle the chicken with the turmeric, the leaves from 1 sprig of thyme, and salt to taste, tossing well so that all the chicken is coated.

2 Heat the oil in a deep skillet or wide pot over high heat. Add the chicken and sauté for 10 minutes, turning often, or until golden brown. You may need to do this in several batches in order not to crowd the skillet. Transfer to a plate or bowl.

3 Add the onions and garlic to the pan and sauté over medium heat for 5 minutes, or until soft. Return the chicken to the pan, add the tomatoes, ginger, and the remaining thyme sprig, and cook for 25 to 30 minutes, until the chicken is cooked through.

4 Just before serving, melt the butter in a large skillet over medium-high heat. Add the bananas, sprinkle with the curry powder and salt to taste, and sauté for 5 minutes, or until slightly crisp. Remove from the heat.

5 Season the chicken stew with the spring onions, more thyme (if desired), and salt to taste. Gently stir in the bananas. Sprinkle with the chopped parsley and serve.

YELLOW RICE

RICE COLORED YELLOW WITH TURMERIC is served everywhere rice is served. The simplest way is just to add a little turmeric to the cooking water and leave it at that. This Balinese version also includes the mild, aromatic flavors of lemongrass, coconut, and, if obtainable, pandan leaves.

Basmati rice is best rinsed and soaked before cooking. This is not necessary if you are using polished or parboiled rice.

Serves 4 as a side dish

1½	cups long-grain rice, such as basmati
1	tablespoon oil, preferably palm oil
3	tablespoons finely chopped shallots
2	cloves garlic, finely chopped
½	cup unsweetened coconut cream (see page 139) or coconut milk
1	stalk lemongrass, green parts removed, bruised
1	pandan leaf, bruised (optional)
1 to 2	teaspoons powdered turmeric

1 If using basmati rice, rinse it in a fine-holed colander or sieve until the water runs clear. Place in a pot, cover with water by at least 2 inches, and let soak for 20 to 40 minutes. Drain.

2 Bring a generous amount of water to a boil in a large pot. Add the rice, bring back to a boil, and boil, covered, for 10 to 15 minutes, until the rice is almost cooked through but still somewhat hard in the middle. (The exact time depends on how long the rice has been soaked and on the hardness of the rice.)

3 Meanwhile, heat the oil in a large skillet over high heat. Sauté the shallots and garlic for 2 minutes. Add the coconut cream, lemongrass, the pandan leaf (if using), and the turmeric and bring to a boil, then reduce the heat and simmer for 5 minutes.

4 Drain the rice well and return it to the pot. Turn the heat to very low, add the coconut mixture, and mix well. Allow to simmer for 15 to 20 minutes, until the rice is cooked through and soft.

5 If you would like the rice to be rather on the dry side, place a folded kitchen towel under the lid and leave to soak up moisture for 5 minutes before serving.

OVEN-BAKED CAPE MALAY CURRY

THIS IS A RECIPE BASED ON A DISH I GOT FROM HARRIET ARENDSE IN CONSTANTIA, on the outskirts of Cape Town. Bobotie is a traditional Cape Malay dish, named after the descendants of the slaves brought to the country by the Dutch East India Company.

In the shadow of the segregation policies of South Africa — where people of different colors and ethnic backgrounds were kept apart at all costs, with brutal and often absurd mechanisms installed to uphold this segregation — food and flavors traveled freely, and Cape Malay cooking became important to all South Africans. The cooking uses a lot of spices but is aromatic rather than hot, and the savory dishes often include dried fruits.

This dish can be prepared a few hours in advance, without the egg mixture. Reheat it, then finish it off with the egg and milk topping just before serving.

Serves 4 to 6 as a main course

2	slices stale bread
1½	cups milk
2 to 3	tablespoons butter
2	onions, chopped
3 to 4	cloves garlic, chopped
2	pounds finely chopped beef or ground beef
1	tablespoon garam masala
2	teaspoons powdered turmeric
2	teaspoons cumin seeds, crushed
2	teaspoons coriander seeds, crushed
3 to 5	cloves, crushed
5	allspice berries, crushed
1	teaspoon dried herb mixture, such as herbes de Provence
2	teaspoons salt, or more to taste
1	teaspoon freshly ground black pepper
½	cup dark or golden raisins
¼	cup finely chopped apricots or figs
¼	cup slivered almonds
2 to 3	tablespoons chutney or apricot jam
6	kaffir lime leaves
3	large eggs, lightly beaten

1 Preheat the oven to 350 degrees F.

2 Soak the bread in ½ cup of the milk.

3 Melt the butter in a large skillet over medium heat. Sauté the onions and garlic for 3 to 5 minutes, until crisp-tender. Remove from the heat.

4 Squeeze the milk from the bread, and tear the bread into smaller pieces. In a large bowl, combine the bread, onions, beef, garam masala, 1 teaspoon of the turmeric, the cumin seeds, coriander seeds, cloves, allspice, mixed herbs, salt, pepper, raisins, apricots, almonds, chutney, and lime leaves. Mix well and place in a baking dish.

5 Bake for 30 minutes.

6 In a small bowl, beat the eggs, the remaining 1 cup milk, and the remaining 1 teaspoon turmeric together. Pour it over the meat mixture. Bake for 15 to 20 minutes longer, until the egg mixture has set. Serve with rice and a green salad.

LEMONGRASS

"FOR THE UNTRAINED EYE, LEMONGRASS MAY INDEED LOOK LIKE A WEED—THE QUEEN OF THAI COOKING PREFERS TO WEAR A MODEST DISGUISE."

STEP ON THE GRASS

It is an everyday situation if there ever was one: a child playing on the porch in a small and dusty Thai village as cars and the three-wheeled tuk-tuks speed by, obviously unconcerned with traffic rules or even etiquette. I am sitting in the shadows watching the world pass by while waiting for a bus that never comes. I look at the child on the porch, trying his best to entertain himself with the extremely limited resources at hand.

Apart from a weed growing on the side of the porch and flowing in through the bars of the railing, there is nothing but a stool and a small cardboard box.

It is hot and damp and the air smells of diesel and fish. A man passes with a prickly durian fruit — the foulest-smelling fruit known to mankind, a vegetable Camembert — and there is that distinctive odor of decay. Then a woman comes out of the house and onto the porch; she talks briefly to the child and then bends down toward where the weeds are growing. She breaks off one of the plumpest weeds, which turns out to be a stalk of lemongrass. With rapid movements, she peels off the outer layers and removes the green part on top before returning to the house.

What she leaves behind is an olfactory revolution. What was only seconds ago a hot and smelly Third World street is now perfumed with the pleasant and fresh-smelling scent of lemongrass. I am not the only one to notice it; the other people waiting for the bus are also now sitting with flared nostrils. And the child is absolutely mesmerized. For a while he just stands there, completely still next to the lemongrass. Then, once the smell begins to wear off, he tries to induce it to return by touching the leaves, but he only reaches the top, green part of the pointy leaves and his sensitive hands are stung by the longitudinal fibers. The child starts crying; a truck puffs by, leaving us in a dark cloud of exhaust; and reality gradually returns to the street.

Lemongrass grows willingly wherever the climate is hot. In Thailand, where it is used most, it can be found at house corners and in gardens, even in big cities. The Thai not only use it in cooking, they also believe it has purifying properties — a claim that is at least partly backed up by modern science. In addition, it is believed that growing lemongrass in the garden helps to keep snakes away, an assertion that modern science would no doubt meet with a healthy dose of skepticism. Snakes are anyway a fairly marginal nuisance, and if growing lemongrass can diminish the *fear* of snakes, it may serve an important purpose for peace of mind.

For the untrained eye, lemongrass may indeed look a like weed — the queen of Thai cooking prefers to wear a modest disguise. She is the most bashful of spices, either disinclined to give herself away or reluctant to intrude. When I was living in Africa, I had lemongrass growing in my garden without realizing it. I passed it every day, sometimes carrying bags full of groceries, including lemongrass. Only when I decided to do something about the mess, to plant an herb garden, and started tearing up the foot-long grass, did it give itself away, and I could return inside to the kitchen as the best-smelling gardener on the continent.

Lemongrass is more lemon than lemon itself. If you add lemon juice to a cup of hot water, the first thing you will notice is that it is tart. If you instead add a bruised stalk of lemongrass — as they do in Zanzibar — you have pure lemon without the sour. And the Thai *tom* soups, *tom kha gai* and *tom yam kung*, where much of the point is the lemony flavor and tangy sourness, lemongrass is used not as a substitute but because, in Thailand, true lemon flavor is what you get when you combine lemongrass and kaffir lime leaves, then add some lime juice just before serving.

Mom, make it smell sweet again: Lemongrass grows everywhere in Thailand. Not only is it used in cooking, but it is also said to help keep snakes away. The top of the grass can be rough; most of the flavor is contained in the stem.

STEAMED FISH
WITH LEMONGRASS AND HERBS

SOME OF THE BEST FISH DISHES I KNOW are two closely related dishes served in Thailand and on Bali — fish wrapped in pandan, or pandanus, leaves or banana leaves and fried, baked, or grilled. No matter what cooking method is used, however, the fish, enclosed inside the leaves, ends up being steamed.

Fresh (or frozen) banana leaves and pandan leaves can be bought in well-stocked Thai shops, but if you cannot find them, a practical although somewhat less stylish alternative is to wrap the fish in baking parchment. Or simply bake in a baking dish or casserole sealed with foil.

I have found that most lean white fish work well in this dish, so go for the freshest fish you can find. Salmon also works surprisingly well.

Serve with rice and sweet chili sauce, preferably Thai-style, or Coriander and Mint Sauce (page 155), or both.

Serves 2 as a main course

2	cloves garlic, sliced
2	cilantro (fresh coriander) roots, crushed and finely chopped, plus 2 tablespoons chopped cilantro
2	teaspoons finely chopped galangal or ginger
4	kaffir lime leaves, preferably fresh, bruised
2	stalks lemongrass, crushed and chopped
2	tablespoons chopped holy basil or 2 tablespoons chopped regular basil plus 1 teaspoon chopped mint
2 to 4	small green chiles, chopped (optional)
1	tablespoon fresh lime juice
1	teaspoon fish sauce (*nam pla*) or salt
2	8-ounce white-fleshed fish fillets
2	pandan or banana leaves, trimmed to 6-inch squares, or baking parchment
	Oil for panfrying, such as canola

1 In a bowl, combine all the ingredients except the fish, pandan leaves, and oil. Rub the fish with this mixture. Place the fish on the leaves or paper, and top with the the the herb mixture remaining in the bowl. Fold the leaves over the fish, enclosing it completely, and tie with cotton string.

2 Heat a little oil in a large nonstick skillet over high heat. Fry the fish packets for 6 minutes on each side. Cut open, and serve.

PORK AND SHRIMP MEATBALLS
WITH LEMONGRASS AND GINGER

SERVING A MIXTURE OF PORK AND SHRIMP ON LEMONGRASS "STICKS," like savory Popsicles, is typical of both Bali and Thailand. The combination of ground pork and shrimp is quite sticky and does not need egg or flour to hold it together. It's best to grind the meat and shrimp yourself using a meat grinder. You can also use a food processor, although the pork and shrimp mixture has a tendency to become quite mushy in the processor.

These are also excellent grilled. Serve with sweet chili sauce.

1 In a food bowl, combine the shrimp, pork, chopped lemongrass, chiles, ginger, sesame oil, and lime leaf. Run the mixture through a meat grinder and return to the bowl. (Or, if using a food processor, pulse to mix. It is better with a rather coarse mixture than a mushy one.)

2 Using a sharp knife, quarter the whole lemongrass stalks lengthwise, making sure that each "skewer" holds together at the bottom. Divide the shrimp mixture into 8 portions. Rub each lemongrass skewer between your palms until it gives off a fresh smell, but not so much as to disintegrate. Wrap one portion of the meat mixture around each piece of lemongrass.

3 Heat a little oil in a large skillet over high heat. Add the skewers and and cook for 6 to 8 minutes, turning several times, until golden brown and cooked through.

VARIATION *If you want more sesame flavor, roll the patties in sesame seeds before frying. This is not recommended if you are grilling, as the sesame seeds have a tendency to pop when exposed to high heat, but frying over medium heat works fine. They will then need a slightly longer cooking time.*

**Serves 4 as a starter,
8 as a canapé**

8	ounces peeled shrimp, minced
4	ounces freshly ground pork, preferably pork belly
2	stalks lemongrass, green parts removed, crushed and finely chopped, plus 2 thick stalks lemongrass
2 to 6	small green chiles
1	tablespoon finely chopped fresh ginger
2	teaspoons light sesame oil
1	kaffir lime leaf, finely chopped if fresh, crumbled if dried
	Oil for panfrying, such as canola

MUSSELS
WITH LEMONGRASS, CHILES, AND HOLY BASIL

IN SOUTHERN THAILAND, many of the lively ferry terminals double as fish markets. Because of their high turnover, that is where you find the freshest seafood.

Although the bright color of green-lip mussels will lend an extra dimension to this dish, it can be made with any type of mussels — use the freshest you can find.

I think this is best as a starter, and I prefer not serving it with rice or vegetables on the side. If anything, I suggest serving with some bread to sop up the cooking juices — even though that is definitely un-Thai.

Because I have noticed that the sweet chili sauce used in Thai recipes is nearly always commercially made, I do not bother making my own either.

Serves 2 as a main course, 4 to 6 as a starter

3	pounds mussels, scrubbed
1	tablespoon vegetable oil
3	shallots, finely chopped
2 to 5	small green Thai or other small hot chiles, finely chopped
2	stalks lemongrass, bruised and finely chopped
1	tablespoon coriander seeds, bruised
⅓	cup seafood, vegetable, or chicken stock
2	tablespoons chopped holy basil for garnish
	Sweet chili sauce for serving

1 Place the mussels in a colander under running water. Discard any mussels with cracked shells, or any that do not close tightly when under the cold water. Pull off any stringy bits, or beards, protruding from the shells. (This should be done just before cooking, as the necessary process of removing the beards can cause the mussels to die, and you want them as fresh as possible.)

2 Heat the oil in a wok or wide pot. Add the shallots and chiles and sauté for 2 minutes, or until slightly softened. Add the lemongrass, coriander seeds, stock, and mussels. Cover and steam for 3 minutes. Turn the shells with a wooden spatula or spoon, cover, and cook for 3 to 5 more minutes, until almost all the mussels have opened.

3 Transfer to deep plates, garnish with holy basil, and serve immediately, with sweet chile sauce for dipping.

VARIATION *This recipe can be made richer and fuller in flavor by using 1 cup unsweetened coconut milk or cream instead of the stock and 1 tablespoon Green Curry Paste (page 161) in addition to the other spices in the cooking liquid.*

NOTE *Cooking the mussels until all the shells have opened will result in overcooking many of them. Discard any unopened mussles as you eat — some will open as they are served — or lift out the opened mussels from the pot and continue cooking the unopened ones for 2 to 3 minutes longer. If there are any that have still not opened, discard them.*

SPICY LEMONGRASS
FISH CAKES

**Serves 2 as a main course,
4 to 6 as a starter**

I	pound mixed white-fleshed fish fillets
3 to 5	tablespoons Green Curry Paste (page 161)
I to 2	kaffir lime leaves, finely chopped, or I teaspoon grated lime zest
I	stalk lemongrass, trimmed and finely chopped
I to 2	small green chiles, finely chopped (optional)
I to 2	large eggs
	Peanut oil for shallow frying
	Bread crumbs or all-purpose flour for dredging

ONE OF THE BEST REASONS FOR MAKING YOUR OWN CURRY PASTES is to be able to use them for more than one purpose. The rich complexity of flavor of homemade curry pastes is best appreciated when they are allowed to display themselves in different settings. Although I love traditional Thai green curries, I am even more excited about my own fish cakes based on the same green curry paste, just spiked up with some more kaffir lime leaves.

If you wrap each fish patty around a slightly bruised stalk of lemongrass, it makes for a nice canapé.

I Rinse the fish thoroughly under cold running water or, preferably, leave it in a bowl of ice water for 10 minutes. (This will help firm the flesh.) Drain and pat dry.

2 Remove any skin, bones, and/or fatty parts, and finely chop the fish using the sharpest knife you have. This is a laborious process, but the results are much better than using a food processor or blender. (You could use a meat grinder, but as this requires cleaning it afterward, it probably won't save you any time.)

3 Combine the fish, curry paste, kaffir lime leaves, lemongrass, and chiles (if desired) in a bowl. Lightly beat I egg, add to the fish mixture, and mix well.

4 In a large nonstick skillet, heat a couple of tablespoons of oil over medium-high heat. Using your hand and a spoon, mold about I tablespoon of the fish mixture into a small ball. Roll in bread crumbs and add to the pan. If the fish ball doesn't hold together, beat the second egg and add some or all of it to the remaining fish mixture and make another test ball. When you have found the right consistency, continue shaping the rest into balls, and fry until golden. You may have to fry the fish cakes in two batches in order not to crowd the pan. Drain on paper towels. Serve with Coriander and Mint Sauce (page 155) or a commercial chili sauce. If served as a main course, serve with rice, preferably jasmine rice.

LEMONGRASS-COCONUT SOUP
WITH SHRIMP

KNOWN AS *TOM YAM KUNG*, THIS IS ONE OF THE MOST IMPORTANT THAI SOUPS, and there are hundreds of ways to make it, with chicken or fish, as well as with, occasionally, tamarind to make a sweet-sour soup.

There is a tradition that the soup, which mainly has mild and aromatic flacors, should also be made with enough chiles to be scorching hot. Crying at the table is something that is highly appreciated in Thailand. Much as the loud discussions around tables in Italian trattorias are a sign of high spirits, constant sniffling and tears at Thai restaraunts mean that everyone is enjoying themselves.

The galangal and lemongrass are left in the soup when served. The lemongrass is never eaten, the galangal rarely.

Serves 2 as a main course

3	cups unsweetened coconut milk
12	thin slices fresh galangal or ginger
2	stalks lemongrass, bruised
6	kaffir lime leaves, bruised
2	small shallots, finely chopped
1	cup vegetable stock
1	pound peeled raw shrimp
2 to 6	small Thai chiles, chopped
2 to 3	spring onions, chopped
2 to 3	tablespoons fish sauce (*nam pla*)
1	teaspoon sugar
2	tomatoes, cut into 8 wedges each
3 to 4	tablespoons fresh lime juice
	Chopped cilantro (fresh coriander) for garnish

1 In a wok or wide, deep skillet, combine the coconut milk, galangal, lemongrass, lime leaves, and shallots, bring to a boil, and boil for 3 to 5 minutes to blend the flavors. Add the stock and return to a boil. Add the shrimp, chiles, spring onions, fish sauce, and sugar and boil for 2 minutes. Add the tomatoes, return to a boil, and take off the heat.

2 Add lime juice to taste, pour into soup bowls, and garnish with cilantro.

LEMONGRASS TEA

LEMONGRASS IS SAID TO HAVE CERTAIN PURIFYING QUALITIES. In addition, it aids digestion. Therefore, this tea is served during festivals and celebrations when one typically eats too much.

You can make it using only lemongrass and water, but I think that it works best together with a small pinch of black tea. Be sure not to use Earl Grey or any other perfumed tea.

Makes 4 cups

4   cups water

2   stalks lemongrass, crushed and chopped, plus lemongrass stalks, quartered lengthwise, for garnish

2   teaspoons black tea leaves

    Sugar (optional)

1 In a small pot, bring the water to a boil. Add the crushed and chopped lemongrass to the water. Allow it to simmer for 5 to 10 minutes, depending on how strong you would like the lemongrass flavor to be. Or, if it becomes too strong, remove the lemongrass and add more water. Add the tea, take the pot off the heat, and let stand for 3 minutes.

2 Serve in heatproof glasses, with sugar (if desired), garnished with the quartered lemongrass stalks.

COCONUT PANNA COTTA
WITH LEMONGRASS, TURMERIC, AND PASSION FRUIT

THAILAND

Serves 4

1 stalk lemongrass, plus additional for garnish (optional)

1 cup heavy cream

1 cup unsweetened coconut cream (see page 139)

¼ cup sugar

2 teaspoons gelatin

2 tablespoons cold water

2 teaspoons finely chopped fresh turmeric or ½ to 1 teaspoon powdered turmeric

4 ripe passion fruit, halved

Lemon verbena or slivers of lemon zest for garnish (optional)

ALTHOUGH NOT A TRADITIONAL THAI DISH, this dessert is inspired by the flavors of Thailand. Use fresh turmeric if you can get it — dried turmeric has a much stronger taste and is somewhat more bitter, so it must be used in moderation.

1 Crush the lemongrass with the back of a knife to help release the flavor, and tie it into a knot. Combine the cream, coconut cream, sugar, and lemongrass in a small pot and bring to a boil. Simmer for 15 minutes.

2 Meanwhile, combine the gelatin and cold water and let stand for 2 minutes to soften.

3 Remove the cream from the heat. Remove the lemongrass and stir in the gelatin mixture and turmeric.

4 Scoop the contents of half a passion fruit into each of four small nonstick metal molds. Pour the lemongrass cream into the four molds, pouring it over the back of a spoon so as to spread the mixture. Refrigerate for at least 3 hours, or up to 24 hours.

5 To serve, dip the molds briefly in hot water, then run a knife around the edges and unmold the panna cotta into individual plates. Scoop the contents of half a passion fruit onto each one, and garnish with lemongrass, lemon verbena, or lemon zest, if desired.

Grate, just grate: The traditional way to grate coconut is labor-intensive and slow. At Time for Lime cooking school in Thailand, one assistant is assigned the task. The grated coconut is later used to make coconut milk.

TAMARIND

"THE SOUR IS WHAT MAKES ALL THE OTHER FLAVORS STAND OUT."

I once risked my life for a tamarind. It was foolish, I admit, but also absolutely irresistible. I had never tasted fresh tamarind, and here I was, less than a hundred feet away from a cluster of majestic trees that were in the process of releasing their ripe fruits.

With every puff of wind through the branches, a handful of tamarind pods would fall down to the ground with a muted thump. They were there for the taking — had it not been for the elephants, which had come out of the deep forest to the shoreline of Lake Kariba, on the Zambezi River in northern Zimbabwe, to refresh themselves on the attractively sour tamarind pulp.

Tamarind, sometimes referred to as "Indian date," is a brown pod with a wobbly, brittle shell, usually about four inches long, that contains up to ten smooth beanlike seeds surrounded by a sticky pulp. It is this pulp, not the seeds, that is the delicacy of tamarind. Containing a high amount of tartaric acid, it is one of the most popular souring agents in the cooking of the Indian Ocean, and indeed most other tropical countries. The tree originated in the inlands of southeastern Africa but soon spread to the shoreline, and from there to India, China, and later on to the West Indies.

The tamarind, like most spices, has been surrounded by legend and superstition. On the west coast of India there was a belief that evil spirits lived in the pods. Taking advantage of this, the British colonialists of the nineteenth century would wear tamarind pods behind their ears when going to the market, so the locals would stay away from them.

I wait until the elephants have turned their attention to another tree. One of the females has found a way to shake the tree, making it rain tamarind pods. After hearing insistent warnings from the others, I take the small rowboat myself. From my vantage point, I can only see the gray behind of one of the elephants, but I know there are more. I leap ashore, struggling to find the exact balance between being efficient and invisible. I reach the pods lying on the ground, grab two, and head back to the boat. My heart pounds heavily, more and more so when I see an elephant heading down to the shoreline. But once back in safety, thrilled by my own successful expedition and the, for me, unusual level of risk taking, I am forced to admit that the elephant hardly noticed me.

My tamarind pods do not contain any evil spirits. However, one of them has been visited by a whole lot of ants. And the tamarind pod that was not almost eaten is so fresh and sour that I too am driven to seek out a quenching drink.

Hiking through the mountains on the island of Réunion, the author suddenly came across a herd of cows grazing in a tamarind forest. He did not tell them about the beef-and-tamarind dish he had eaten a few nights before.

TAMARIND-GLAZED FRUITS
WITH STAR ANISE

THE SWEET AROMAS OF VANILLA AND THE COOLING FLAVORS OF STAR ANISE need something pleasantly tart, and it is the flavor of tamarind that makes this dish come together. This recipe was inspired by British chef Paul Gayler's beautiful book *Flavors of the World.*

Serves 4 to 6

1 Preheat the oven to 350 degrees F.

2 Using a spoon or a butter knife, scrape the seeds out of the vanilla pod, and reserve the seeds. Place the scraped-out pod in a small pot and add 6 tablespoons sugar, the lemongrass, ginger, star anise, tamarind, and water. Bring to a boil and let boil uncovered for about 10 minutes, allowing the flavors to be released and about half of the water to evaporate.

3 Meanwhile, rub all the fruits with the vanilla seeds. Melt the butter in a large skillet over medium-high heat, add the fruits and rum (if desired) and cook for 5 to 7 minutes, until the fruits are slightly caramelized. If they are still very pale, add 2 tablespoons sugar, increase the heat to high, and cook for 2 minutes, stirring frequently to make sure the fruits do not burn.

4 While the fruits are cooking, place a baking dish in the oven to preheat.

5 Transfer the fruits to the hot baking dish, add the tamarind and spice syrup, and stir well. Bake for 7 to 10 minutes. For extra glazing, use the broiler for a minute or two — but pay close attention so the fruits do not burn. The fruits and sauce should be sweet-and-sour with an emphasis on the sweet, so you might want to adjust with a little more sugar to taste.

1	vanilla bean, halved lengthwise
6 to 10	tablespoons palm sugar or brown sugar
2	stalks lemongrass, green parts removed, crushed, and finely chopped
2	teaspoons finely chopped fresh ginger
4	star anise
2	tablespoons tamarind paste
½	cup water
4	½-inch-thick pineapple slices
2	apples, peeled, cored, and quartered
2	pears, peeled, cored, and quartered
8	dried figs, halved
8	dried apricots, halved
4	tablespoons (½ stick) butter
3 to 4	tablespoons dark rum (optional)

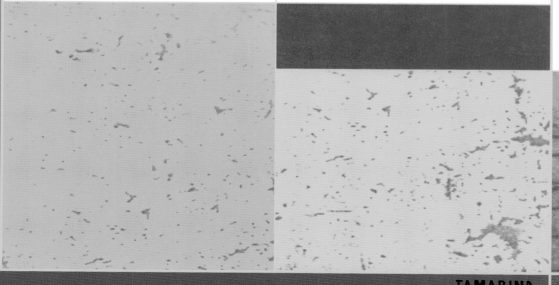
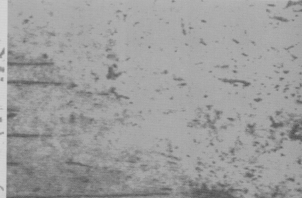

ENTRECÔTE
WITH ONION, GINGER, AND TAMARIND

IN THE MOUNTAINS OF RÉUNION there is an ancient tamarind forest, and in between the trees there are cows grazing, as if presenting a live version of this dish.

This dish is fairly close to your ordinary steak with caramelized onions, but while it has in my opinion all of the fine qualities of that international classic, at the same time it shows off some of the unique qualities of the Réunionnaise kitchen, adding Creole flavors and colors to classical French cooking.

Serves 2 as a main course

2	1-inch-thick 8-ounce entrecôte (rib) or sirloin steaks
	Salt and freshly ground black pepper
1	tablespoon vegetable oil or ghee
2 to 3	tablespoons tamarind paste
1	teaspoon ground ginger
1	tablespoon finely chopped fresh ginger
3	tablespoons butter
6	onions, sliced
1 to 2	tablespoons sugar
⅓	cup beer, dry white wine, or water

1 Heat a large cast-iron skillet over high heat. Season the meat generously with salt and pepper. Rub with the oil. Sear the meat for 2 minutes on each side. Transfer to a plate to rest.

2 Add 1 tablespoon of the tamarind paste and 3 tablespoons water to the skillet and bring to a simmer, stirring to scrape up the browned bits from the bottom of the pan. When most of the liquid has evaporated, pour the remaining mixture over the steaks. Season them with half the ground ginger and 1 teaspoon of the fresh ginger.

3 Reduce the heat under the skillet to medium, add the butter and onions, and season with a little salt to help start the browning. Cook for 10 minutes, or until the onions have started to brown nicely. Add the remaining 1 to 2 tablespoons tamarind paste and ground and fresh gingers, the sugar, and beer and cook uncovered until the onions are soft and light brown and almost all the liquid has evaporated. Transfer the onions to a serving bowl, and cover to keep warm.

4 Add the steaks to the pan and cook over medium-high heat for 4 to 6 minutes, depending on desired doneness. Serve with the onions.

SWEET-AND-SOUR VEGETABLE SOUP
WITH PEANUTS

INDONESIAN SWEET-AND-SOUR SOUPS are very different from the Chinese versions, lighter and fresher-tasting. This one can be made with all sorts of vegetables — a balance of green beans, spinach, and scallions works well, or use what you have at hand. It can also be served with shrimp, fish, or chicken added for a more substantial soup.

Serves 4 as a starter or light lunch

1 Soak the tamarind pulp (if using) in the boiling water for 15 minutes. Remove the seeds and stir until you have an even, smooth sauce.

2 Using a mortar and pestle, crush the shallots, garlic, galangal, turmeric, coriander seeds, chile, one-third of the peanuts, and the shrimp paste until you have a fine paste.

3 In a wok or deep skillet, toast the remaining peanuts over high heat for 3 to 5 minutes, stirring constantly to prevent burning. Add the stock and the spice paste and bring to a boil. Add half the tamarind and half the sugar, then add more of either one to taste, until you have a pleasant sweet-and-sour balance.

4 Add the vegetables and the noodles (if desired) and bring to a boil. Reduce the heat and simmer for 3 to 5 minutes, until the vegetables are cooked but still firm.

1	tablespoon tamarind pulp or 1 teaspoon tamarind paste
¼	cup boiling water (if using tamarind pulp)
4	shallots, sliced
3	cloves garlic, chopped
1	1-inch piece of galangal
2	teaspoons finely chopped fresh turmeric or 1 teaspoon powdered turmeric
1	teaspoon coriander seeds
1	large red chile, seeded and sliced
½	cup raw peanuts, coarsely chopped
1	teaspoon shrimp paste
5	cups lightly salted vegetable stock
2	tablespoons brown sugar, or to taste
1	pound assorted vegetables, trimmed as necessary and cut into equal slices or pieces
8	ounces rice noodles (optional)

ZANZIBAR – LIFE AQUATIC

Kizimkazi is a sad village on the south side of Zanzibar, a place of dark secrets. At night, bats patrol the streets and even the hotel corridors, and strange sounds can be heard – of drumming and dancing and shouting, up until it is nearly time for morning prayer.

In the daytime, when I inquire about these nocturnal activities, their very existence is vigorously denied, and people sit tired and apathetically watching Dirty Harry movies. On my favorite island, this is certainly not my favorite place to go, and had it not been for the life aquatic, I would not have bothered coming here again.

But this is where you can meet and swim with the dolphins. I dive into the warm ocean and swim with a dolphin mother and her young child. For a few minutes, the whole world is bathed in blue through the clear light, with the soft movements of the gray dolphins casting long shadows in the water, as in an indescribably beautiful underwater ballet. Then suddenly, without warning, the dolphins decide to go somewhere else and I am left floating alone in the deep blue sea – a tiny dot in nature's infinite, three-dimensional Yves Klein painting.

Closer to the shoreline are coral reefs encircling the island. And while the deep sea, where the dolphins hang out, is mysterious and minimalist blue, the area around the reef is an explosion of colors and life. Some of the mussels have large violet mouths and are making strangely suggestive kissing motions. A parrot fish floats by. Some pink fish are teasing a hermit crab, while a small black fish goes wild when it sees its own reflection in my diving mask. It charges toward me, trying to attack its potential rival. But the rival in the mirror is just as brave and strong, if not stronger, and just before it smashes into my mask, the fish loses its courage. A small snapping sound can be heard as it rapidly turns around. If I continue looking at it when it turns to see what happened, it gains confidence by seeing that it's adversary swam away cowardly, and it charges again.

I am not the only human down here. A local fisherman has landed his boat by the same reef. The boat is a dug-out tree trunk, his anchor merely a stone with a rope around it, and his only fishing equipment is a stick with a nail driven through it. Even on Zanzibar this is very primitive, and it demands luck, concentration, and the occasional show of courage from the fisherman. Fortunately the fisherman is not disturbed by his pinkish white observer; instead he proudly volunteers to show me the secrets of his work. We soon develop a wordless communication where he points at some diffuse and inert object at the bottom of the sea, giving me time to affirm that I cannot see anything there except a bump in the sand, before he swims down, sticks his nail into the object, and comes up with a small stingray that has been hiding there, or some other exotic fish. At one point I alert him to a barracuda that swims by, but the fish is too fast. The fisherman is visibly disappointed at having missed such a valuable

LEFT: The traditional *dhow* boats have been of tremendous importance to the spice trade. Long before globalization, the triangular sails of the *dhows* could be seen all over the Indian Ocean.
RIGHT: Boiled octopus at a market on Zanzibar.

catch, and the opportunity of showing off his real skills, but you cannot achieve everything with a stick and a nail.

Soon after, he directs my attention to a small hole in a group of stones, about seven feet under the sea surface. When I look, I can barely glimpse something moving, but I cannot see what it is. The fisherman dives down and reaches his hand inside, and immediately the water is black, a thick, semitransparent fog. Now he is just a shadow within the shadowy dark. After what seems like an eternity, he surfaces, gasping for air, holding up a hand that is completely covered by the many arms of a bravely fighting octopus that he alternates between punching with his hand and poking with the nail. The fight takes several minutes, and when he finally can place the octopus in his boat, he is covered with ink and his arm is covered with loveless hickeys. He pulls his boat up onto land and commences to beat the octopus against the sand for half an hour, and even though I know that this is what is normally done to tenderize the sometimes impossibly chewy meat, I cannot help but think that it must also feel like a somewhat reassuring ritual: "The beast is really dead and I am the stronger man for it."

Not much to worry about: A hammock tempts one to a bit of laziness on the east coast of Zanzibar.

TURMERIC SQUID
WITH TAMARIND SAUCE

THIS IS CALAMARI ASIAN-STYLE, with lots of temperament and fresh flavors. The sweet-and-sour tamarind sauce makes the dish light and fresh-tasting, so that it is perfect as a snack or an appetizer.

Serve with salad or steamed vegetables. This recipe also works well with fish instead of squid; a similar dish with sea bass is common in Thailand.

Serves 2 as a main course, 6 as a starter

2	tablespoons tamarind pulp or 2 to 3 teaspoons tamarind paste
1	tablespoon palm sugar or brown sugar, or more to taste
1	tablespoon fish sauce (*nam pla*), or more to taste
¼	cup water
2 to 3	dried chiles, plus a few for garnish
¼	cup all-purpose flour
1	tablespoon powdered turmeric
½	teaspoon ground cardamom
	Vegetable oil for deep-frying
1	pound cleaned squid, bodies sliced, tentacles left whole
	Fried onions or scallions for garnish (optional)

1 In a small pot, combine the tamarind, sugar, fish sauce, and water and bring to a boil. Remove the tamarind seeds if you used tamarind pulp. Add the dried chiles and boil over low heat for 15 minutes, or until you have a smooth sauce. Adjust the sauce for sweetness and saltiness with more palm sugar and/or fish sauce to taste.

2 In a shallow bowl, combine the flour, turmeric, and cardamom.

3 Heat oil in a deep-fryer, or heat at least 1 inch of oil in a deep skillet over high heat. Working in batches, dredge the squid in the flour, shake to remove excess flour, and add to the hot oil. Fry until golden and crispy, and drain on paper towels. Garnish with dried chiles and fried onions, if desired. The sauce can be either served on the side or poured over the fried squid.

VARIATION *This dish can be expanded upon by including vegetables. Typical Thai vegetables would include spring onions, tomatoes, cucumber, and bell peppers or mild chiles. If serving with vegetables, toss the vegetables in the hot sauce and serve with the squid on top.*

OCTOPUS CURRY

THIS IS A TRADITIONAL ZANZIBARI CURRY, hotter and spicier than most other dishes from the island and with a sharp, tart edginess to it. Octopus can be tough and needs a little rougher treatment to show off its real qualities. The curry can also be made with chicken or fish, but in that case I prefer cutting down a bit on the tamarind.

1 Boil the octopus in lightly salted water for 20 to 25 minutes, until tender or nearly tender. Drain.

2 Crush the dry spices and garlic using a mortar and pestle, or coarsely grind in a small blender.

3 If using tamarind pulp, dissolve it in the boiling water, then remove the seeds.

4 Heat a little oil in a deep skillet and sauté the onions over medium-high heat for 3 to 5 minutes, until lightly browned. Add the octopus and the spice mixture and sauté for 5 minutes. Add the tomatoes, coconut cream, tomato paste, half the tamarind, and 1 teaspoon of the sugar, reduce the heat to medium, and let simmer for 10 to 15 minutes.

5 Add more tamarind and sugar to taste, if desired. Sprinkle with cilantro before serving.

Serves 4 as a main course

1½	pounds octopus, cleaned and sliced into 1-inch slices
2	teaspoons coriander seeds, slightly bruised
2 to 3	teaspoons cumin seeds
2 to 3	small dried chiles, bruised, or 3 to 4 fresh red chiles, chopped
2	teaspoons powdered turmeric
2	cloves garlic, chopped
2 to 3	tablespoons tamarind pulp or 2 to 4 teaspoons tamarind paste
½	cup boiling water (if using tamarind pulp)
	Oil for panfrying, such as canola
1 to 2	onions, chopped
3	tomatoes, chopped
1	cup unsweetened coconut cream (see page 139)
1	tablespoon tomato paste
2	teaspoons sugar
	Chopped cilantro (fresh coriander) for garnish

SHRIMP BALLS
WITH TAMARIND SAUCE

**Serves 4 as a main course,
10 as a starter**

3	tablespoons tamarind pulp
1	cup boiling water
2	pounds shrimp, shelled and deveined
2	teaspoons coarsely ground coriander seeds
1	teaspoon powdered turmeric
½	teaspoon ground ginger
½	teaspoon grated black lime or regular lime zest
½	cup cooked rice
3	tablespoons finely chopped cilantro (fresh coriander)
2	onions, finely chopped
1	tablespoon butter or ghee
¼	teaspoon freshly grated nutmeg
½	teaspoon ground cinnamon, preferably freshly ground
1	cardamom pod, bruised
1	large tomato, finely chopped
1	dried chile, slightly bruised
1	teaspoon sugar, or more to taste
	Salt

IF THE DIFFERENT CUISINES ALONG THE INDIAN OCEAN ARE COUSINS, then the kitchens of the Persian Gulf states are like brothers. This is a festive dish that has close relatives in many of the Gulf states. The combination of the sweet shrimp meat with the sour tamarind is also reminiscent of some of the more eastern Asian sweet-and-sour dishes. However, here the sweetness is not so pronounced, and the emphasis is more on fragrance than on the sugar. In Oman, lime was, for a long time, considered a spice more than a vegetable, and dried lime fruits — referred to as "black lime" — are still used in cooking.

This is a great starter or snack. For a main course, serve with rice.

1 Soak the tamarind in the boiling water.

2 Meanwhile, combine the shrimp, coriander, turmeric, ginger, lime zest, rice, cilantro, and 2 tablespoons of the onions. Grind the mixture in a meat grinder, or alternatively, pulse in a food processor (make sure that it is not too finely processed; it is better to have some chunks left than to have a mushy mixture).

3 In a medium pot, heat the butter and sauté the rest of the onions for 3 to 5 minutes, until soft. Remove from the heat.

4 Press the tamarind mixture through a sieve into the pot, pressing on the tamarind with the back of a spoon to release as much liquid as possible. Discard the seeds and stringy fibers left in the sieve. Add the nutmeg, cinnamon, cardamom pod, tomato, chile, and sugar to the pot and bring to a boil. Let simmer for 15 minutes. Season with salt and more sugar to taste, if necessary.

5 Using a tablespoon dipped in water, form the shrimp mixture into balls and drop the balls into the tamarind sauce. Roll them around in the hot sauce so they firm up, then simmer gently for about 20 minutes, until cooked through.

NOTE *The shrimp balls can be made up to 24 hours in advance and reheated just before serving.*

The giant shrimp that swim in the Indian Ocean are great for treats small and large. The largest and best shrimp are found off the coast of Mozambique.

Fresh shells at a market in southern Thailand. Some of the best seafood markets can be found at ferry landings, where there are always lots of people.

Crabs in a market on Zanzibar.

The characteristic Thai longboats, like these in Lobahra Village, use old, modified car engines.

A fisherman on Bali studies his catch. Since the introduction of modern offshore trawlers, local fishermen claim that fish resources have been depleted.

LEFT: Covering one's head is normal, if not mandatory, for women in many Muslim countries. The many interpretations of Islam on Zanzibar lead to many different fashions. RIGHT: A fisherman rinsing his catch before bringing it to market.

LEFT: Octopus is delicious but has a tendency to be tough. Therefore fishermen on Zanzibar often beat them against the ground to tenderize them.

RIGHT: The waters on the east coast of Zanzibar are shallow. During low tide, one can walk a long way and still only have water up to the ankles. Growing seaweed is an important household industry on the east coast of Zanzibar, and is important for empowering women.

The outskirts of Muscat, Oman, stretching into the desert.

A man at the port in Muscat.

The local mode of transport is often the same today as it was centuries ago. This boat off the coast of Zanzibar is an example of limited interest in modern technology; it has an outboard engine, but doesn't use it.

The coconut palm can grow more than 80 feet, a fact as impressive as the men who climb to the top to cut down the nuts.

NUTMEG & CLOVES

"THE HISTORY OF CLOVES AND NUTMEG IS THE HISTORY OF HOW THE WORLD CAME TO BE ONE—AND TO TASTE A WHOLE LOT BETTER AT THE SAME TIME."

MISSIONARY OF SPICES

At first I do not notice him where he stands, rigid, surrounded by tropical plants and a small flock of ducks. And when I do notice him, I am surprised to find that he looks like such a small man, wearing an apologetic look on his verdigris-coated face.

It seems as if he is leaning to his left, as if he were wishing to be somewhere else than in this lush garden in Mauritius that he himself helped establish. But then there was always something slightly odd about him, always wishing to be somewhere else. Intriguing yet anonymous, charismatic yet friendless, cunning yet in many ways unsuccessful, a man who changed world history but who has still managed to be ignored by history books — and even *almost* overlooked by those who have come a very long way just to see him.

It is only appropriate that someone named Pierre Poivre — Peter Pepper in English — should grow up to change, even revolutionize, the history of spices. And it is fitting for his strange blend of awkwardness and deceitfulness that the spice with which he shares a name is the one that he had nothing to do with.

I have come to Mauritius in search of Poivre's legacy, some small trace of a man that the world has not quite figured out — grand or insignificant, hero or villain, hustler or visionary? This lush botanical garden outside Pamplemousse, Mauritius, is one of the most visible results of his passion and unceasing activity. Poivre, great missionary of spices and liberator of flavor, is the man responsible for breaking the Dutch spice monopoly in the eighteenth century. I find that there is something poetic about Poivre: the man named pepper liberated nutmeg and cloves and made them available to the world at affordable prices.

While pepper at the time of Poivre was already being grown in several places, resulting in drastically lowered prices, the two most sought after spices of the time, nutmeg and cloves, were still almost as expensive as before the discovery of the sea route to India — when goods changed hands dozens of times and were taxed at all ports of call and cities along the way. The continued high prices were largely due to the monopolistic practices of the Dutch East India Company. Up until the sixteenth century, the Arab merchants who controlled the spice trade had managed to keep the origins of the spices a secret — saying only that they came from faraway, dangerous places, the lands of dragons and snakes. In fact, both nutmeg and cloves came from the Moluccas, also known as the Spice Islands and now a part of Indonesia.

By the seventeenth century, though, the Arabs had been outmaneuvered, the Portuguese were on the run, and the Dutch controlled the Spice Islands with supreme, tyrannical powers. The Dutch understood that the only way they could keep the prices high, making as much as 10,000 percent profit, was to guard their nutmeg and clove monopoly jealously. And, in contrast to modern-day capitalists, who are ever increasing production in order to chase expanding markets, the Dutch strategy was to keep supply down in order to keep prices up.

Cloves and nutmeg would grow on several of the small islands in the Moluccas — sometimes slightly different species on each island. This

Few spices have been surrounded by as much drama and mystique as nutmeg and mace. For centuries, whoever controlled the Moluccas, in what is now Indonesia, tried to keep the spices' origins a secret. The nutmeg is the kernel of the seed, while mace is the aril, or cap, surrounding it. The fruit, however, is not very good.

diversity was not of much interest to the Dutch, who were rightly worried that if a single tree or seedling were to be lost, they would no longer be able to hold the world ransom for the commodities it most longed for. Therefore, they decided that cloves and nutmeg should only be allowed to grow in highly restricted areas, where they could be guarded by armed troops. With the profit-hungry conqueror's usual heavy-handedness, they burned all the spice trees that grew outside the designated areas — and in the process scorched several villages. Before the nutmegs were shipped, they were roasted and dipped in lime in order to prevent germination, and there were strict requirements that no clove seeds were to be exported — the spice clove is actually the bud of a flower and thus useless for planting.

Poivre, no philanthropist himself, felt that it was wrong that the riches of the Dutch were not in the hands of the French. He also understood that with France's weak army and a fractious and inefficient overseas administration in the form of the French East India Company, it was not possible to conquer the Dutch. They had to be conned.

Originally a philosopher and missionary from a well-to-do family, Poivre had an artistic streak and a penchant for traveling. It was only after he, as a result of mistaken identity, was arrested by the Chinese and held captive for a year that he became an adventurer. After that point, his life reads like an almost too-fully packed adventure novel, with a somewhat anticlimactic ending. In captivity, he learned fluent Chinese and endeared himself to the royal court at Cochin China, in what is now Vietnam. He set up a trading post but then alienated the king when he kidnapped a young local man to have him serve as interpreter. As a result he was expelled, and with him all the other Europeans in the country.

On his way back through enemy territories, Poivre's right arm was ripped off by a cannonball, and he was taken hostage by the English, who then gave their wounded prisoner away to the Dutch. He developed gangrene and barely survived. During his subsequent convalescence while in Dutch custody, he managed to learn Malay fluently and also developed an interest in the lucrative spice trade. On his return to France, he published his colorful autobiography, *Voyages of a Philosopher*, and he used his new eminence to gain a royal appointment. In 1749 — only thirty years old — he returned to the East, only to meet a disillusioned, largely broke, and definitely hostile French administration in India and the Far East.

Despite the Dutch iron grip on the Moluccas and lack of support from his own countrymen, Poivre, using all his skill and cunning, managed to go behind enemy lines in a daredevil operation, get hold of nutmeg and clove seedlings, and smuggle them out — at one point even raising a Dutch flag to avoid detection by a patrol ship.

He planted the seedlings on Île de France, which today is Mauritius. And here the story of Poivre enters a new, almost tragic phase. Because of neglect, and possibly also sabotage by colleagues at the French East India Company, all the plants died. Poivre, bitter and angry but not one to give up, returned to the Moluccas, once again risking his life for spices and fatherland — only to see the same thing happen again. At that point, he moved back to France, married, and settled in Lyon — a visionary in his mid-forties with not much to show for it.

Clove for sale: When they are picked, the cloves are red to purple. They have to be dried before they can be used, and during that process, the color changes to dark brown.

French politics — and at this stage in history, spices were politics — is equally famous for intrigue and second chances, and when the ailing French East India Company was finally dissolved and the overseas territories set under the administration of the government, Poivre was appointed governor of Île de France and neighboring Île de Bourbon, now Réunion.

This time he did everything right. He had entered a new phase in his life. Gone was the overenergetic adventurer; enter the administrator with a vision. He built a mansion on the hill overlooking what is now the botanical garden at Pamplemousse. Here he gathered one of the largest collections of tropical plants in the world and established himself as one of history's first modern conservationists. He also transformed the island into a model agricultural community; in only a few years, the five thousand French soldiers stationed on the island were self-sufficient, able to manage without the usual supplies from the fatherland. Then he charged one of his closest associates to go to the Moluccas one last time, and in June 1770 he could finally reap the fruits of a lifetime of labors: four hundred rooted nutmeg trees and seventy rooted clove trees were planted in the garden in Pamplemousse, and from there, they were distributed to the rest of the world. The time of monopoly was over and the spice trade finally truly globalized. Soon there were successful nutmeg and clove plantations all over the world, from Zanzibar and Madagascar in the Indian Ocean to Grenada and Martinique in the New World.

Poivre had fulfilled his ambition of breaking the monopoly, and after him no one person would have such a singular impact on the world spice trade — he was the last in a long line that included Marco Polo and Vasco da Gama.

Today, however, wandering around the garden in Pamplemousse does not instill a clear feeling of walking in Pierre Poivre's footsteps. As nutmeg and cloves have gone from being the most sought after ingredients in the world to something that is taken for granted, or ignored, Poivre's footprints have been gradually erased. The garden he helped establish is now named the Sir Seewoosagur Ramgoolam Botanical Garden, in honor of Mauritius's first prime minister, and the small statue of Poivre is so modest and tucked away that it is not hard to miss. The moment Poivre left Mauritius in 1773, the forces within the French administration who had always objected to his style, methods, and unaristocratic background began chipping away at his legacy. The garden fell into neglect — there was even talk of abandoning it altogether — and while the offspring from the clove and nutmeg trees Poivre had smuggled out of the Moluccas were blooming on Zanzibar and Grenada, the ones growing in Pamplemousse fell into neglect, and most of them died.

I leave the garden somewhat disappointed that there is not more of Poivre left. But then, a couple of days later, I suddenly feel the whiff of Poivre's legacy when I am invited to the home of Jeanette Lequin, just a few miles south of Pamplemousse. There, in her small kitchen in her meticulously well-kept house in a modest neighborhood outside Bois Rouge, she prepares a mild and aromatic chicken curry, spiked up with more than just a hint of cloves, and I look at the back of the small tin of curry powder, made in India and on Zanzibar, and costing less than a dollar. This is Poivre's legacy, I think.

Heavy duty: It takes a hard head to carry 100-pound bags of cardamom. This picture shows spice traders in Kerala, India. The weakling on the right was fired soon after for being "unfit for real work."

PERSIAN RICE PILAF
WITH SAFFRON AND POMEGRANATES

PERSIAN PILAFS PLAY WITH THE CONTRAST BETWEEN SWEET AND SAVORY FLAVORS. Here the rice is first cooked, then fried to get a nice crust, referred to as *tah dig*, that is highly appreciated.

It works very well with aromatic meat dishes, such as Grilled Sirloin with Pepper and Cinnamon (page 264), the Omani classic from the other side of the Persian Gulf, and with poultry dishes like Squab with Coriander, Cumin, and Apricots (page 157), also from Iran. It can also easily be expanded to a main course itself by adding cooked meat, fish, or poultry and more vegetables.

Serves 6 to 8 as a side dish

1½	cups basmati rice
2 to 3	tablespoons vegetable oil
1	onion, chopped
¼	cup coarsely chopped apricots
1	½-inch piece of cinnamon stick
2 to 3	cardamom pods, lightly bruised
4	cups boiling water
2	tablespoons butter
2	tablespoons plain yogurt
	A small pinch of saffron threads (approximately ⅓ gram)
1	teaspoon powdered turmeric
1	teaspoon paprika (optional)
	Salt
¼	cup finely chopped spring onions
¼	cup pomegranate seeds

1 Soak the rice in water, either placing it in a small-holed colander under running water or placing it in a pot full of water, stirring well and changing the water two or three times. This removes the surface starch and prevents it from sticking and clumping.

2 In a wide nonstick pot, heat the oil over medium heat. Sauté the onion and apricots for 4 to 5 minutes. Using a slotted spoon, transfer to a bowl.

3 Add the rice, cinnamon, and cardamom to the oil remaining in the pot and cook, stirring, for 2 to 3 minutes. Add the boiling water and let the rice boil uncovered over medium-low heat for 20 minutes, or until almost cooked through.

4 Drain the rice, reserving the cooking water, and return the rice to the pot. Turn up the heat to high and add the butter, yogurt, saffron, turmeric, paprika (if desired), and the onion and apricot mixture. Cook for 5 to 7 minutes, stirring to prevent scorching.

5 Add the reserved water (and more, if needed) little by little and continue to cook, stirring occasionally, until the rice is cooked through.

6 Remove the rice from the heat and season with salt to taste. Stir in the spring onions and pomegranate seeds, and serve.

FARMER'S SAUSAGE
WITH CLOVES AND CORIANDER

Serves 8 to 10 as a main course

3	**pounds beef, preferably shoulder, chopped or minced**
1	**pound pork, preferably neck, chopped or minced**
2	**pounds pork fat (belly or back fat) or sheep fat, chopped or minced**
1 to 2	**tablespoons coriander seeds, crushed**
2	**teaspoons ground cloves, preferably freshly ground**
2	**tablespoons salt**
2	**teaspoons freshly ground black pepper**
2	**teaspoons chili powder (optional)**
	Vegetable oil or butter for panfrying
	Sausage casings, soaked in cold water for at least 15 minutes

THE BOERS, OR FARMERS, THE WHITE SOUTH AFRICAN AFRIKANERS OF DUTCH ORIGIN, are not known for their embrace of exotic food traditions or use of spices. They pride themselves on their carnivorous capacity, and their favorite mode of cooking is grilling, or *braii*, as it is called in Afrikaans. However, the sausages that are a much-loved part of the *braii* are often seasoned liberally with cloves, coriander, and/or nutmeg, spices that are normally not allowed to play leading roles, and during my visits to South Africa, *boerwors* — farmer's sausage — with cloves and coriander became one of my favorites.

The *boerwors* are almost always made with beef; the more rustic varieties are mixed with sheep fat, while for a finer flavor, pork fat and occasionally also some pork meat are used. If possible, you should chop the meat; if using a meat grinder, grind it as coarse as you can. The sausages are typically made into one long coil and not twisted into links. This works best if you are preparing them for a big party — I usually divide them into several individual sausages, often with slightly different flavors (see the variation below).

They can also be frozen for up to 3 months.

1 Combine the meats and fat in a large bowl. Add the coriander seeds, cloves, salt, pepper, and chili powder, if desired.

2 Heat a little oil in a small skillet. Using a teaspoon, shape a small ball of the meat mixture, sauté it, and taste. Adjust the flavor with more spices to taste if necessary.

3 Stuff the meat mixture into the sausage casings, using the sausage maker attachment of your food processor or electric mixer or a sausage horn. Or, if you lack any kind of special equipment, a sausage horn can be emulated with reasonable results using a large funnel and the back of a large wooden spatula to cram the meat mixture into the casings; this, however, will demand the concentration and cooperation of two people and a willingness to accept a result that is often somewhat less than perfect.

4 Grill or fry the sausages without piercing the skin — the fat should not be allowed to run out.

5 Serve with mustard and potatoes, or, somewhat contrary to tradition but delicious nonetheless, with nan bread (such as one of the variations on page 48) or Rice Pilau (page 243).

VARIATION *Since making sausages can be quite laborious, I normally make two or three different varieties in addition to the one above, such as one seasoned with nutmeg or mace; one with garlic, orange zest, and sage; and one flavored with crushed red pepper flakes or piri piri and cumin.*

NOTE *If you cannot find sausage casings or cannot be bothered with the laborious process required to make link sausages, this recipe can also be used to make good farm-style sausage patties. In that case, you may want to add ½ cup potato flour or 2 eggs to the recipe to prevent the sausage from falling apart.*

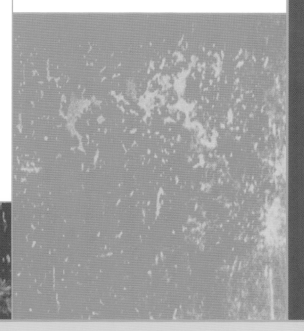

RICE PILAU
WITH CASHEWS AND CORIANDER

RICE PILAU CAN BE FOUND IN MANY DIFFERENT VERSIONS, from the Middle East and Iran to India and Zanzibar. *Pilau* is both a way to cook rice that ensures a fluffy, nonsticky result and the name of several related dishes made with rice cooked that way. The first written description of a pilau turns up in the thirteenth-century Arabic cookbook *Kitab al-Tabikh*, published in Baghdad. Pilau is also variously known as pilaf, pilav, pulaw, palaw, or pulao, depending on the language into which it has been integrated.

This rice pilau can be served as a side to fish, poultry, or meat dishes and can easily be expanded into a main dish itself — just add meat, fish, or poultry, and more vegetables.

Of all the pilaus I have had in the countries around the Indian Ocean, I like this Zanzibari version best. That said, it seems to me that often the differences in pilau making within one community may be greater than those among different countries.

1 Soak the rice in water, either placing it in a small-holed colander under running water or placing it in a pot full of water, stirring well and changing the water two or three times. This removes the surface starch and prevents the rice from sticking or clumping.

2 In a wide pot, heat the oil over medium heat. Sauté the onion and garlic with all the spices for 5 to 7 minutes, until the onion is soft. Drain the rice well, add to the pot, and cook, stirring, for 2 to 3 minutes, until shiny.

3 Add the boiling water, reduce the heat, and allow to boil gently, uncovered, for 25 minutes, or until the rice is soft. Taste the rice a couple of times while it cooks, and if you feel that one spice is in the process of becoming too predominant, fish it out using a fork.

4 When the rice is cooked, remove it from the heat and cover with a folded kitchen towel and a lid. Let stand for 5 minutes. The kitchen towel will absorb the steam and leave the rice nice and fluffy.

5 Add the nuts. Season with salt, stir in the butter (if desired), and garnish with cilantro.

Serves 6 to 8 as a side dish

1½	cups basmati rice
2	tablespoons vegetable oil
1	onion, chopped
2	cloves garlic, finely chopped
2	teaspoons coriander seeds, crushed
1	teaspoon mild curry powder
1	½- to 1-inch piece of cinnamon stick, broken into smaller pieces
1	teaspoon black peppercorns
2 to 3	cardamom pods, lightly bruised
3 to 4	cloves
3	cups boiling water
3 to 4	tablespoons cashews, coarsely broken into smaller pieces
	Salt
1 to 2	tablespoons butter or ghee (optional)
	Chopped cilantro (fresh coriander) for garnish

KINGFISH
WITH ORANGE, CLOVES, AND GINGER

NOTHING SAYS ZANZIBAR LIKE CLOVES! Since the introduction of the clove tree there in the eighteenth century, the production of cloves has been one of the island's most important sources of income, and since the end of the slave trade in the mid-nineteenth century, in fact, it has been the single most important industry. For a while, at the end of the 1880s, cloves made Zanzibar one of the wealthiest countries in the region, and Stone Town was the first city in Africa to be fully electrified.

This is one of my favorite modern Zanzibari dishes, inspired by one served by Masoud Salim and Judi Palmer at Archipelago restaurant in Stone Town. Judi is from that vast continent on the other side of the Indian Ocean, Australia, and the food at Archipelago manages to combine the contemporary influences of Australian cooking with the flavors of traditional Zanzibari cooking.

It's best to use a white game fish of some kind, such as kingfish, marlin, yellowtail, or swordfish, but you can use the fillets of any white firm-fleshed fish, such as halibut. If you want the sauce to be somewhat thicker in consistency, you can add a small pinch of cornstarch at the last minute and boil just until the sauce thickens. If you would like it richer, you can whisk in a small amount of butter just before serving. I like the clear flavors of the fish, orange, and spices and leave it as it is; although the sauce then looks short of perfect, the flavor is, in my opinion, best.

Serve with a simple salad and rice, preferably Rice Pilau (page 243).

Serves 4 as a main course

4	8-ounce white-fleshed fish fillets, such as kingfish
1	teaspoon ground ginger
¼	teaspoon freshly ground cloves, plus 2 to 3 whole cloves
1	tablespoon finely grated orange zest, or more to taste
2 to 3	tablespoons oil, such as canola, plus more for panfrying
1	small onion, finely chopped
1	cup fresh orange juice
2	teaspoons finely chopped fresh ginger, or more to taste
2 to 3	tablespoons brown sugar
	Salt and freshly ground black pepper
1	teaspoon cornstarch (optional)
1	tablespoon butter (optional)

1 Wash the fillets and pat dry with a paper towel. Season with the ground ginger, ground cloves, and half the orange zest.

2 In a small pot, heat a small amount of oil and sauté the onion for 2 to 3 minutes, until soft. Add the orange juice, fresh ginger, whole cloves, 1 to 2 tablespoons sugar, and the rest of the orange zest and bring to a boil. Boil until reduced to about ¼ cup, then reduce the heat and let simmer gently, uncovered, while you cook the fish. Taste the sauce every now and then, and remove the cloves if you feel that the clove flavor is getting too penetrating.

3 Season the fish fillets with salt and pepper and sprinkle with the remaining 1 tablespoon sugar. Heat 2 to 3 tablespoons oil in a large nonstick skillet over medium-high heat. Sauté the fish for 3 to 5 minutes until golden brown, then turn and continue cooking for 3 to 5 minutes, depending on the thickness of the fillet. To test for doneness without ruining the appearance of the fillets, stick a fork into the thickest part of one fillet and hold it there for 10 seconds: the fork should come out warm. Or, if using an instant-read thermometer, the interior temperature should be about 160 degrees F.

4 Just before serving, bring the sauce to a boil. Season with salt and pepper. If you want the sauce to be somewhat thicker, whisk in the cornstarch, return to a boil, and boil for 1 minute. If you want the sauce to be richer, whisk in the butter and remove from the heat.

5 Arrange the fillets on plates, pour the sauce over them, and serve.

NUTMEG-AND-GINGER SPINACH SOUP
WITH SOY SAUCE-BAKED SWEET POTATO

THIS DISH IS TYPICAL OF THE MODERN AND COLORFUL SOUTH AFRICAN APPROACH TO COOKING — where food from all over the world meets up, and European and African cooking meets the flavors and spices of the Indian Ocean.

In the seventeenth century, nutmeg was one of the most rare and expensive spices. It is still an interesting and difficult spice. When used in moderation, it lends an intensely aromatic spiciness to the food; when used in excess, it overpowers everything else. The essential oils that give off flavors are very fragile and evaporate and oxidize fast, so you should use only freshly grated nutmeg.

Serves 4 to 6 as a starter

I	medium sweet potato (8 ounces), cut into ¼-inch dice
2	tablespoons sunflower oil
I	teaspoon soy sauce
½	teaspoon freshly grated nutmeg, or more to taste
2	tablespoons butter
2	onions, finely chopped
II	ounces spinach, washed and dried
I	medium russet potato, peeled and cut into 1-inch dice
2	teaspoons finely chopped fresh ginger
4	cups chicken stock
	Salt and freshly ground black pepper
6	tablespoons yogurt
I	teaspoon ground ginger

I Preheat the oven to 400 degrees F.

2 In a small bowl, toss the sweet potato with the oil, soy sauce, and ¼ teaspoon of the nutmeg. Spread the sweet potatoes on a baking sheet. Bake in the middle of the oven for 25 minutes, or until soft and almost caramelized. Remove and keep warm.

3 Meanwhile, melt the butter in a medium pot over medium heat. Sauté the onions for 5 minutes, or until soft and shiny. Add the spinach, russet potato, fresh ginger, and stock and bring to a boil, then let simmer for 15 to 20 minutes, until the potato is cooked.

4 Season the spinach mixture with salt and pepper to taste. Transfer to a blender or food processor and process until smooth.

5 Pour the soup into soup bowls. Garnish with the sweet potato and yogurt, and sprinkle with the ground ginger and the remaining ¼ teaspoon nutmeg.

STEWED OXTAIL
WITH NUTMEG SAUCE

ONE OF MY FAVORITE PLACES ON BALI IS, SOMEWHAT SURPRISINGLY, RUN BY A SWISS CHEF. Heinz von Holzen is originally from Switzerland but has lived on the island for twenty years, and with a restaurant, cooking school, and "cultural village," where visitors are invited to learn about Balinese food and handicraft traditions, he is one of the most important figures on the Balinese culinary scene. Heinz uses ox tongues in this dish and makes it more full-flavored by adding stock; I use oxtails, in which case it is not necessary to add stock. In either case, the meat is simmered for hours until it is very tender, close to the point where it starts falling apart.

Remove the seeds from the chiles if you would like a milder dish.

1 Using a small sharp knife, trim the oxtails of excess fat.

2 Crush the chiles, garlic, shallot, ginger, galangal, peppercorns, coriander seeds, and sugar using a mortar and pestle; or coarsely grind in a food processor or through a meat grinder.

3 Heat a little oil in a wide pot over medium-high heat. Sear the oxtails, in batches, until well browned on all sides, about 10 minutes. Return all the meat to the pot, add the spice mixture, and sauté with the meat for 5 to 7 minutes.

4 Add half the nutmeg and enough water to cover the meat by 1 inch. Bring to a boil, then reduce the heat and simmer, uncovered, for approximately 2½ hours, until the meat is falling-apart tender. Make sure the pot does not boil dry; add a little more water if necessary. (If you must leave the meat to cook unsupervised, you will have to cover the pot; in which case you should remove the lid toward the end and boil until the consistency is that of a thick sauce. You may want to remove the bones; I prefer to leave them in.)

5 Add the potatoes, lime leaves, and soy sauces, mix well, and simmer until the potatoes are tender. Season with the remaining nutmeg and salt and pepper to taste. Serve with rice, preferably a fragrant basmati or jasmine.

NOTE *I like the nutmeg flavor in this dish to be fairly pronounced, but it is a spice that can easily overpower all other flavors, so use moderation. You may instead want to add the last of the nutmeg when the dish is served – grating a small amount of nutmeg over each serving at the table will perfume the room, and this will influence the interpretation and appreciation of the dish.*

Serves 4 to 6 as a main course

3	pounds oxtails, cut into 1½-inch-thick slices (you can ask your butcher to do this)
1	large red chile, seeded if desired and finely chopped
2	small red bird's-eye chiles, Thai chiles, or piri piri chiles, preferably fresh, seeded if desired and finely chopped or crushed
1	clove garlic, crushed
1	shallot, crushed
1	teaspoon finely chopped fresh ginger
2 to 3	teaspoons finely chopped galangal or ginger
1	teaspoon black peppercorns, crushed
1	teaspoon coriander seeds, crushed
2	teaspoons palm sugar or brown sugar
	Oil for panfrying, preferably palm oil
⅔	teaspoon freshly grated nutmeg, or more to taste
1 to 2	pounds potatoes, peeled and cut into 1-inch cubes
4	kaffir lime leaves, slightly bruised
3	tablespoons sweet soy sauce or *kecap manis*
1	tablespoon dark soy sauce
	Salt and freshly ground black pepper

VANILLA

"IT TOOK A SLAVE TO LIBERATE THE FINEST SPICE ON EARTH."

HEAVEN CAN'T WAIT

I have just left Réunion's capital, Saint-Denis, when the sky opens up. Within a quarter of an hour, there are rivers crossing the road and reddish brown water flowing in from the sugar fields. Schoolchildren on their way home take off their shirts and play in the rain.

I manage to leave the main road just before it is closed down, taking a narrow, winding road surrounded by endless rows of sugarcane. Then I pass the vast fields of turmeric growing on the slopes of the mountain. The water here seems more yellow. No, it can't be, can it? Suddenly the already heavy rain intensifies and I can't see more than ten feet ahead of me. Slowly, slowly I drive to the next town and wait for the rain to stop.

On a cool day, of which Réunion has quite a few, while sipping your espresso or eating your *confit de canard* at a sidewalk café, you may be excused for thinking that you are in France. Yellow La Poste cars pass by with uniformed mailmen; there is an endless stream of "Bonjour, madames," "Bonjour, monsieurs," wherever people come into greeting distance of each other; and elderly men in berets pass you by with an issue of *Le Monde* under one arm and a baguette under the other. It is all *tres gentil*, like small-town life somewhere in rural France, in Provence, perhaps? And true, the island — first a possession of the French East India Company, then a colony — is still a part of France, technically a *département*, with representation in parliament and daily flights to Paris Orly's domestic terminal.

But when the elements set their mark on life, you realize that although you are officially in a part of France and the European Union, reality puts you in a different place, a tropical island five hundred miles off the coast of Madagascar in the Indian Ocean, more than five thousand miles from the French mainland. Tropical rain is nothing like normal rain. It gets everywhere, it is everywhere. There is nothing to do but wait. Let

the rain kiss you and tap you on your head like silver drops, let the rain play a lullaby on your roof when you go to bed. Tap tap tap, a thousand different rhythms, a long-lost blues that turns the rivers red. Not even indoors is dry — the humidity knows no walls, no doors. You have to shower to get dry, and drink rum to assure yourself that not everything around you is water.

It takes three days before the rain stops, and by then it has rained almost five feet. It must be the heaviest rain that man has seen since the days of Noah. But it is not. Réunion holds the world record for precipitation; in the Cilaos area in the middle of the island, it once rained more than six feet in one day.

This climate has, despite its occasional extremity, a mild friendliness to it – a Garden of Eden without snakes, wild animals, or dangerous insects, but with plenty of temptations. And when the rain has more or less stopped, I drive past the sugarcane and turmeric fields again — they are not what interest me the most. I venture into the rain forest at the foot of the Piton de la Fornaise volcano. Here, in the thick green lushness of the rain forest, is the plant that made Réunion the sweetest place on earth.

The island of Réunion — formerly known as Île de Bourbon — is the vanilla capital of the world, home to the much-sought-after Bourbon vanilla, arguably the best. No other spice, no other food, can match the complex aromas and sweetness of vanilla.

The rain forest smells of the wet soil, rusty and slightly sulfurous. When I pass a cinnamon tree, slightly bruising a few of the leaves, there

When first picked, the vanilla pods are flavorless. Only after a long period of fermentation do they develop the fine, sweet aromas that make vanilla the most aromatic spice.

is a faint whiff of cinnamon in the air. Yet the cinnamon and the other trees play only supporting roles in this forest — they all provide protection for the vanilla, which thrives in the humid shade. The forest is full of climbing vanilla orchids that are carefully tied up on everything that can support them. Fat green pods are hanging from the beautiful vines, looking more like long beans than a valuable spice. At this point the vanilla gives off no fragrance whatsoever — just the promise of the magic to come.

When the green pods are picked, they are still odorless. Only after weeks of curing are the flavors released. By then the pods have a wonderful smell composed of thousands of different odorants, making a complex sweetness that cannot be matched.

Vanilla is used all over the world, in everything from Coca-Cola to crème brûlèe to ice cream. The difference between vanilla proper and artificial vanillin — a by-product of the cellulose industry — is well known to anyone who has tasted real homemade vanilla ice cream with its tiny black seeds and compared it to the artificial stuff that has plenty of sweetness but very little elegance and depth.

I spend the next days in sweet, fragrant bliss, driving from one vanilla plantation to another and experiencing the almost intoxicating smell coming from the curing sheds. Some farms are just small patches on a field, with a shady cover. Others are huge plantations — like Vanilla, the large cooperative of vanilla growers in the Bras-Panon region, where the director refuses to meet with any foreigners because he claims that they do not appreciate the true value of vanilla.

And life is very sweet. The sun has just set, a full moon is barely visible through the thin veil of skies over Piton de la Fornaise. I am sipping a *rhum arrangé* infused with vanilla on the veranda of a small Creole bar in Saint-Philippe. Inside the bar, someone has just started dancing to the slow reggae rhythms.

Then the heavens open their gates again. And this time it is for real. The clouds over Piton de la Fornaise turn crimson red. Soon there are rivers of lava running down the mountainside. Réunion is a relatively new island, and it is still in the making. Every year or so there are new eruptions from the island's only active volcano. It is frightening and wonderful to behold — like seeing both the beginning and the end of time.

The next day, people flock to the volcano to see and admire this force of nature. The lava has crossed the road, blocking the main route between Saint-Denis and Saint-Philippe. With the help of a guide, I climb the mountain up toward the molten lava that is still slowly pouring down the hill, but I turn back when my shoes start melting.

There are so many indications that this is paradise that it is sometimes easy to forget the brutality that lies below. The dodo, the national bird of Réunion, was so trustful that it became extinct within a few years of the arrival of man. Now it smiles happily at you from the label of the local beer. Human enterprise was not always built on respect for nature — or indeed humankind itself.

The volcano eruption — and lingering smell of sulfur in the air for days afterward — is a reminder that all is not just sweet here on this paradise island, that a dark history, still molten, hides beneath the lush and fertile surface.

Much of what is now sweet — the sugar, rum, and vanilla the island prides itself on — is based on great injustices that leave a bitter aftertaste.

The sugar industry, which supported the island for a long time and is still one of the most important industries, depended on the brutality of slavery. And the vanilla industry would have been nothing were it not for a young slave named Edmond Albius.

Vanilla is one of the few tropical spices to have originated in the New World, and it has always been the one most surrounded with mystery. In Central America, it would yield regular — albeit small — crops, but whenever growing it was attempted in other places, it was a fruitless endeavor. What people did not know then was that the vanilla flower is normally pollinated by a large bee. When left untouched and virginal, the flower will bloom for six to eight hours and then wither away — it needs the impurity of outside intervention to bear fruit.

Vanilla was brought to Réunion in 1822 and planted on a large scale. But twenty years later, most farmers had all but given up on the new plant. It was then that the young slave Edmond, by sheer ingenuity, found a way to artificially pollinate the vanilla flowers. He peeled back the lip of the blooming vanilla flower and, with the aid of a small stick, lifted the rostellum out of the way and pressed the anther and the stigmatic surfaces together. Seven years later, the island sent its first hundred kilos of dried and cured vanilla pods to France. When Edmond died in 1880, as a miserable and impoverished freed slave in a still heavily segregated society, the island was one of the largest vanilla producers in the world. And in the 1890s, it surpassed Mexico and became the world's largest vanilla producer.

Partly because of the abundance of vanilla, but also, perhaps, because the Réunionnaises themselves have experienced the injustice of confinement, they allow the spice to play a more complex and active role than in the rest of the world. Vanilla is not only used in desserts and in the aromatic *rhum arrangé*. Just as often it pops up in savory dishes — to complement and elaborate on the intrinsic sweetness of fine white chicken meat or crustaceans, for example, or to give depth of flavor to salty pork stews and gamey duck, with lots of mild curry.

Today Réunion mourns the inhumane treatment of Edmond and the many others who helped make the island what it is, and it actively embraces mixing of all kinds. People take pride in the varieties of their origins and the riches these bring to their culture. The island thrives on a Creole mixture of African, French, Indian, Malay, Malagasy, Chinese, and many others, reflected in everything from architecture to gastronomy — making Réunion a paradise of diversity, taking the bitter and salty with the sweet and mixing it together to make something more wonderful and interesting in its lively impurity.

TROUT
WITH RUM AND VANILLA

THE SWEETEST WOMAN ON EARTH MUST BE OCTOGENARIAN SCHOLASTIQUE "MAMIE" JAVEL IN THE VILLAGE OF HELL-BOURG in the mountains of Réunion. Even though the island lies in the Indian Ocean, five hundred miles off the coast of Madagascar, it is still a French *département*, and when entering Hell-Bourg, you are reminded that it has been named "one of the most beautiful towns in France." The combination of French and Creole styles is obvious everywhere: in the beautiful buildings, in the people, and in the cooking. Swimming in a nearby river are trout imported from Europe, and lovely Scholastique – who describes herself as a "mix of this and that" – combined the fish with the two archetypeal Réunionnaise ingredients, vanilla and rum.

I find that it is best to serve this sweet and aromatic dish with relatively neutral flavors, nothing to compete with the lovely sweet-savory balance. Rice and Pearl Onions with Coriander and Mint (page 154) would work well.

Serves 4 as a main course

2	1½-pound trout, Arctic char, or other firm-fleshed fish, cleaned, scaled, rinsed, and patted dry
½	vanilla bean, preferably Bourbon, halved lengthwise, seeds scraped out and reserved, bean cut into smaller pieces
	Salt
½	cup all-purpose flour for dredging
2	teaspoons yellow curry powder or powdered turmeric
3	tablespoons butter
3 to 5	tablespoons dark rum

1 Rub the fish with the vanilla seeds and season with salt. On a plate, combine the flour and curry powder. Dredge the fish in the flour.

2 Melt 2 tablespoons of the butter in a large skillet over medium heat. Add the trout and vanilla bean and cook, turning once, for 8 to 10 minutes, until the fish is cooked through. To test for doneness, insert a fork into the thickest part of the fish: if it comes out warm after 10 seconds, the fish is done.

3 Meanwhile, have long matches or a lighter ready for flambéing the fish, and select a good spot to do this. You will need at least three feet of clearance above the pan for the flames; and bear in mind that a kitchen fan often contains a significant amount of grease and, in the worst-case scenario, may catch fire.

4 Add the rum to the pan and carefully set it alight. Allow the flames to die out before transferring the fish to serving plates. Cook the sauce for 1 more minute to make sure the alcohol has evaporated, then stir in the remaining 1 tablespoon butter. Pour the sauce over the fish and serve.

 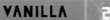

CURRIED DUCK
WITH VANILLA

WHEN I FIRST HEARD OF THE RÉUNIONNAISE TRADITION OF USING VANILLA AS A SPICE IN SAVORY DISHES, I thought the result would be too much, too sweet — something like the fusion chefs of the 1990s serving steaks with a vanilla custard sauce. But, as it turned out, my reservations were just prejudice. The sweet aromas of vanilla should not be misused, but when used in moderation with duck, chicken, or fish the spice shows off a side of itself that is capable of more than just contributing to the world's best-loved ice cream.

In this curry, the vanilla is allowed to interact and blend with more flavors. The dish can also be made with pork.

Serves 4 as a main course

4	duck thighs
½	vanilla bean, halved lengthwise, seeds scraped out, seeds and bean reserved
2	teaspoons mild curry powder
	Salt
2 to 3	tablespoons butter or palm oil
3	onions, chopped
2	tomatoes, chopped
1	cup diced butternut squash, peeled and seeded
2 to 3	sun-dried tomatoes, finely chopped
1	clove

1 Rub the duck with the vanilla seeds, curry powder, and salt to taste. Cut the vanilla bean in smaller pieces.

2 Heat the butter in a large, deep skillet or a wide pot over medium heat. Add the duck and vanilla bean and sauté for 15 minutes, turning occasionally. Add the onions and cook for 5 to 10 minutes. Add the rest of the ingredients and cook for 20 minutes, or even longer for falling-apart-tender duck thighs. Serve with rice, such as Yellow Rice (page 189), or Rice Pilau (page 243).

FLAMBÉED BANANAS
WITH VANILLA AND RUM CARAMEL

THIS DESSERT COMBINES THREE OF THE MOST IMPORTANT RÉUNIONNAISE INGREDIENTS: bananas that grow willingly in the rich, volcanic soil and tropical climate; rum, an important by-product of the sugar industry; and vanilla, for a long time the island's most valuable commodity.

Although this recipe calls for rum, the alcohol is burned off before the dish is served. If you are intending to serve it to children — they love to watch the flambéing — you can continue cooking the sauce for a couple of minutes to ensure that all the alcohol evaporates.

The rum that is normally used in cooking in Réunion is called *rhum agricole* and is a pale dark rum made from the molasses that is left after refining sugar. If you cannot find *rhum agricole*, use an inexpensive dark rum.

Serve with whipped cream or Bourbon Vanilla Ice Cream (facing page).

Serves 4

3	tablespoons butter
1	vanilla bean, preferably Bourbon, halved lengthwise, seeds scraped out, seeds and bean reserved
3	tablespoons brown sugar, or more to taste
4	large bananas
1	tablespoon fresh lemon juice
¼	cup fresh orange juice
2	teaspoons grated orange zest
1	teaspoon grated lemon zest
¼	cup dark rum (see headnote)

1 In a large skillet, melt the butter over medium-high heat. Add the vanilla bean, vanilla seeds, and sugar and cook, stirring with a wooden spatula or spoon, until the sugar dissolves and you have a light brown caramel. Be careful that it does not burn.

2 Add the bananas and cook for 4 minutes, turning them a couple of times and spooning over the caramel to make sure the bananas are coated. Add the lemon and orange juices and continue cooking until most of the citrus juice has evaporated. Add the orange and lemon zests.

3 Meanwhile, have long matches or a lighter ready for flambéing the bananas. and select a good spot to do this. You will need at least three feet of clearance above the pan for the flames; and bear in mind that a kitchen fan often contains a significant amount of grease and, in the worst-case scenario, may catch fire.

4 Add the rum to the pan and set it alight. Allow the flames to die out, then carefully transfer the bananas to serving plates. Pour over the caramel and serve.

BOURBON VANILLA
ICE CREAM

CONSIDERING HOW WONDERFUL REAL VANILLA ICE CREAM CAN BE, I am surprised how few have actually tasted it. With lots of cream and egg yolks and the finest vanilla in the world, this is an ice cream that makes no compromises or excuses.

It is easy to make your own ice cream if you have your own ice-cream machine, but it is by no means impossible if you don't — it just takes more time, as you will have to stir frequently along the way to prevent the ice from freezing into one solid block.

Commercial ice cream is often pumped full of air to make it softer and to increase its volume. Homemade ice cream is not filled with air — so it goes a lot farther. Leaving the vanilla bean in for as long as possible infuses the ice cream mixture with many of the finer and more subtle aromas.

Makes about 1½ quarts

10	large egg yolks
1	cup sugar, or more to taste
1	fat vanilla bean, preferably Bourbon, halved lengthwise, seeds scraped out, seeds and bean reserved
2	cups milk
2	cups heavy cream

1 In a large pot, whisk the egg yolks, sugar, and vanilla seeds until you have a pale mixture speckled with small black spots. Add the milk, cream, and vanilla bean and heat over low heat, stirring constantly with a wooden spoon, until the mixture has thickened enough to coat the back of the spoon. Remove from the heat but continue stirring energetically for another 2 minutes, so the egg yolks don't curdle. Transfer to a bowl, preferably stainless steel, and let cool to room temperature.

2 Cover, place in the refrigerator, and leave until cold.

3 If you have an ice-cream maker, remove the vanilla bean and process the ice cream as usual. If you do not have an ice-cream maker, place the bowl in the freezer for 45 minutes to 1 hour. Take out the bowl and stir the mixture with a spatula, making sure to scrape well along the edges. Return to the freezer for 30 minutes, and repeat until the mixture begins to thicken. Then stir every 15 minutes until it is too hard to stir, at which point you have ice cream.

4 Transfer the ice cream to a freezer container and freeze (if you intend to serve the ice cream in several batches, transfer to several smaller containers). If the ice cream is frozen hard, leave it in the refrigerator for 30 minutes to 1 hour before serving.

NOTE *When heating an egg-and-cream mixture directly over heat, there is always a danger that the eggs will curdle, so be very careful. If you want to be extra careful, use a double boiler. It may also be helpful to keep two ice cubes or ½ cup of cold milk by the side of the stove. If there is any sign of curdling, immediately remove the pot from the heat and stir in the ice cubes or cold milk.*

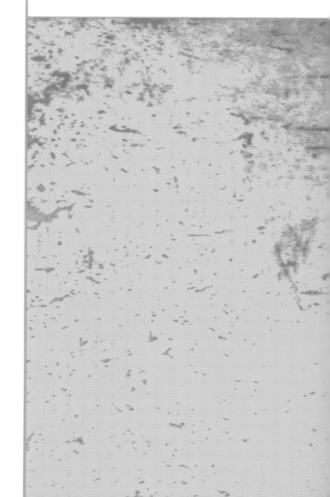

CINNAMON

"THE SECRET ABOUT CINNAMON IS THAT THE MORE SECRETIVE YOU ARE, THE SWEETER IT TASTES."

COOKING UNDER PRESSURE

Imagine sitting with a cinnamon stick in your hand for the first time and hearing the unlikely story of its origin: Cinnamon comes from a land far away, you will be told. No one knows exactly where – not even the Arab traders who specialize in bringing it to you. All they know is that the cinnamon sticks are brought to the Arabian Peninsula by large birds that use them to build their nests.

Both cinnamon and cassia are the bark of trees. When fresh, they are more fresh-tasting but less aromatic than after drying.

The imposing but fragile nests are high up on mountain precipices that no man can climb. The only way to get hold of the cinnamon is by fooling the large birds. It is all quite ingenious and more than a little macabre. Cattle are taken from the nearby oasis, brought into the valley, and slaughtered, as the birds watch from a distance. The carcasses are then cut up, the cinnamon hunters go into hiding, and the birds come to collect the meat and place it in their nests, one piece at a time. But the birds are greedy, and the nests are too weak to bear the weight, so eventually they collapse, and everything crashes to the ground. The men come and collect the cinnamon, fighting off the furious birds. Is it easy? No. Is it dangerous? Definitely.

This was the story told by the Arab tradesmen bringing cinnamon to Europe two thousand years ago. There are good reasons to believe that they did not really know where cinnamon came from and they just constructed a story that would serve their purpose as merchants. Because, as you were sitting there, looking at the cinnamon stick, perhaps trembling just a little, thinking about all it had taken to bring the spice to you, they could add:

"So you do understand that this cannot come cheap. But it makes for a wonderful lamb stew, and some quite delicious desserts."

With most spices, learning the truth about their origins and history, peeling off layer upon layer of superstition and myths, results in a *more*

colorful and fascinating story. Learning how piri piri traveled from the New World to Africa and became African, for example, or how the secret of vanilla was discovered by a young slave boy; seeing cardamom being picked by the women of Kerala; or cutting open a fruit and beholding for the first time the mace-covered nutmeg that is hidden within: these are worth more than most fairy tales and myths. Learning the truth about the spices I use in my cooking makes me feel a richer person, lucky not to be living in the Dark Ages, when spices were readily available but expensive and surrounded by mystery; no one knew where they came from.

But I am not so sure when it comes to cinnamon. Once you know the truth about cinnamon, you know that it is only the bark of a tree, cut off, rolled up, and dried. There is not much more to it, there is no secret of fermentation, and no longer the mystique of rarity. Cinnamon, with its happy and carefree sweetness, could well need some secrets and myths to cover the fact that it is neither rare nor mysterious.

It is therefore a fitting coincidence that cinnamon is particularly popular in countries where facts do not always triumph over myths and secrets are part of everyday life, where truth and lies are not always easy to tell apart. The countries around the Persian Gulf — where a large part of the population lives behind a veil and there tends to a be a veil of secrecy over both matters of state and of family life — use cinnamon in a variety of dishes, from savory stews and meat dishes to drinks and desserts.

In Oman's capital, Muscat, the smell of cinnamon followed me everywhere. It was there on the small pieces of sweet halvah given to me by my friendly handlers from the Ministry of Information, who were there to make sure that I, a journalist and therefore both a potential asset and hazard, saw most of what was agreeable and not much of the disagreeable (of which, of course, there is none). Cinnamon also perfumed the air of the hospitable home of my friend the sheik, when we, with hushed voices and in very general terms, discussed the possibilities of *even more* democracy in the sultanate with a friend of his who had just recently lost his place in the nonlegislative parliament. And it was there when I dined at the strangest and most secretive restaurant I have ever been to, the Bin Ateeq Restaurant for Traditional Omani Food. There, every room is a *chambre privée*; you and your friends dine sitting on the floor of a large austere room with no chairs or tables, and you never see any of the other guests. The only way to tell whether there is a mixed-sex group inside one of the rooms is to look at the shoes standing outside. But have the women take their shoes inside with them, and it all looks very respectable.

There is no doubt that the feeling of secrecy added to the experience — as if the halvah is more than just sweet, the beef is not so tough and the lamb stew has a different layer of flavor that I cannot fully comprehend — an intriguing difference between what the sweet smell promises and the savory spiciness that greets me when I bite into the stew.

But there is one thing you *should* know about cinnamon that is likely to improve your impression of it greatly, and that is the sad but also promising fact that you may not ever have tasted it. Most of the cinnamon that is sold on the world market

— including that in the United States — is in fact not true cinnamon but an inferior relative, cassia, or, if bought powdered, often a combination of the two. There is nothing wrong with cassia, from *Cinnamonum cassia* and a few other trees in the *Cinnamonum* family — it just lacks some of the finer nuances of true cinnamon, *Cinnamonum verum*, which originated in Sri Lanka.

Cinnamon and cassia are among the oldest spices traded. In the land of the Pharaohs there are references going back 2,500 years, perhaps as much as 4,000 years, depending on how you read the hieroglyphs. Up until the nineteenth century, all cinnamon was grown on what is now Sri Lanka. But the trade was never handled by the locals — it was outsourced to merchants with a strong interest in keeping secret the origin of the spice — so it took a long time for the world to figure out where it originated. The main types of cassia originated in the Far East.

The distinction between the two has been known ever since antiquity, but only a few countries have bothered to set up regulations to sort out the misunderstanding. And then spice merchants have an interest in keeping the price up, and therefore they tend to label their cassia as cinnamon if they can. Cassia, you see, is *not* taken from the nests of giant birds. It is merely picked in a shallow lake in a faraway country where there are giant batlike birds that give off terrible shrieks and try to attack the eyes of the cinnamon pickers. But as long as they cover their faces, they are safe, so it is not all that difficult.

Note: I always prefer to buy cinnamon sticks, not ground cinnamon. The sticks keep well, so I buy a large quantity whenever I find good-quality cinnamon that I am fairly sure is not cassia. For most recipes, I break up the cinnamon into smaller pieces or crush it coarsely; I rarely bother to crush it to a powder, except for some desserts.

Cassia quills neatly tied up at a market on Bali.

RICE FLOUR DUMPLINGS
IN SWEET COCONUT-CINNAMON SAUCE

THIS BALINESE RECIPE CAN BE FLAVORED WITH VARIOUS SPICES, or even with pandan (screw pine) leaves. I think it works best as a dessert, but on Bali I was surprised to experience how often it was served as breakfast — and not so surprised to learn that diabetes is rampant on the island.

The dumplings are somewhat rubbery and jellylike and the sauce is very sweet. It takes a little effort to master the first time you make it, but after that it is really not a big deal. I got this recipe from Heinz von Holzen, a Swiss chef who has lived on the island for twenty years and is one of the most important custodians of Balinese cuisine.

Serves 4

For the dumplings

5 ounces glutinous (sweet) rice flour

2 ounces tapioca flour, plus more for rolling out dumplings

¼ teaspoon salt

⅔ cup water

For the sauce

½ cup water

½ cup unsweetened coconut cream (see page 139)

½ cup palm sugar or packed brown sugar

1 ½-inch piece of cinnamon stick, crushed

¼ teaspoon salt

Grated or shredded coconut for garnish (optional)

1 To make the dumplings, combine the rice flour, 2 ounces tapioca flour, and salt in a bowl. Add the ⅔ cup water little by little, working it into the flour, and knead until you have a smooth dough.

2 Dust a work surface with tapioca flour. Using your hands, roll the dough into small dumplings, approximately ⅓ inch in diameter.

3 Bring a large pot of lightly salted water to a boil. Add the dumplings and bring back to a boil, then turn down the heat and simmer for 5 to 7 minutes, until the dumplings are firm.

4 Meanwhile, fill a bowl with cold water and ice cubes.

5 With a slotted spoon, remove the dumplings from the hot water and add to the ice water to cool.

6 To make the sauce, combine all the ingredients in a small pot and bring to a boil. Reduce the heat and let simmer, stirring, for 3 minutes, or until the sugar is completely dissolved.

7 Drain the dumplings and add them to the sauce. Simmer over very low heat for 15 minutes. Remove from the heat and allow to cool to room temperature before serving.

8 Divide the dumplings among serving bowls and pour over the sauce. Garnish with grated coconut, if desired.

THE FIRST TIME I TASTED THE TRADITIONAL OMANI COMBINATION of pepper and cinnamon, I was surprised and somewhat disappointed with myself — why didn't I think of this? After all, I have had *almost* the same dish hundreds of times.

While I have noticed that most Omanis like their meat to be thoroughly cooked through, I like to make this dish much the same way I would any steak — medium-rare and juicy. In Oman, it is typically served with an aromatic rice dish, such as a Rice Pilau (page 243), but I also serve it in a Western style, with a sauce and potatoes alongside.

Serves 2 as a main course

2	1-inch-thick 8-ounce sirloin steaks
2	teaspoons salt
1	tablespoon freshly ground black pepper, or more to taste
1	½- to 1-inch piece of cinnamon stick, coarsely ground, or more to taste
About 1	tablespoon butter

1 Let the steaks stand at room temperature for 30 minutes before cooking.

2 Season the steaks with the salt, pepper, and cinnamon. Heat a large cast-iron or other heavy skillet over high heat. Sear the steaks for 2 minutes on each side. Transfer the steaks to a plate and let rest for 5 minutes.

3 Melt the butter in the skillet over medium heat. Cook the steaks for 3 to 5 minutes on each side, depending on how done you would like them. Allow the steaks to rest for 5 minutes before serving.

4 Just before serving, sprinkle the steaks with a little more freshly ground pepper and salt and cinnamon to taste, if desired.

NOTE *You can make a simple sauce by adding ⅓ cup cream and 2 tablespoons finely chopped shallots to the skillet after you remove the steaks. Bring to a simmer, stirring to scrape up the browned bits from the bottom of the pan. This works well in itself, but if you add a couple of handfuls of spinach and a pinch of cinnamon, grated nutmeg, or freshly ground cardamom, it makes a nice side dish.*

LAMB
WITH SPINACH AND CINNAMON

THIS IS A DELICIOUS LAMB STEW related to dishes served in several countries around the Indian Ocean, and as far away as the highlands of Afghanistan, where the dish is called *kourma challow*. The Iranians have more of a sweet tooth, so they are more likely to add dried fruits as well — I alternate between adding them or not.

Serve with plain rice or rice seasoned with cumin.

Serves 4 to 6 as a main course

I Heat the oil in a large pot over medium-high heat and brown the meat, in batches if necessary, on all sides. Transfer the meat to a plate. Add the onions and garlic to the pot and sauté for 5 minutes, or until soft and lightly browned.

2 Return the meat to the pot, add the turmeric, cinnamon, tomatoes, tomato paste (if using), and beef stock, and bring to a simmer. Reduce the heat and simmer, uncovered, over low heat for 1 hour, or until the meat is falling-apart tender and the cooking juices are reduced.

3 If the cooking juices still seem thin, continue cooking over medium heat until reduced to the desired consistency. Season with salt, and stir in the spinach, yogurt, and honey.

4 Meanwhile, in a small dry skillet, toast the pine nuts over medium-high heat until light brown.

5 Sprinkle the lamb stew with the pine nuts and lemon zest and serve.

¼	cup olive oil
2	pounds lamb or mutton stew meat, preferably from the shoulder
1	pound onions, chopped
3	cloves garlic, chopped
2	teaspoons powdered turmeric
1	2-inch cinnamon stick
1	14½-ounce can tomatoes
1	tablespoon tomato paste (optional)
⅔	cup beef stock
	Salt
8	ounces spinach, washed and stemmed
⅓	cup plain yogurt
2	teaspoons honey
⅓	cup pine nuts
2	teaspoons grated lemon zest

RHUM ARRANGÉ

THE ISLAND OF RÉUNION IS IN MANY WAYS A PARADISE ON EARTH, a tropical island with no malaria, no snakes, and no dangerous predators, a place with a combination of Creole hospitality and French sophistication. The only danger, one might claim, is the *rhum arrangé* — a hazard mainly because it is so pleasant and because it is served everywhere. *Rhum arrangé* literally means "arranged rum," coarse cheap rum that has been made palatable by the addition of various fruits and spices. No meal is complete without a small glass of sweet and spicy homemade *rhum arrangé*, and few meals commence without a glass of a slightly fresher-tasting variety. If you visit someone, a bottle will pop up on the table next to the tea or coffee. And it can be very hard to say no, both for fear of offending the host and for curiosity; every home has its own recipe — I have come across some people who make up to twenty different varieties. During my stay in Réunion, I never had two glasses that tasted the same.

There is a general rule to begin with: the rum should be light brown and it should be cheap. The drink is normally made with *rhum agricole* — agricultural rum — made from the molasses that is left after refining sugar. Rum of the "agricultural" quality is available in well-stocked liquor stores. I normally look to see if they have rum from Réunion, but that is mainly for sentimental reasons; it may just as well be made with rum from the West Indies.

Recipes are of little use, except as pointing out a direction. Apart from that, you must taste your way to the final result, and if this is not a process you take pleasure in, then much of the pleasure of making your own *rhum arrangé* is lost.

I almost always make several different varieties. I make spicy and fruity varieties separately — they release flavors differently, and the best way to get a well-balanced result is to combine them afterward. That also gives you more to play with: I am a great fan of a pineapple and vanilla version, but pineapple and cinnamon is also very good.

Add sugar to taste. Some dark rums owe their color to caramel that has been used as a sweetener and so need almost nothing more.

Makes I bottle

- **6**   **fresh cinnamon leaves, slightly bruised, or a 1½-inch piece of cinnamon stick**
- **I**   **bottle pale dark rum**

     Sugar to taste (optional)

I Place the cinnamon leaves or cinnamon stick in the rum and leave for 3 to 4 days. Taste a small mouthful every evening.

2 Once the cinnamon taste is strong enough, transfer the rum to another bottle, or remove the cinnamon leaves (leave one for decorative purposes) or cinnamon stick. Add sugar to taste, if necessary.

VARIATIONS

Rum with Pineapple *Add 1 cup finely chopped pineapple, preferably fresh, to a bottle of rum. Let stand for 2 days to several weeks. Add sugar to taste.*

Rum with Vanilla *Add ½ vanilla bean (it may well be a scraped-out bean, with the seeds used for another recipe; there will still be enough flavor left) to a bottle of rum and let stand for 3 to 4 days. Taste every evening, and remove when the vanilla flavor is strong enough — or drink some of it and add more rum.*

Rum with Lemongrass and Lime Leaf *Crush 1 stalk lemongrass with the back of a knife, and crush 1 fresh kaffir lime leaf gently in your hand. Add both to a bottle of rum, and let stand for 3 to 5 days. Add sugar to taste.*

Rum with Passion Fruit *This is one of my favorites. Add the seeds and pulp from 2 to 3 passion fruits to a bottle of rum. Shake well. This can be drunk immediately or infused with the passion fruit for several weeks.*

Rum with Flowers *On Réunion they make a rhum arrangé with a local orchid, but it can also be made with other edible flowers, like jasmine or briar rose.*

ORANGES WITH CINNAMON

Serves 4

4 to 6   oranges

4   teaspoons ground cinnamon,
      or more to taste

12   mint leaves for garnish (optional)

THIS IS PROBABLY THE WORLD'S SIMPLEST DESSERT, and one of the best examples of how one spice can make a whole lot of difference. It is fresh tasting, with a wonderful balance between sweetness and acidity, perfect after a heavy meal, or when you don't think you have time to make dessert – this only takes a minute.

Occasionally it is served with an orange syrup made with orange water, orange juice, orange zest, and sugar, but I am of the opinion that this does little to improve the dish.

As there are only two ingredients, the quality of the cinnamon is of crucial importance – crush a cinnamon stick yourself using a mortar and pestle, or at least use freshly bought ground cinnamon.

1 Prepare the dish immediately before serving: Using a sharp knife, peel the oranges. Slice them into ½-inch slices and arrange them on four plates.

2 Sprinkle with the cinnamon. (If you have ground your own cinnamon and want to make sure that there are no large pieces, sift it though a sieve.) Garnish with the mint leaves, if desired.

ZANZIBAR COFFEE

DRINKING STEAMING-HOT, GENTLY SPICED COFFEE on the corner at the end of Sokomohogo Street in Zanzibar is one of the rituals I make sure not to miss when I visit the island. I must admit, though, that I never quite get used to the fact that the coffee is not filtered in any way, so I always end up with my mouth full of grounds when I take the last swallow of the first cup. The only remedy is to order another thirty shillings' worth of coffee to clear my mouth.

The cardamom and cinnamon add sweet aromas to counter the intrinsic bitterness of the coffee, along with a generous dose of sugar, while the ginger ensures a clear, cool aftertaste.

Makes 6 to 8 small cups

2	cups water
3	cardamom pods, gently bruised, or more to taste
I	⅔-inch piece of cinnamon stick
4 to 5	tablespoons coarsely ground coffee beans
I	teaspoon ground ginger
	Sugar to taste

I Bring the water to a boil in a small pot, add the cardamom and cinnamon, and simmer for a couple of minutes. Add the coffee and bring to a boil, then turn off the heat and let the grounds settle. Repeat at least twice.

2 Add more cardamom, if desired, then add the ginger and sugar. Pour into cups and leave for a couple of minutes in order to let the coffee clear before you drink.

VARIATIONS *Once you get used to spiced coffee, there are many different versions you can make with very little effort, deconstructing or elaborating on the Zanzibari version. I sometimes add a sprinkle of nutmeg when I'm using steamed milk, and a small piece of a scraped-out vanilla bean adds a little sweetness to regular filtered coffee without adding any sugar.*

BAKED ALMOND CUSTARD
WITH CINNAMON AND RAISINS

THIS IS A TRADITIONAL EGYPTIAN DESSERT — *UM ALI* — the Arabic equivalent of crème brûlée — but it is now commonplace all over the Middle East. It can be made in several different ways, from just simmering raisins and almonds in cream to more elaborate versions, sometimes flavored with cardamom, sometimes cinnamon, and occasionally also with rosewater. This recipe resembles one commonly served in Iraq.

According to legend, this is a dish that was served by Ali's mother (that is what *Um Ali* means), but no one seems to know quite who Ali was. The only thing I think we can say with absolute certainty is that he must have had a sweet tooth.

Serves 4

1	large sheet puff pastry (about 10 inches square)
1	1-inch piece of cinnamon stick
1	cup milk
1	cup heavy cream
½	cup sugar
1	large egg
1	cup slivered almonds
3 to 4	tablespoons unsalted pistachios, slivered or chopped (optional)
3 to 4	tablespoons raisins

1 Preheat the oven to 375 degrees F. Grease four individual ovenproof dishes.

2 Cut the puff pastry into 4 squares and line the ramekins with the pastry. Bake for 15 minutes, until brown and puffed.

3 Meanwhile, using your hands, break the cinnamon stick into smaller pieces. In a pot, combine the milk, cream, sugar, and cinnamon and heat until almost boiling. Reduce the heat and let simmer gently for a couple of minutes.

4 In a bowl, beat the egg. Add the cinnamon cream little by little while whisking energetically. Add ⅔ cup of the almonds, the pistachios (if desired) and the raisins.

5 Push down some of the puffed pastry in the middle of each individual mold to make room for the cinnamon cream mixture. The flakes that result will help thicken the custard. Add the custard to the dishes and sprinkle with the remaining ⅓ cup almonds.

6 Bake on the middle oven rack for 20 to 25 minutes, until golden brown on top. Serve hot.

SOURCES: WHERE TO BUY YOUR SPICES

MOST SPICES ARE READILY AVAILABLE IN SUPERMARKETS, and as long as they are bought whole and kept in tightly sealed containers away from direct daylight, these everyday spices will probably fulfill most of your needs. All rarer spices that are not often used should be bought in relatively small containers. If any spice develops "off notes" or smells rancid, it should be discarded. If you have a local spice shop, it should be supported and their knowledge taken advantage of. The well-stocked spice shop is also the place to find your own favorite spices — to smell the difference between cassia and true cinnamon, and between different types of black pepper.

There are also high-quality mail-order sources. I've listed my favorite ones.

ADRIANA'S CARAVAN

A renowned Manhattan spice shop with a useful and extremely well stocked online outlet.

Web site: www.adrianascaravan.com

CHEFSHOP.COM

A large online food source with a nice selection of spices, among them the relatively rare cubeb pepper.

Web site: www.chefshop.com

Phone: 1-800-596-0885

GET SPICE — THE ONLINE SPICE SHOP

A U.K.-based spice shop, specializing in organic spices, Get Spice also ships to the United States.

Web site: www.getspice.com

HERBIE'S SPICES

An Australia-based spice shop owned and run by renowned spice specialist Ian Hemphill, offering lots of useful tips and high-quality spices and spice mixtures; ships internationally. Highly recommended.

Web site: www.herbies.com.au

KALUSTYAN'S SPICES & SWEETS

A New York institution, Kalustyan's is one of the best spice shops in the world, with a great online store, offering the widest variety of spices and spice blends imaginable — their list of spices, spice mixtures, and herbs includes nearly one thousand items. Lots of useful kitchen utensils, some very reasonable. Highly recommended.

Web site: www.kalustyans.com

Phone: 1-800-352-3451

McCORMICK

With a basic range of spices available in most supermarkets, giant McCormick also has a useful Web site for finding your nearest food store along with some information on spices, storage and use.

Web site: www.mccormick.com

PENZEYS SPICES

A Wisconsin-based spice purveyor with branches in more than fifteen states and a well-stocked online store with a wide assortment of spices and spice blends.

Web site: www.penzeys.com

Phone: 1-800-741-7787

SAVORY SPICE SHOP

A small, well-stocked Denver-based spice shop with an online store. The helpful owners, Mike Johnston and Janet Chambers, also publish a newsletter. They make their own spice blends and will prepare custom-made blends upon request.

Web site: www.savoryspiceshop.com

Phone: 1-888-677-3322

FURTHER READING

THE LITERATURE ON SPICES STRETCHES BACK almost as long as the history of the written word. Spices have been an intrinsic part of religious discourse and have been desired by explorers. Greek, Roman, Arab, Indian, and Chinese historians gave us some of the first, sometimes spectacularly ill-founded, sometimes surprisingly accurate, accounts of the history and origin of spices.

In working on this book, I have used – in addition to oral sources and personal experience – a wide array of written sources, both cookbooks and historical works. The history of spices and the story of the cooking of the different countries in the region around the Indian Ocean and the people living there can indeed offer enough reading for a lifetime of studies. However, any reader who ventures out into this exciting field will soon realize that the accounts differ dramatically in many important aspects. Information must be interpreted and reevaluated, assessed, and weighed.

In this process, a few important works have meant more to me than any others. Ian Hemphill's wonderful book *The Spice and Herb Bible* has been a constant companion and point of reference, and I am greatly indebted to Hemphill's pioneering work and inspirational presentation. Alan Davidson's *The Oxford Companion to Food* from 1999 (also published as *The Penguin Companion to Food*) is another invaluable companion for both reference and inspirational reading.

Battutah, Ibn, *The Travels of Ibn Battutah*, London: Picador.

Boxer, Arabella, *The Hamlyn Spice Book*, London: Hamlyn.

Cheifitz, Phillippa, *Cape Town Food*, Cape Town: Struik.

Corn, Charles, *The Scents of Eden – A History of the Spice Trade*, New York: Kodansha International.

Dalby, Andrew, *Dangerous Tastes – The Story of Spices*, Berkeley: University of California Press.

Dassanayaka, Channa, *Sri Lankan Flavors*, Melbourne: Hardie Grant Books.

Davidson, Alan, *The Oxford Companion to Food*, New York: Oxford University Press.

De Neefe, Janet, *Fragrant Rice – My Continuing Love Affair with Bali*, Sydney: Harper Perennial.

Ecott, Tim, *Vanilla*, London: Michael Joseph.

Gélabert, Serge, *La Réunion des Mille et Une Saveurs*, Réunion: Éditions Serge Gélabert.

Halford, Katie, and Shapi, Fatma, *A Lamu Cookbook*, Lamu, Kenya: The Manu Society.

Hamilton, Cherie, *Cuisines of Portuguese Encounters*, New York: Hippocrene Books.

Harrison, Mike, *From Tagine to Masala*, United Arab Emirates: Zodiac Publishing.

Hemphill, Ian, *The Spice and Herb Bible*, Sydney: Pan Macmillan; Toronto: Robert Rose.

Hobson, Wendy (ed.), *The Classic 1000 Indian Recipes*, London: Foulsham.

Hourani, George F., *Arab Seafaring*, Princeton, N.J.: Princeton University Press.

Iva, Carole, *La Cuisine Réunionnaise*, Réunion: Orphie.

Jafferji, Zarinan, *A Taste of Zanzibar*, Zanzibar: The Gallery Publications.

Kannampilly, Vijayan, *The Essential Kerala Cookbook*, New Delhi: Penguin Books India Ltd.

Mallos, Tess, *Cooking of the Gulf*, London: Parkway Publishing.

McNair, James, *James McNair Cooks Southeast Asian*, San Francisco: Chronicle Books.

Milton, Giles, *Nathaniel's Nutmeg*, New York: Penguin Books.

Norman, Jill, *Herbs & Spices*, New York: DK Publishing.

Roy, Nilanjana S. (ed.), *A Matter of Taste – The Penguin Book of Indian Writing on Food*, New Delhi: Penguin Books India Ltd.

Sadler, Bea, *The African Cookbook*, New York: Citadel Press.

Swahn, J. O., *The Lore of Spices*, London: Senate Publishing Ltd.

Turner, Jack, *Spice – The History of Temptation*, New York: Knopf.

Von Holzen, Heinz, *Bali Unveiled*, Singapore: Times Editions.

THE HOTNESS OF CHILES IS MEASURED BY SCOVILLE UNITS, named after a system developed by the American chemist Wilbur Scoville in 1912. The chart is in no way concise, as the actual hotness of one variety can vary by as much as tenfold, according to the subvariety (which is often not stated), soil, and other growth conditions. It does give a rough map of the world of chiles and a vivid illustration of the enormous differences in the level of capsaicin levels of different chiles — some of which may look very similar.

0	BELL PEPPER
100 to 500	PIMENTO
100 to 500	PEPERONCINI
100 to 700	SANTA FE GRANDE
500 to 800	NEW MEXICO
500 to 2,500	ANAHEIM
1,000 to 2,000	ANCHO
2,500 to 8,000	JALAPEÑO
5,000 to 12,000	CHIPOTLE
5,000 to 23,000	SERRANO
30,000 to 50,000	TABASCO
30,000 to 50,000	CAYENNE
40,000 to 68,000	PEQUÍN
50,000 to 100,000	CHILTEPÍN
75,000 to 150,000	THAI
95,000 to 110,000	BAHAMIAN
100,000 to 125,000	CAROLINA CAYENNE
100,000 to 225,000	PIRI PIRI OR BIRD'S-EYE
100,000 to 325,000	SCOTCH BONNET
100,000 to 580,000	HABANERO
2,000,000 to 5,300,000	PEPPER SPRAY
15,000,000	PURE CAPSAICIN DIHYDROCAPSAICIN

COLOR BARS REPRESENT MINIMUM FIGURE ONLY.

TABLE OF EQUIVALENTS

The exact equivalents in the following tables have

been rounded for convenience.

LIQUID/DRY MEASUREMENTS

U.S.	METRIC
¼ teaspoon	1.25 milliliters
½ teaspoon	2.5 milliliters
1 teaspoon	5 milliliters
1 tablespoon (3 teaspoons)	15 milliliters
1 fluid ounce (2 tablespoons)	30 milliliters
¼ cup	60 milliliters
⅓ cup	80 milliliters
½ cup	120 milliliters
1 cup	240 milliliters
1 pint (2 cups)	480 milliliters
1 quart (4 cups; 32 ounces)	960 milliliters
1 gallon (4 quarts)	3.84 liters
1 ounce (by weight)	28 grams
1 pound	448 grams
2.2 pounds	1 kilogram

LENGTHS

U.S.	METRIC
⅛ inch	3 millimeters
¼ inch	6 millimeters
½ inch	12 millimeters
1 inch	2.5 centimeters

OVEN TEMPERATURES

Fahrenheit	Celsius	Gas
250	120	½
275	140	1
300	150	2
325	160	3
350	180	4
375	190	5
400	200	6
425	220	7
450	230	8
475	240	9
500	260	10

[MINIMUM LENGTH: EIGHTEEN FEET]

[MINIMUM LENGTH: ONE HUNDRED TWENTY-SIX FEET]

BEING A TRAVELER IS, MORE THAN ANYTHING, ABOUT BEING DEPENDENT ON THE KINDNESS OF STRANGERS. The writing that follows, on the other hand, is a solitary process but one that is no less dependent on kindness — that of those you know and love, and who support you and endure you.

This book is the fruit of the close and enduring cooperation with my photographer, Mette Randem, who makes it all come alive: the food, the landscape, and the people. You are a dream to work with!

My thanks go out to my partner, Vibeke Maria Larsen, and her unique combination of patience, enthusiasm, and support. Without her love and her interest in sharing the food and traveling together, the process would not have been the same.

My agent, Lisa Ekus, has been a steadfast supporter and, as ever, a joy to work with. You're the top!

At Chronicle Books, I would especially like to thank Bill LeBlond for believing in the project and for his enthusiasm, commitment, and professionalism. I would like to thank Amy Treadwell and Judith Sutton for their invaluable comments and hard work, never resting in their efforts to improve the quality and accuracy of the recipes and essays. I would also like to thank Vanessa Dina and Marc English Design for turning the text and pictures into one living whole. It looks like magic, but I know it's hard work.

I would like to thank my travel companions Ingeri Engelstad, Bjørn Gabrielsen, Guro Fløgstad, and Jørn Middelborg, with a special thanks to Silje Sibel, who also took some of the photos in India. All my friends and colleagues who tested recipes and evaluated my results, and who gave me important input along the way, deserve a special thanks, not least Erik Røed, Christopher Sjuve, Jon Krog Pedersen ("Jon the Young"), and Craig Whitson. And a special thanks to Magnus Castracane for testing and styling, and to Vemund Blumkvist for his important input on linguistic questions.

During the making of this book. I have traveled distances equaling four times around the world to some rather remote places, and thanks to Line Langfjæran at www.tasteandtravel.no, who has organized most of my trips, I have been able to do so without worry.

In South Africa, the friendship and generosity of Wiggo Andersen and Tomm Kristiansen made an enormous difference, as did the help from many chefs, food professionals, and enthusiasts — among them chef Peter Pankhurst and everyone else at Savoy Cabbage, and Harriet Arendse for her generous introduction to the many colors of South African home cooking. The cooperation and friendship of Paul Cluver and the Cluver family will be sure to make South Africa more and more important in my life in the years to come.

On Zanzibar, Emerson Skeens, "Babu," has been an important figure for me ever since I first visited the island in 1992, and staying in an apartment in his house in Sokomohogo Street, a place where a piece of my heart will always remain, allowed me unique insight into Zanzibari life. Zanzibar would also not have been the same without Asaa Faki Iddi, Maria Barretto, Lesley Lobo, George Shum, Masoud Salim, and Naila Gidawi.

In Maputo, Mozambique, I would like to extend my deepest thanks to the lively and hospitable Ardnt family, who allowed me to use their house overlooking the Indian Ocean as an inspirational study, and to my longtime friend and former professor Helge Rønning and his wife, Mette Mast. In Oman, Asma Al Hajri at the Oman Tourism Office, Rosemary Hector at the Royal Omani Ministry of Information, and Khalid Al Jadidi at the Oman *Daily Observer* helped me with information and facilitated my travels. In Thailand, my thanks go especially to Orr and everyone at the Costa Lanta Resort, to Junie Kovacs at Time for Lime Cooking School, and to Jørn Middelborg at Thavibu gallery in Bangkok — and a special thanks to Hilde Hirai and Thai Air. In Indonesia, Marte Gerhardsen was of great help, as was Heinz von Holzen, the godfather of Balinese cooking and chef-proprietor of Bumbu Bali Restaurant and Cooking School. On La Réunion, I am greatly indebted to Madame Mogalia and her son, Orwa, and to Scholastique "Mamie" Javel and her son, François, and to Michèle Benard for facilitating the trip and introducing me to important people on the culinary scene; and to Air France; and, in Oslo, to Rikke Dobloug at the French embassy. On Mauritius, things would not have been the same without Jeanette Leguin. In India, Sunil Varghese and everyone at the Brunton Boatyard and Rajesh Davis were among the many that went the extra mile for me, as did Roma Singh at Indian Tourism in Amsterdam; and a special thanks to the State Government of Kerala.

My travels the last few years have been an adventure, and, I know, also just the beginning of a great adventure. I will always return.

INDEX

A

Afghanistan
Lamb with Spinach and Cinnamon, 265
Allspice, 28
Almonds
Baked Almond Custard with Cinnamon and Raisins, 271
Cumin-Carrot Soup with Almonds and Nigella, 46
Lamb Korma, 146
Oven-Baked Cape Malay Curry, 191
Aniseed, 20
Apricots
Coriander Lamb Skewers with Grilled Peppers, 156
Oven-Baked Cape Malay Curry, 191
Persian Rice Pilaf with Saffron and Pomegranates, 241
Squab with Coriander, Cumin, and Apricots, 157
Tamarind-Glazed Fruits with Star Anise, 209
Aromatic Cardamom Lamb with Saffron Carrots, 127
Australia
Cardamom Mangoes, 121
Kingfish with Orange, Cloves, and Ginger, 245
Austronesians, 89
Avocado, Spice-Dusted, with Mango and Crab, 59

B

Baked Almond Custard with Cinnamon and Raisins, 271
Bali, Indonesia
Balinese Suckling Pig, 183
cuisine of, 19
food transportation in, 111, 112
galangal and, 23
ginger and, 23
markets in, 4, 13, 16, 70, 99, 164, 166, 172, 176, 260
Pork and Shrimp Meatballs with Lemongrass and Ginger, 197
rice and, 111, 114
Rice Flour Dumplings in Sweet Coconut-Cinnamon Sauce, 263
Spicy Lemongrass Fish Cakes, 200
Stewed Oxtail with Nutmeg Sauce, 247
street food in, 179–80
temple offerings in, 112, 169, 171
Yellow Rice, 189
Bananas
Bananas with Coconut and Cardamom, 125
Flambéed Bananas with Vanilla and Rum Caramel, 256
Réunionnaise Yellow Chicken and Banana Curry, 188

Beans
Cumin-Curry Tuna Salad with Dates and Chickpeas, 45
Green Curry with Chicken, 160
Green Papaya Salad, 109
Beef
Entrecôte with Onion, Ginger, and Tamarind, 210
Farmer's Sausage with Cloves and Coriander, 242
Grilled Sirloin with Pepper and Cinnamon, 264
Kerala Spicy Beef Curry, 145
Mussaman Beef Curry, 149
Oven-Baked Cape Malay Curry, 191
Spicy Beef Salad with Green Peppercorns, 81
Stewed Oxtail with Nutmeg Sauce, 247
Bell peppers
Coriander Lamb Skewers with Grilled Peppers, 156
Sor Patel, 137
Beverages
coffee, 16
Lemongrass Tea, 203
Rhum Arrangé, 267
Rum with Flowers, 267
Rum with Lemongrass and Lime Leaf, 267
Rum with Passion Fruit, 267
Rum with Pineapple, 267
Rum with Vanilla, 267
tea, 69
Zanzibar Coffee, 269
Black Pepper Crabs, 83
Bourbon Vanilla Ice Cream, 257
Bread
Nan with Cumin, Raisins, and Onions, 48
Nan with Dried Fruits, 48
Nan with Sesame Seeds, 48
Nan with Spicy Ground Meat, 48
Spicy Honey Bread, 57

C

Cake, Coconut Curry, 147
Cape Malay, South Africa, 191
Cape Town, South Africa, 82, 85, 87, 129
Cardamom, 20, 117–19
Aromatic Cardamom Lamb with Saffron Carrots, 127
Bananas with Coconut and Cardamom, 125
Cardamom Mangoes, 121
Chicken Cardamom Masala with Cashews, 122
Coconut Pancakes with Cardamom, 126

Persian Rice Pilaf with Saffron and Pomegranates, 241

Red Coconut Rice, 162

Rice Pilau with Cashews and Coriander, 243

Zanzibar Coffee, 269

Cardamom Hills, India, 117–19

Carrots

Aromatic Cardamom Lamb with Saffron Carrots, 127

Carrots with Ginger and Soy Sauce, 95

Cumin-Carrot Soup with Almonds and Nigella, 46

Cashews

Chicken Cardamom Masala with Cashews, 122

Rice Pilau with Cashews and Coriander, 243

Cassia, 21, 259–60

Chicken

Chicken Cardamom Masala with Cashews, 122

Chicken Piri Piri, 103

Cumin Toasted Chicken Drumsticks with Honey, 47

Green Curry with Chicken, 160

Indian Pepper Chicken, 79

Lemon Pepper Chicken, 86

Réunionnaise Yellow Chicken and Banana Curry, 188

Rice Noodles with Squid, Shrimp, and Chicken, 141

Chickpeas, Cumin-Curry Tuna Salad with Dates and, 45

Chiles, 20–21, 99–100

Balinese Suckling Pig, 183

Black Pepper Crabs, 83

Chicken Piri Piri, 103

Chiles with Hot Tuna Stuffing, 107

Chili Potatoes, 108

flakes, 21

Goan Fish Cakes, 93

Green Curry Paste, 161

Green Curry with Chicken, 160

Green Papaya Salad, 109

heat levels of, 20, 107, 274

Kerala Spicy Beef Curry, 145

Lemongrass-Coconut Soup with Shrimp, 201

Mussaman Curry Paste, 142, 165

Mussels with Lemongrass, Chiles, and Holy Basil, 199

Octopus Curry, 219

Piri Piri Sauce, 105

Pork and Shrimp Meatballs with Lemongrass and Ginger, 197

Shrimp Piri Piri, 106

Spicy Beef Salad with Green Peppercorns, 81

Stewed Oxtail with Nutmeg Sauce, 247

Chili powder, 21

Chocolate Pepper Cookies, 87

Cinnamon, 21, 259–60

Baked Almond Custard with Cinnamon and Raisins, 271

Grilled Sirloin with Pepper and Cinnamon, 264

Lamb with Spinach and Cinnamon, 265

Nan with Dried Fruits, 48

Oranges with Cinnamon, 268

Rhum Arrangé, 267

Rice Flour Dumplings in Sweet Coconut-Cinnamon Sauce, 263

Zanzibar Coffee, 269

Cloves, 21, 96, 235–36, 238

Farmer's Sausage with Cloves and Coriander, 242

Kingfish with Orange, Cloves, and Ginger, 245

Soothing Clove and Yogurt Dip, 104

Cochin, Kerala, India, 66, 151, 153

Coconut

Bananas with Coconut and Cardamom, 125

Coconut Curry Cake, 147

Coconut Pancakes with Cardamom, 126

Coconut Panna Cotta with Lemongrass, Turmeric, and Passion Fruit, 204

cracking, 139

cream and milk, 139

Fish in Coconut Curry, 138

grating, 204

Green Curry with Chicken, 160

Lemongrass-Coconut Soup with Shrimp, 201

Mauritian "Bouillabaisse," 185

Mussaman Beef Curry, 149

Octopus Curry, 219

Red Coconut Rice, 162

Rice Flour Dumplings in Sweet Coconut-Cinnamon Sauce, 263

Yellow Rice, 189

Coffee, 16

Zanzibar Coffee, 269

Constantia, South Africa, 191

Cookies, Chocolate Pepper, 87

Coriander, 22

Coriander and Mint Sauce, 155

Coriander Lamb Skewers with Grilled Peppers, 156

Farmer's Sausage with Cloves and Coriander, 242

Fresh Yogurt-Cucumber Soup with Coriander and Cumin, 43

Green Curry Paste, 161

Kerala Jewish Fish with Green Herbs and Spices, 153

Pearl Onions with Coriander and Mint, 154

Rice Pilau with Cashews and Coriander, 243

Squab with Coriander, Cumin, and Apricots, 157

Crab

Black Pepper Crabs, 83

Mauritian "Bouillabaisse," 185

Spice-Dusted Avocado with Mango and Crab, 59

Cubeb pepper, 22

Cubeb Pepper Figs Cooked in Red Wine, 85

Oysters with Cubeb Pepper and Lemongrass Vinaigrette, 62

Cucumbers

Fresh Yogurt-Cucumber Soup with Coriander and Cumin, 43

Oysters with Malay Masala and Cucumber Relish, 62

Tomato and Cucumber Salad with Cumin Salt, 41

Cumin, 22

Cumin-Carrot Soup with Almonds and Nigella, 46

Cumin-Curry Tuna Salad with Dates and Chickpeas, 45

Cumin Toasted Chicken Drumsticks with Honey, 47

Fresh Yogurt-Cucumber Soup with Coriander and Cumin, 43

Lemon-and-Cumin-Grilled Fish, 42

Nan with Cumin, Raisins, and Onions, 48

Squab with Coriander, Cumin, and Apricots, 157

Stuffed Onions with Ginger and Lamb, 94

Tomato and Cucumber Salad with Cumin Salt, 41

Curries, 129

Coconut Curry Cake, 147

Cumin-Curry Tuna Salad with Dates and Chickpeas, 45

Curried Duck with Vanilla, 255

Fish in Coconut Curry, 138

Green Curry Paste, 161

Green Curry with Chicken, 160

Grilled Green Fish with Red Rice, 159

Kerala Spicy Beef Curry, 145

Mussaman Beef Curry, 149

Mussaman Curry Paste, 142, 165

Octopus Curry, 219

Oven-Baked Cape Malay Curry, 191

Réunionnaise Yellow Chicken and Banana Curry, 188

Curry leaves, 23

Custard, Baked Almond, with Cinnamon and Raisins, 271

D

Dahab, Egypt, 37–38, 41

Dates, Cumin-Curry Tuna Salad with Chickpeas and, 45

Dill, 28

Dip, Soothing Clove and Yogurt, 104

Duck, Curried, with Vanilla, 255

Dumplings, Rice Flour, in Sweet Coconut-Cinnamon Sauce, 263

Durban, South Africa, 51

E

Eggplant

Green Curry with Chicken, 160

Egypt

Baked Almond Custard with Cinnamon and Raisins, 271

cuisine of, 37–38, 46

Lemon-and-Cumin-Grilled Fish, 42

Tomato and Cucumber Salad with Cumin Salt, 41

Entrecôte with Onion, Ginger, and Tamarind, 210

Ethiopia

history of, 57

Spicy Honey Bread, 57

F

Farmer's Sausage with Cloves and Coriander, 242

Fennel, 28

Fenugreek, 28

Figs

Cubeb Pepper Figs Cooked in Red Wine, 85

Oven-Baked Cape Malay Curry, 191

Tamarind-Glazed Fruits with Star Anise, 209

Fish

Chiles with Hot Tuna Stuffing, 107

Cumin-Curry Tuna Salad with Dates and Chickpeas, 45

Fish in Coconut Curry, 138

Goan Fish Cakes, 93

Grilled Green Fish with Red Rice, 159

Grilled Tuna with Zanzibar Spices, 63

Grouper with Ginger and Spring Onion, 91

Kerala Jewish Fish with Green Herbs and Spices, 153

Kingfish with Orange, Cloves, and Ginger, 245

Lemon-and-Cumin-Grilled Fish, 42

Mauritian "Bouillabaisse," 185

Pepper-Crusted Fish with Watercress and Spring Onion Sauce, 82

Spicy Lemongrass Fish Cakes, 200

Steamed Fish with Lemongrass and Herbs, 195

Trout with Rum and Vanilla, 253

Flambéed Bananas with Vanilla and Rum Caramel, 256
Forodhani Gardens, Zanzibar, 30
Fresh Yogurt-Cucumber Soup with Coriander and Cumin, 43
Fruits. *See also individual fruits*
    Nan with Dried Fruits, 48
    Tamarind-Glazed Fruits with Star Anise, 209

G

Galangal, 23
Garlic, 28
Ginger, 23–24, 89
    Carrots with Ginger and Soy Sauce, 95
    Chicken Cardamom Masala with Cashews, 122
    Cumin Toasted Chicken Drumsticks with Honey, 47
    Entrecôte with Onion, Ginger, and Tamarind, 210
    Goan Fish Cakes, 93
    Grouper with Ginger and Spring Onion, 91
    Kingfish with Orange, Cloves, and Ginger, 245
    Nutmeg-and-Ginger Spinach Soup with Soy Sauce-Baked
        Sweet Potato, 246
    Oysters with Ginger and Sweet Chili Sauce, 62
    Piri Piri Sauce, 105
    Pork and Shrimp Meatballs with Lemongrass
        and Ginger, 197
    Potato Croquettes with Ginger and Honey, 96
    Shrimp Piri Piri, 106
    Stuffed Onions with Ginger and Lamb, 94
Goan Fish Cakes, 93
Green Curry Paste, 161
Green Curry with Chicken, 160
Green Papaya Salad, 109
Grilled Green Fish with Red Rice, 159
Grilled Sirloin with Pepper and Cinnamon, 264
Grilled Tuna with Zanzibar Spices, 63
Grouper with Ginger and Spring Onion, 91

H

Hell-Bourg, Réunion, 253

I

Ice Cream, Bourbon Vanilla, 257
India
    cardamom and, 15, 66, 117–19, 238
    Chicken Cardamom Masala with Cashews, 122
    chiles and, 20
    Chili Potatoes, 108

Coconut Curry Cake, 147
Coconut Pancakes with Cardamom, 126
    coriander and, 22
Coriander and Mint Sauce, 155
    cubeb pepper and, 22
    cuisine of, 46, 96, 122
    dill and, 28
    fennel seeds and, 28
    ginger and, 23, 66, 89
Goan Fish Cakes, 93
Grouper with Ginger and Spring Onion, 91
Indian Pepper Chicken, 79
Kerala Jewish Fish with Green Herbs and Spices, 153
Kerala Spicy Beef Curry, 145
Lamb Korma, 146
    markets in, 66
    mustard seeds and, 29
Nan with Cumin, Raisins, and Onions, 48
Nan with Dried Fruits, 48
Nan with Sesame Seeds, 48
Nan with Spicy Ground Meat, 48
Pearl Onions with Coriander and Mint, 154
    pepper and, 15, 25, 66, 73–74, 76
Pepper Tandoori Potato Chips, 56
Potato Croquettes with Ginger and Honey, 96
Spicy Deep-Fried Vegetables, 65
    tamarind and, 26
    tea and, 69
    turmeric and, 27, 175–76
Indonesia
    Balinese Suckling Pig, 183
    cloves and, 21, 235–36
    Cubeb Pepper Figs Cooked in Red Wine, 85
    cuisine of, 19
    food transportation in, 111, 112
    galangal and, 23
    ginger and, 23, 89
    mace and, 24
    markets in, 4, 13, 16, 70, 99, 164, 166, 172, 176, 260
    nutmeg and, 24, 235–36
    Pork and Shrimp Meatballs with Lemongrass and Ginger, 197
    rice and, 111, 114
    Rice Flour Dumplings in Sweet Coconut-Cinnamon Sauce, 263
    Spicy Lemongrass Fish Cakes, 200
    Stewed Oxtail with Nutmeg Sauce, 247
    street food in, 179–80

Sweet-and-Sour Vegetable Soup with Peanuts, 211

temple offerings in, 112, 169, 171

Yellow Rice, 189

Iran

cuisine of, 46

Lamb with Spinach and Cinnamon, 265

Persian Rice Pilaf with Saffron and Pomegranates, 241

Squab with Coriander, Cumin, and Apricots, 157

Stuffed Onions with Ginger and Lamb, 94

Iraq

Baked Almond Custard with Cinnamon and Raisins, 271

J

Java, Indonesia, 23

K

Kaffir lime, 24

Kerala, India

cardamom and, 15, 76, 117–19, 238

cuisine of, 122, 126

ginger and, 23

Kerala Jewish Fish with Green Herbs and Spices, 153

Kerala Spicy Beef Curry, 145

pepper and, 15, 73–74, 76

spice trade and, 151

tea and, 69

turmeric and, 27, 175

Kingfish with Orange, Cloves, and Ginger, 245

Kizimkazi, Zanzibar, 132, 213–14

Ko Lanta, Thailand, 142, 160, 165, 166

Korma, Lamb, 146

Krabi region, Thailand, 4, 91, 142, 287

L

Lamb

Aromatic Cardamom Lamb with Saffron Carrots, 127

Coriander Lamb Skewers with Grilled Peppers, 156

Lamb Korma, 146

Lamb with Spinach and Cinnamon, 265

Nan with Spicy Ground Meat, 48

Slow-Cooked Leg of Lamb, 143

Stuffed Onions with Ginger and Lamb, 94

Lemongrass, 24, 193

Balinese Suckling Pig, 183

Coconut Panna Cotta with Lemongrass, Turmeric, and
Passion Fruit, 204

Lemongrass-Coconut Soup with Shrimp, 201

Lemongrass Tea, 203

Mussels with Lemongrass, Chiles, and Holy Basil, 199

Oysters with Cubeb Pepper and Lemongrass Vinaigrette, 62

Pork and Shrimp Meatballs with Lemongrass and Ginger, 197

Rum with Lemongrass and Lime Leaf, 267

Spicy Lemongrass Fish Cakes, 200

Steamed Fish with Lemongrass and Herbs, 195

Tamarind-Glazed Fruits with Star Anise, 209

Lemons

Lemon-and-Cumin-Grilled Fish, 42

Lemon Pepper Chicken, 86

M

Mace, 24–25, 235

Madagascar, 27

Malaysia

Black Pepper Crabs, 83

fennel seeds and, 28

galangal and, 23

tamarind and, 26

Tamarind-Glazed Fruits with Star Anise, 209

Mangoes

Cardamom Mangoes, 121

Oysters with Piri Piri and Mango, 62

Spice-Dusted Avocado with Mango and Crab, 59

Mangosteens, 70

Maputo, Mozambique, 99–100

Masala, 129

Mauritius

cloves and, 235–36, 238

cuisine of, 15, 185

Grouper with Ginger and Spring Onion, 91

history of, 185

Mauritian "Bouillabaisse," 185

nutmeg and, 235–36, 238

Melaka, Malaysia, 83

Melon with Pepper, 61

Middle East. *See also individual countries*

Aromatic Cardamom Lamb with Saffron Carrots, 127

Coriander and Mint Sauce, 155

Lemon-and-Cumin-Grilled Fish, 42

Oranges with Cinnamon, 268

Soothing Clove and Yogurt Dip, 104

Moghul cooking, 141

Moluccas, Indonesia, 21, 24, 235–36, 238

Mozambique
    Chicken Piri Piri, 103
    crabs and, 59
    cuisine of, 99–100
    Piri Piri Sauce, 105
    Shrimp Piri Piri, 106
Muscat, Oman, 45, 156, 231, 260
Mussaman Beef Curry, 149
Mussaman Curry Paste, 142, 165
Mussels with Lemongrass, Chiles, and Holy Basil, 199
Mustard, 29

N

Nan
    Nan with Cumin, Raisins, and Onions, 48
    Nan with Dried Fruits, 48
    Nan with Sesame Seeds, 48
    Nan with Spicy Ground Meat, 48
Nigella, 29
Noodles, Rice, with Squid, Shrimp, and Chicken, 141
Nutmeg, 24–25, 235–36, 238
    Nutmeg-and-Ginger Spinach Soup with Soy Sauce-Baked
        Sweet Potato, 246
    Oysters with Spinach and Nutmeg, 62
    Stewed Oxtail with Nutmeg Sauce, 247

O

Octopus Curry, 219
Oman
    cinnamon and, 260
    Coriander Lamb Skewers with Grilled Peppers, 156
    Cumin-Curry Tuna Salad with Dates and Chickpeas, 45
    fish and, 45
    Grilled Sirloin with Pepper and Cinnamon, 264
    Lamb with Spinach and Cinnamon, 265
    Shrimp Balls with Tamarind Sauce, 220
    Slow-Cooked Leg of Lamb, 143
    Stuffed Onions with Ginger and Lamb, 94
    Zanzibar Coffee, 269
Onions
    Entrecôte with Onion, Ginger, and Tamarind, 210
    Lamb with Spinach and Cinnamon, 265
    Nan with Cumin, Raisins, and Onions, 48
    Pearl Onions with Coriander and Mint, 154
    Stuffed Onions with Ginger and Lamb, 94

Oranges
    Kingfish with Orange, Cloves, and Ginger, 245
    Oranges with Cinnamon, 268
Oven-Baked Cape Malay Curry, 191
Oxtail, Stewed, with Nutmeg Sauce, 247
Oysters
    Oysters with Cubeb Pepper and Lemongrass Vinaigrette, 62
    Oysters with Ginger and Sweet Chili Sauce, 62
    Oysters with Malay Masala and Cucumber Relish, 62
    Oysters with Piri Piri and Mango, 62
    Oysters with Spinach and Nutmeg, 62

P

Pakistan
    Lamb Korma, 146
    Lamb with Spinach and Cinnamon, 265
    Spicy Deep-Fried Vegetables, 65
Pakora, 65
Pamplemousse, Mauritius, 235
Pancakes, Coconut, with Cardamom, 126
Panna Cotta, Coconut, with Lemongrass, Turmeric, and Passion
    Fruit, 204
Papayas, 162
    Green Papaya Salad, 109
Paprika, 25
Passion fruit
    Coconut Panna Cotta with Lemongrass, Turmeric, and
        Passion Fruit, 204
    Rum with Passion Fruit, 267
Peanuts
    Green Papaya Salad, 109
    Pineapple with Minced Shrimp and Peanut Topping, 55
    Sweet-and-Sour Vegetable Soup with Peanuts, 211
Pearl Onions with Coriander and Mint, 154
Pepper, 25–26, 73–74, 76, 173. *See also* Cubeb pepper
    Black Pepper Crabs, 83
    Chocolate Pepper Cookies, 87
    Grilled Sirloin with Pepper and Cinnamon, 264
    Indian Pepper Chicken, 79
    Lemon Pepper Chicken, 86
    Melon with Pepper, 61
    Pepper-Crusted Fish with Watercress and Spring
        Onion Sauce, 82
    Pepper Tandoori Potato Chips, 56
    Spicy Beef Salad with Green Peppercorns, 81
Persian Rice Pilaf with Saffron and Pomegranates, 241

Pineapple, 51
    Pineapple with Minced Shrimp and Peanut Topping, 55
    Rum with Pineapple, 267
    Spicy Pineapple Skewers, 53
    Tamarind-Glazed Fruits with Star Anise, 209
Piri piri, 99–100
    Chicken Piri Piri, 103
    Piri Piri Sauce, 105
    Shrimp Piri Piri, 106
Poivre, Pierre, 235–36, 238
Pomegranates, Persian Rice Pilaf with Saffron and, 241
Pork
    Balinese Suckling Pig, 183
    Farmer's Sausage with Cloves and Coriander, 242
    Pineapple with Minced Shrimp and Peanut Topping, 55
    Pork and Shrimp Meatballs with Lemongrass
        and Ginger, 197
    Sor Patel, 137
Potatoes
    Chiles with Hot Tuna Stuffing, 107
    Chili Potatoes, 108
    Goan Fish Cakes, 93
    Mussaman Beef Curry, 149
    Pepper Tandoori Potato Chips, 56
    Potato Croquettes with Ginger and Honey, 96
    Spicy Deep-Fried Vegetables, 65
    Stewed Oxtail with Nutmeg Sauce, 247

R

Raisins
    Baked Almond Custard with Cinnamon and Raisins, 271
    Nan with Cumin, Raisins, and Onions, 48
    Oven-Baked Cape Malay Curry, 191
Rambutans, 164
Red Coconut Rice, 162
Red Sea, 37
Réunion
    Bourbon Vanilla Ice Cream, 257
    cuisine of, 15, 251
    Curried Duck with Vanilla, 255
    Entrecôte with Onion, Ginger, and Tamarind, 210
    Flambéed Bananas with Vanilla and Rum Caramel, 256
    Réunionnaise Yellow Chicken and Banana Curry, 188
    Rhum Arrangé, 267
    tamarind and, 207
    Trout with Rum and Vanilla, 253

    turmeric and, 27, 175, 188
    vanilla and, 27, 249–51
Rhum Arrangé, 267
Rice, 114
    Grilled Green Fish with Red Rice, 159
    Persian Rice Pilaf with Saffron and Pomegranates, 241
    Red Coconut Rice, 162
    Rice Flour Dumplings in Sweet Coconut-Cinnamon Sauce, 263
    Rice Noodles with Squid, Shrimp, and Chicken, 141
    Rice Pilau with Cashews and Coriander, 243
    Yellow Rice, 189
Rum
    Flambéed Bananas with Vanilla and Rum Caramel, 256
    Rhum Arrangé, 267
    Rum with Flowers, 267
    Rum with Lemongrass and Lime Leaf, 267
    Rum with Passion Fruit, 267
    Rum with Pineapple, 267
    Rum with Vanilla, 267
    Trout with Rum and Vanilla, 253

S

Saffron, 29
    Aromatic Cardamom Lamb with Saffron Carrots, 127
    Persian Rice Pilaf with Saffron and Pomegranates, 241
Saint-Denis, Réunion, 249
Salads
    Cumin-Curry Tuna Salad with Dates and Chickpeas, 45
    Green Papaya Salad, 109
    Spicy Beef Salad with Green Peppercorns, 81
    Tomato and Cucumber Salad with Cumin Salt, 41
Sauces
    Coriander and Mint Sauce, 155
    Piri Piri Sauce, 105
Sausage, Farmer's, with Cloves and Coriander, 242
Scoville units, 274
Sharm el-Sheikh, Egypt, 37
Shellfish. *See also individual shellfish*
    Mauritian "Bouillabaisse," 185
    Simple Shellfish Stock, 187
Shrimp
    Lemongrass-Coconut Soup with Shrimp, 201
    Mauritian "Bouillabaisse," 185
    Pineapple with Minced Shrimp and Peanut Topping, 55
    Pork and Shrimp Meatballs with Lemongrass and Ginger, 197
    Rice Noodles with Squid, Shrimp, and Chicken, 141

Shrimp Balls with Tamarind Sauce, 220

Shrimp Piri Piri, 106

Simple Shellfish Stock, 187

Shuwa, 143

Simple Shellfish Stock, 187

Sinai Desert, Egypt, 37, 41

Slow-Cooked Leg of Lamb, 143

Soothing Clove and Yogurt Dip, 104

Sor Patel, 137

Soups

Cumin-Carrot Soup with Almonds and Nigella, 46

Fresh Yogurt-Cucumber Soup with Coriander
and Cumin, 43

Lemongrass-Coconut Soup with Shrimp, 201

Nutmeg-and-Ginger Spinach Soup with Soy Sauce—Baked
Sweet Potato, 246

Sweet-and-Sour Vegetable Soup with Peanuts, 211

South Africa

Carrots with Ginger and Soy Sauce, 95

Chocolate Pepper Cookies, 87

Cubeb Pepper Figs Cooked in Red Wine, 85

cuisine of, 15, 51, 129

Farmer's Sausage with Cloves and Coriander, 242

Grouper with Ginger and Spring Onion, 91

Lemon Pepper Chicken, 86

Nutmeg-and-Ginger Spinach Soup with Soy Sauce-Baked
Sweet Potato, 246

Oven-Baked Cape Malay Curry, 191

Oysters with Malay Masala and Cucumber Relish, 62

Pepper-Crusted Fish with Watercress and Spring
Onion Sauce, 82

Spicy Pineapple Skewers, 53

Spice-Dusted Avocado with Mango and Crab, 59

Spices. *See also individual spices*

definition of, 19

history of, 14

importance of, 14, 19

listing of, 20–29

sources of, 272

storing, 19

Spicy Beef Salad with Green Peppercorns, 81

Spicy Deep-Fried Vegetables, 65

Spicy Honey Bread, 57

Spicy Lemongrass Fish Cakes, 200

Spicy Pineapple Skewers, 53

Spinach

Lamb with Spinach and Cinnamon, 265

Nutmeg-and-Ginger Spinach Soup with Soy Sauce—Baked
Sweet Potato, 246

Oysters with Spinach and Nutmeg, 62

Spicy Deep-Fried Vegetables, 65

Squab with Coriander, Cumin, and Apricots, 157

Squid

Rice Noodles with Squid, Shrimp, and Chicken, 141

Turmeric Squid with Tamarind Sauce, 217

Sri Lanka

Chiles with Hot Tuna Stuffing, 107

cinnamon and, 260

Grilled Green Fish with Red Rice, 159

Red Coconut Rice, 162

Star anise, 26

Tamarind-Glazed Fruits with Star Anise, 209

Steamed Fish with Lemongrass and Herbs, 195

Stewed Oxtail with Nutmeg Sauce, 247

Stock, Simple Shellfish, 187

Stone Town, Zanzibar, 34, 111, 121, 125, 131–32, 134, 137, 245

Stuffed Onions with Ginger and Lamb, 94

Sweet-and-Sour Vegetable Soup with Peanuts, 211

Sweet Potato, Soy Sauce—Baked, Nutmeg-and-Ginger Spinach
Soup with, 246

T

Tamarind, 26, 207

Entrecôte with Onion, Ginger, and Tamarind, 210

Octopus Curry, 219

Shrimp Balls with Tamarind Sauce, 220

Sweet-and-Sour Vegetable Soup with Peanuts, 211

Tamarind-Glazed Fruits with Star Anise, 209

Turmeric Squid with Tamarind Sauce, 217

Tea, 69

Lemongrass Tea, 203

Thailand

Coconut Panna Cotta with Lemongrass, Turmeric, and
Passion Fruit, 204

coriander and, 22

cuisine of, 15

galangal and, 23

Green Curry Paste, 161

Green Curry with Chicken, 160

Green Papaya Salad, 109

Grilled Green Fish with Red Rice, 159

Grouper with Ginger and Spring Onion, 91

lemongrass and, 193

Lemongrass-Coconut Soup with Shrimp, 201

markets in, 4, 38, 166, 222, 287

Mussaman Beef Curry, 149

Mussaman Curry Paste, 142, 165

Mussels with Lemongrass, Chiles, and Holy Basil, 199

Spicy Beef Salad with Green Peppercorns, 81

Spicy Lemongrass Fish Cakes, 200

Steamed Fish with Lemongrass and Herbs, 195

tamarind and, 26

Turmeric Squid with Tamarind Sauce, 217

Thekkady, India, 69, 73

Tomatoes

Aromatic Cardamom Lamb with Saffron Carrots, 127

Fresh Yogurt-Cucumber Soup with Coriander and Cumin, 43

Green Papaya Salad, 109

Lamb with Spinach and Cinnamon, 265

Mauritian "Bouillabaisse," 185

Réunionnaise Yellow Chicken and Banana Curry, 188

Spicy Beef Salad with Green Peppercorns, 81

Tomato and Cucumber Salad with Cumin Salt, 41

Trout

Kerala Jewish Fish with Green Herbs and Spices, 153

Trout with Rum and Vanilla, 253

Tuna

Chiles with Hot Tuna Stuffing, 107

Cumin-Curry Tuna Salad with Dates and Chickpeas, 45

Grilled Tuna with Zanzibar Spices, 63

Turmeric, 27, 175–76

Balinese Suckling Pig, 183

Chili Potatoes, 108

Coconut Panna Cotta with Lemongrass, Turmeric, and Passion Fruit, 204

Mauritian "Bouillabaisse," 185

Oven-Baked Cape Malay Curry, 191

Réunionnaise Yellow Chicken and Banana Curry, 188

Stuffed Onions with Ginger and Lamb, 94

Turmeric Squid with Tamarind Sauce, 217

Yellow Rice, 189

U

Ubud, Bali, Indonesia, 13, 16, 70, 164, 179

V

Vanilla, 27, 249–51

Bourbon Vanilla Ice Cream, 257

Curried Duck with Vanilla, 255

Flambéed Bananas with Vanilla and Rum Caramel, 256

Rum with Vanilla, 267

Tamarind-Glazed Fruits with Star Anise, 209

Trout with Rum and Vanilla, 253

Vegetables. *See also individual vegetables*

Spicy Deep-Fried Vegetables, 65

Sweet-and-Sour Vegetable Soup with Peanuts, 211

W

Watercress, Pepper-Crusted Fish with Spring Onion Sauce and, 82

Y

Yellow Rice, 189

Yogurt

Chicken Cardamom Masala with Cashews, 122

Fresh Yogurt-Cucumber Soup with Coriander and Cumin, 43

Lamb Korma, 146

Lamb with Spinach and Cinnamon, 265

Nan with Cumin, Raisins, and Onions, 48

Soothing Clove and Yogurt Dip, 104

Z

Zanzibar

Bananas with Coconut and Cardamom, 125

cardamom and, 126

cloves and, 21, 34, 96, 245

cuisine of, 14, 15, 131–32, 134

Fish in Coconut Curry, 138

ginger and, 89

Grilled Tuna with Zanzibar Spices, 63

Grouper with Ginger and Spring Onion, 91

history of, 34

Kingfish with Orange, Cloves, and Ginger, 245

Lemongrass Tea, 203

markets in, 30, 111, 121, 125, 213, 223

Octopus Curry, 219

Rice Noodles with Squid, Shrimp, and Chicken, 141

Rice Pilau with Cashews and Coriander, 243

Sor Patel, 137

Spice-Dusted Avocado with Mango and Crab, 59

Zanzibar Coffee, 269

Mom and pop on the road, from the Krabi region of southern Thailand.